KONSEP BOOKS
KONSEP LAGENDA SDN BHD
Kuala Lumpur 59100
MALAYSIA
FAX: 60 3 282 1348

ISBN 983 9778 00 5

First Published May 1996
Second printing August 1996
Third Printing December 1996

Cover Design: L. Too
Type set by Konsep Lagenda Sdn Bhd

Printed by
Ritz Print Sdn Bhd

CHINESE ASTROLOGY FOR ROMANCE & RELATIONSHIPS

USE THE CHINESE ASTROLOGICAL SCIENCES TO ENHANCE YOUR LOVE LIFE AND IMPROVE ALL YOUR RELATIONSHIPS.

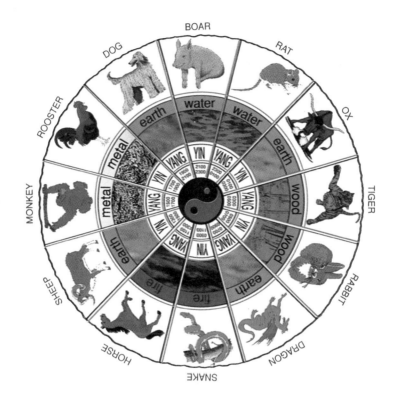

LILLIAN TOO

bestselling author of the feng shui classics

A KONSEP BOOK

Other books by the author:
Feng Shui
Applied Pa Kua Lo Shu Feng Shui
Practical Applications of Feng Shui
Chinese Numerology in Feng Shui
Water Feng Shui for Wealth
The Chinese Dragon
Strategies for Career Success
Creative Visualization
Making your First Million
Tap the Power Inside You
Explore the Frontiers of your Mind

Audio Cassettes by the author:
Creative Visualization
Developing Success habits
Positive Affirmations
Making your First Million

A Short Note to readers ...

In the old days, our ancestors believed totally in the wisdom of arranged marriages. The suitability of eligible young men or women were judged not merely on the basis of their family's social status and their physical attributes ... but often, compatibility was a prime consideration. Dates of birth and element charts were drawn up by soothsayers and fortune tellers who were consulted to determine the compatibility of young couples ...

Much of the matchmaking part of those old practices have since been discarded ... thank heavens ! Neither mine nor my daughter's generation would, I am certain, have any inclination to revive that particular old practice. Indeed, as bona fide members of the twentieth century, we are believers in romance and love. We choose our own mates ... thank you very much !

And yet ... much can be said for the old practice of determining compatibility between young couples. Looking at all my married friends, most now in the prime of their years, and many even already have grand children; I see marriages which have been deliriously happy and fruitful ... and equally also I observe those that somehow went horribly wrong ... and almost always, upon checking their dates of birth I have discovered how their respective animal signs and elements, and often their feng shui have conflicted or harmonized beautifully, as a result affecting the quality of their relationships in no small measure. In my own experience also, I have been pleasantly surprised at how uncannily accurate the astrological readings on compatibility have been. Indeed, these readings have accurately explained relationships that somehow went wrong, and those which somehow seemed blessed by some intangible luck.

Perhaps we should revive the old practice of investigating compatibility, and seriously study the Chinese Astrological Sciences. There is much in our culture and tradition we can use to investigate the intangible forces that seem to affect our love life and our relationships. If it makes for increased happiness, why not indeed.

It is with these thoughts in mind that I was prompted to write this book. A great deal of serious research has gone into this user friendly guide to relationships. I hope it will prove useful for old and young alike. I know I loved writing it ... and I have had a wonderful time checking out relationships, investigating the feng shui of my many friends, and consulting the wonderful I Ching to point me in the right directions.

But I also hope you have fun with this book ... don't be startled by the uncanny accuracy of descriptions, and of characteristics and attributes ...
Chinese Astrological Sciences have after all been around for centuries, and the seasoned wisdom of the ages has much to offer us .....

Lillian Too
March 1996

... dedicated to Darling Jennifer,
Now, more than ever,
May you have lots of fun with this book !

CONTENTS

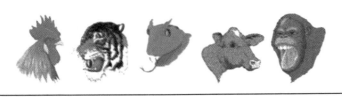

64. HOROSCOPE COMPATABILITIES

The affinity triangles

65. RAT/DRAGON: an absolutely delicious marriage
66. RAT/MONKEY: Fun & games on a roller coaster ride
67. MONKEY/DRAGON: bringing out the best in each other

68. SNAKE/OX: a deeply abiding love match
69. SNAKE/ROOSTER: eyes only for each other
70. OX/ROOSTER: a match made in heaven

71. DOG/TIGER: Quite adorably perfect !
72. DOG/HORSE; Durable & solid but a trite dull ?
73 HORSE/TIGER: an auspicious & volcanic passion

74. BOAR/SHEEP: happy, mellow & smooth together
75. RABBIT SHEEP: wobbly start but a solid relationship
76. RABBIT/BOAR almost custom made for each other

77. OTHER COMPATIBLE PAIRINGS

78. RAT/RAT: enriching each other's lives
89. RAT/OX: guarantee of marital stability
80. RAT/TIGER: initial enthusiasm could waver
81. RAT/BOAR: these two make marvelous mates

82. OX/OX: hugely successful & productive
83. OX/RABBIT: a cozy, cuddly pair
84. OX/MONKEY: a promise of much happiness
85. OX/DOG: rocky start deepens into true love
86. OX/BOAR: getting along famously

87. BOAR/BOAR: not exactly th best, but OK
88. TIGER/BOAR: loving and very romantic pair
89. RABBIT/RABBIT: a mutual admiration society
90 RABBIT/SNAKE: not the best but could work.
91. RABBIT/MONKEY: Intellectually well matched
92. RABBIT/DOG: an OK match - dull but solid
93. DRAGON/SNAKE: a brilliant, scorching pair
94. DRAGON/HORSE: a highly physical, electrifying union.

FUNDAMENTALS OF CHINESE ASTROLOGY

Chinese astrology has little to do with the sun, moon or stars directly. Unlike Western or Indian astrology, it does not look heavenward to chart the movement of the constellations, either to draw up a personality composite of an individual, or to predict that person's destiny. Chinese astrology is all about understanding Chinese philosophical and cultural systems, and comprehending the Chinese view of the Universe.

Chinese astrological sciences make specific references to the balance of Yin and Yang, and draw conclusions on destiny and personality profiles according to the cycles of relationships of the Five Elements. Chinese horoscopes are drawn up and interpreted according to the Chinese Ganzhi lunar Calendar, which measures time according to sixty year cycles. The use of Chinese astrology must thus start by converting your western day of birth to its Chinese equivalent.

The nearest thing to a Chinese astrological chart is the *Tzu Wei* or Purple Star system, which arranges an individual's destiny according to twelve houses, and this, like all other branches of Chinese astrology is based on the <u>exact time, day, month and year</u> of birth. The *stars* described in the *Tzu Wei* system are all imaginary and were used by ancient astrologers to make up a person's destiny chart. The *Tzu Wei* system is in turn based on the *Paht Chee* or 8 characters chart. Both charts are laborious to calculate and draw up; and even more difficult for the uninitiated to interpret. This book does <u>not</u> refer either to the *Tzu Wei* system, or to the *Paht Chee* chart. This is not a fortune telling book on destiny.

But it IS a book about character traits and personality profiles. Using the Chinese date of birth, and referring to more easily accessible portions of the Chinese astrological sciences, it is easy to examine compatabilities and investigate what makes someone tick and how best to read his/her character. This is what this book is about ⁻ a reference aid for the reader to discover his/her most compatible and perfect partner ! This book is about romantic and business relationships, and how anyone can better understand AND enhance these relationships. You will find, as you check through the descriptions, how uncannily accurate they are. Chinese astrology really does work, as does *feng shui,* the science of positively activating the invisible energy lines of the atmosphere to your advantage. As also does the *I Ching,* this wonderful ancient divination system which answers all your specific questions about the future. This book tells you how to investigate the character of your friends and potential partners, and how to use *feng shui* and the *I ching.* But first, it is necessary to understand the various concepts that make up Chinese astrology.

THE YIN YANG CONCEPT

This is the principle of dualism which underpin all Chinese belief. Yin and Yang are the negative and positive principles which together symbolize perfect harmony. They are opposites but they are complementary rather than opposing forces.

YIN is female, dark, passive, cold and soft. It symbolizes the earth and the moon and is also representative of death. Yin is negative energy.
YANG is male., light, active, warm and strong. It symbolizes the heaven and the sun, and is representative of life. Yang is positive energy.

Yin and Yang together is pictorially represented by the universal symbol which depicts an egg showing the black and white strongly differentiated. Yin and Yang together are believed to constitute the TAO, the eternal principle of heaven and earth; life and death; the sun and the moon, one unable to have meaning without the other. Yin and Yang depend on each other, and together they give meaning to the existence of Man. Thus without dark, there can be no light; without hot there is no cold; without day there can be no night, and without stillness there can be no movement. Yin and yang continually interacts, thereby creating change. Thus summer (yang) gives way to winter (yin). Night (yin) follows day (yang). The moon (yin) gives way to the sun (yang) and darkness (yin) becomes light (yang).

Applying the Yin/Yang concept to human relationships, one sees that in the interaction of two individuals one should ideally be aggressive and other passive; one initiates and is assertive while one follows and is passive. Together the two symbolize a perfect whole and there is balance. Every relationship contains varying degrees of Yin and Yang; and in the Yang there is a bit of Yin, just like in the Yin there is a bit of Yang. In relationships there should be a balance of these two forces. Neither too much Yang nor too much Yin is good. Thus when both parties are hard and cold, the relationship will flounder. Similarly when both persons are weak and passive, it cannot be auspicious. When both parties are too *male* or too *female* the relationship also cannot succeed. (the words *male* and *female* here does not refer to gender).

In the Chinese system of categorizing individuals according to their year of birth, each year is considered either a YIN or a YANG year, and this is one of the attributes to check when investigating compatabilites between partners. Thus all even years are Yang years while all odd years are Yin years ! Thus 1995 is a Yin year while 1996 is a Yang year. A yin/yang match is thus preferred to a yin/yin or a yang/yang match !

# THE FIVE ELEMENTS THEORY

The evolution of Time and Man, according to the Chinese, is brought about by the dynamic interactions of the five elements - WOOD, FIRE, EARTH, METAL and WATER. Every one of the Chinese astrological sciences depend on five element analysis for interpretation. It is the central theme which permeates the understanding of time, of space and of human interactions. Thus each hour, day, month and year is categorized as one of the elements. Later, as we delve deeper into the heavenly stems and the earthly branches that make up the Chinese calendar, we shall see that every stem and every branch has an element. Everyone of the twelve animals of the Chinese zodiac also has an element. Indeed, everything on Earth is categorized as belonging to one of the five elements.

It is in understanding the true nature of the element interactions that we can accurately surmise the outcome of relationships and destiny cycles ! There are two primary cycles, one productive and the other destructive:

THE PRODUCTIVE CYCLE:
WOOD produces FIRE which produces EARTH which produces METAL which produces WATER which in turn produces WOOD. From this productive Cycle we can also see that WOOD exhausts WATER which exhausts METAL which exhausts EARTH which exhausts FIRE which in turn exhausts WOOD !

THE DESTRUCTIVE CYCLE
WOOD destroys EARTH which destroys WATER which destroys FIRE which destroys METAL which in turn destroys WOOD.

When investigating compatabilities of loved ones and partners, it is absolutely vital that the relevant element balances be thoroughly analyzed, since these offer clues on interactive behavior patterns. It is however important to note that every person's date of birth comprise several elements, and it is the *basket of elements* which must be analyzed. Thus a person born in a wood year may have other elements represent his day, month or hour ! Also, although the primary element cycles offer important clues to interactions, one must also go deeper to investigate the true nature of the interaction. For example, while water destroys fire, small water is turned by fire into steam signifying power and energy ! Similarly, while metal destroys wood, small metal can convert wood into furniture thereby making the wood more valuable !! Thus the obvious may not always be the case. One must instead see the quantities of elements present in a date of birth before drawing conclusions about compatibilities !

THE CHINESE CALENDAR

The Chinese calendar is totally different from the western calendar ! It is made up of 60 year cycles which are differentiated according to *heavenly stems* and *earthly branches* ! There are ten stems and twelve branches. In the 60 year cycle, the stems comprise the five elements while the branches are the twelve animals. Every 60 year cycle is made up of the combinations of elements and animals. Thus 5x12=60 years. This system of stems and branches comprehensively signify the interaction of heavenly and earthly forces, and are supposed to reflect the character and destiny of all mankind. They thus form the basis of Chinese astrology.

The branches in this system are the Horoscope animals, and there are twelve animals to represent twelve years of the cycle. In every 60 year cycle, the elements work by dominating each animal sign once only. There is thus e.g. only one Fire Snake and one Water Horse in every 60 year cycle. There is also a yin and a yang aspect to the elements, and this also gets reflected in the 60 year cycles according to whether the year is odd or even.

In addition, there are also the month (season) and time (hour) considerations which are thought to exert their influences. Thus a midnight Rat is cheekier & braver than a daytime Rat. And a Wood Rooster born in winter is deemed to be weaker than the Wood Rooster born during the summer ! Each of the animals born in different element years is also different e.g. an Earth Boar is quite different from a Metal Boar ! Calculations of the permutation of character/personality types indicate that only two people in a million will show identical personalities and this too without taking the differences of the 60 year cycles into account !

To get the most out of this book, which focuses on the earthly branches (i.e. the animals) and their respective compatibilites in great depth, readers should always take note of the influence of the elements when comparing birthcharts. These often offer clues to the long- term prospects of any relationship, and will also suggest the better way of dealing with the individual concerned. They should also factor in the implication of yin/yang balances, seasonal scrutiny (month of birth), and hourly aspects when investigating individual compatibilites. When drawing conclusions about compatibilties, also do not forget to investigate Compass Feng Shui calculations to determine the Compass compatibilities.

Finally, remember that it is seldom possible to get the most perfect match. But to ensure a reasonably good union, neither the earthly branches (the animals) nor the elements should clash too badly !

THE HEAVENLY STEMS & EARTHLY BRANCHES

The 10 stems and 12 branches are the pillars of the Chinese Astrological Sciences. In the annual calendar of the sixty year cycle, each of the stems feature six times while each of the branches feature five times.

Under the Chinese system, each year has a name which has two characters. One character refers to the stem while the other character refers to the branch. The name of the year also represents the YEAR CHARACTERS of the *Paht Chee* system of destiny analysis. In this book of relationships however, the name of the year is used to determine the elements which dominate a person's year of birth. The name of the year has been included in the tables on pages 8-11 . By referring to these tables, readers can determine the respective elements of both the stem and the branch as indicated in each of the names by comparing them with the keys below. These element indications are so central to destiny analysis that they are vital ingredients for comprehensive readings of Chinese birthcharts.

TEN HEAVENLY STEMS

1. CHIA = Wood
2. YI = Wood
3. PING = Fire
4. TING = Fire
5. MOU = Earth
6. CHI = Earth
7. KEN = Metal
8. SIN = Metal
9. ZEN = Water
10. KWAY =Water

TWELVE EARTHLY BRANCHES

1. TZU = RAT = Water
2. CH'OU = OX = Earth
3. YIN = TIGER = Wood
4. MAO = RABBIT = Wood
5. CHEN = DRAGON = Earth
6. SZU = SNAKE = Fire
7. WU = HORSE = Fire
8. WEI = SHEEP = Earth
9. SHEN = MONKEY = Metal
10. YU = ROOSTER = Metal
11. HSU = DOG = Earth
12. HAI = BOAR = Water

The next thing to understand is the Chinese lunar month. Because the lunar month theoretically has 29.5 days, the lunar year has big months (30 days) and small months (29 days). In addition, the lunar year can comprise either 12 months or 13 months. This happens every two to three years when one of the months will get repeated. Every month has its own combination of heavenly stem and earthly branch. The same is also true for each day of the month, and each hour of the day. The combination of the stems and branches of a person's year, month, day and hour of birth thus adds up to eight characters made up from the list above. This is the famous *Paht Chee* system of destiny analysis that is so potent and accurate. However the formulas for diagnosing what these 8 characters are, requires the Chinese *thousand year calendar* which is not reproduced here. For relationships analysis, it is sufficient to examine the year elements.

THE STEMS & BRANCHES OF FORTUNE

While it is not within the scope of this book to delve too deeply into destiny analysis, we are however investigating characteristics and personalities of individuals, and for this analyses to be comprehensive, it is vital that the interaction of the stems and branches for the YEAR of birth be properly understood.

Basic personality traits are categorized initially according to the earthly branch (i.e. the animals) of the year of birth. Thus if the person being investigated is born in a year when the ruling branch is TZU, then that person is deemed to have been born in a RAT year and will exhibit the general characteristics that rule the RAT personality.

However, in any 60 year cycle, the RAT year appears five times, each time with a different heavenly stem ! Thus one can be a WOOD RAT, a FIRE RAT, an EARTH RAT. a METAL RAT or a WATER RAT. The attributes, temperaments and personalities of these five different rats will differ. The same is true for all twelve animals.

When investigating compatibilities therefore, it is necessary to first investigate affinity according to earthly branch alone. This is to obtain a generalized but complete first impression, and then later to extend it to both heavenly stem and earthly branch. To do this successfully, it is necessary only to read the sections on the twelve animals, and to investigate the two characters that make up the NAME of the year. With the addition of the heavenly stem, the all important element analysis will have been added to the compatibility readings. Here compatibility is taken to mean whether the person in question *will be good for you* in the long run, and not whether the temperaments are suited. For attunement of temperaments, the earthly branch characteristics are sufficient.

To investigate longer term prospects of potential partners, it is also recommended that their month and time of birth be examined. This is easily done because the relevant tables and information for analysis is quite easily reproduced in this book, and indeed have been included in the following pages. What has NOT been included however are the characters on stems and branches that apply to the DAY of birth. This has been left out simply because it is impossible to address the individual day combinations for all the days of the past hundred years ! And since the DAY stems & branches add only marginally to the analysis, their exclusion should not affect the main part of the analysis, which is based on the characteristics affected by the year of birth.

THE CHINESE HOROSCOPE ANIMALS

The popular view of Chinese Astrology is the categorization of years according to each of twelve animals. These animals, in their order of appearance are the Rat, the Ox, the Tiger, the Rabbit, the Dragon, the Snake, the Horse, the Sheep, the Monkey, the Rooster, the Dog, and the Boar.

There have been many legends and explanations surrounding the choice of the animals featured in the Chinese Horoscope. One popular version describes the anointing of these animals by the Lord Buddha as reward for their respectful presence at his birthday party. Another story has it that the Heavenly Jade Emperor, bored of life in heaven specifically asked to meet with twelve earthly creatures, and were presented with these twelve animals. Yet a third version talks of a competition organized by the King of Heaven where all animals were invited to cross the fast moving Lo river, and the first twelve that reached the other side of the river were selected to represent the years of the calendar then being designed. The order of appearance in the cycle was usually explained by their sequential appearance before the exalted personality who selected them. There are, special stories to explain the Rat being the first animal of the Chinese Zodiac, and these usually explain his craftiness in achieving first place. The Rat, apparently did not run all the way to beat the rest. Instead he hitched a ride from the ox and just before the finishing line merely jumped ahead and landed in front of the ox ! That he was not censured for his craftiness, the story goes, reflects heaven's approval of those who use their head !

The above notwithstanding, I prefer to view the selection of animals as reflecting the wisdom of the ancients, particularly as it applied to the mainly agricultural and superstitious society of ancient China. Thus the Rat being the all important king during times of famine comes first in the Cycle because food is all important for survival. Being aggressive and clever, he is also deemed a *yang* animal. The slow moving, hardworking ox is made a *yin* animal. The festive fifth year, tumultuous and exciting is given over to the dragon while the boisterous seventh year is deemed the year of the horse ! The tenth year belongs to the proud rooster, strutting around, while the twelfth year belongs to the slow indolent Boar ! And so it goes. These animals in Chinese Astrology have been in use since time was first officially recorded under the reign of the emperor Huang Ti - around the year 2637 BC - and has thus been around for forty six centuries ! The cycle always starts with the Rat and ends with he Boar. This century, 1900 started with the Rat year, and next year - 1996, we begin the eighth cycle of the Zodiac for this century.

LUNAR BIRTH YEAR TABLES 1912 to 1947

ANIMAL	WESTERN CALENDAR DATES	YEAR NAME	HS/EB ELEMENT
RAT (water)	Feb 18, 1912 - Feb 5, 1913	Zen Tzu	water/water
OX (earth)	Feb 6, 1913 - Jan 25, 1914	Kway Chou	water/earth
TIGER (wood)	Jan 26, 1914 - Feb 13, 1915	Chia Yin	wood/wood
RABBIT (wood)	Feb 14, 1915 - Feb 2, 1916	Yi Mao	wood/wood
DRAGON (earth)	Feb 3, 1916 - Jan 22, 1917	Ping Ch'en	fire/earth
SNAKE (fire)	Jan 23, 1917 - Feb 10, 1918	Ting Szu	fire/fire
HORSE (fire)	Feb 11, 1918 - Jan 31, 1919	Mou Wu	earth/fire
SHEEP (earth)	Feb 1, 1919 - Feb 19, 1920	Chi Wei	earth/earth
MONKEY (metal)	Feb 20, 1920 - Feb 7, 1921	Ken Shen	metal/metal
ROOSTER (metal)	Feb 8, 1921 - Jan 27, 1922	Sin Yu	metal/ metal
DOG (earth)	Feb 28, 1922 - Feb 15, 1923	Zen Szu	water/earth
BOAR (water)	Feb 16th 1923 - Feb 4, 1924	Kway Hai	water/water

ANIMAL	WESTERN CALENDAR DATES	YEAR NAME	HS/EB ELEMENT
✪ start of 60 year Cycle			
RAT (water)	Feb 5th 1924 - Jan 23, 1925	Chia Tzu	wood/water
OX (earth)	Jan 24, 1925 - Feb 12, 1926	Yi Chou	wood/earth
TIGER (wood)	Feb 13, 1926 - Feb 1, 1927	Ping Yin	fire/wood
RABBIT (wood)	Feb 2, 1927 - Jan 22, 1928	Ting Mao	fire/wood
DRAGON (earth)	Jan 23, 1928 - Feb 9, 1929	Mou Ch'en	earth/earth
SNAKE (fire)	Feb 10, 1929 - Jan 29, 1930	Chi Szu	earth/fire
HORSE (fire)	Jan 30 1930 - Feb 16, 1931	Ken Wu	metal/fire
SHEEP (earth)	Feb 17 1931 - Feb 5 1932	Sin Wei	metal/earth
MONKEY (metal)	Feb 6, 1932 - Jan 25, 1933	Zen Shen	water/metal
ROOSTER (metal)	Jan 26, 1933 - Feb 13, 1934	Kway Yu	water/metal
DOG (earth)	Feb 14, 1934 - Feb 3, 1935	Chia Hsu	wood/earth
BOAR (water)	Feb 4, 1935 - Jan 23, 1936	Yi Hai	wood/water

ANIMAL	WESTERN CALENDAR DATES	YEAR NAME	HS/EB ELEMENT
RAT (water)	Jan 24, 1936 - Feb 10, 1937	Ping Tzu	fire/water
OX (earth)	Feb 11, 1937 - Jan 30, 1938	Ting Chou	fire/earth
TIGER (wood)	Jan 31, 1938 - Feb 18, 1939	MouYin	earth/wood
RABBIT (wood)	Feb 19, 1939 - Feb 7, 1940	Chi Mao	earth/wood
DRAGON (earth)	Feb 8, 1940 - Jan 26, 1941	Ken Ch'en	metal/earth
SNAKE (fire)	Jan 27, 1941 - Feb 14, 1942	Sin Szu	metal/fire
HORSE (fire)	Feb 15, 1942 - Feb 4, 1943	Zen Wu	water/fire
SHEEP (earth)	Feb 5, 1943 - Jan 24, 1944	KwayWei	water/earth
MONKEY (metal)	Jan 25 1944 - Feb 12 1945	Chia Shen	wood/metal
ROOSTER (metal)	Feb 13, 1945 - Feb 1, 1946	Yi Yu	wood/metal
DOG (earth)	Feb 2, 1946 - Jan 21, 1947	Ping Hsu	fire/earth
BOAR (water)	Jan 22, 1947 - Feb 9, 1948	Ting Hai	fire/water

LUNAR BIRTH YEAR TABLES 1948 to 1983

ANIMAL	WESTERN CALENDAR DATES	YEAR NAME	HS/EB ELEMENT
RAT (water)	Feb 10, 1948 - Jan 28, 1949	Mou Tzu	earth/water
OX(earth)	Jan 29 1949 - Feb 16, 1950	Chi Chou	earth/earth
TIGER (wood)	Feb 17, 1950 - Feb 5, 1951	Ken Yin	metal/wood
RABBIT (wood)	Feb 6, 1951 - Jan 26, 1952	Sin Mao	metal/wood
DRAGON (earth)	Jan 27, 1952 - Feb 13, 1953	Zen Ch'en	water/earth
SNAKE (fire)	Feb 14, 1953 - Feb 2, 1954	Kway Szu	water/fire
HORSE (fire)	Feb 3, 1954 - Jan 23, 1955	Chia Wu	wood/fire
SHEEP (earth)	Jan 24, 1955 - Feb 11 1956	Yi Wei	wood/earth
MONKEY (metal)	Feb 12, 1956 - Jan 30 1957	Ping Shen	fire/metal
ROOSTER (metal)	Jan 31, 1957 - Feb 17, 1958	Ting Yu	fire/metal
DOG (earth)	Feb 18, 1958 - Feb 7, 1959	Mou Hsu	earth/earth
BOAR (water)	Feb 8, 1959 - Jan 27, 1960	Chi Hai	earth/water
RAT (water)	Jan 28, 1960 - Feb 14, 1961	Ken Tzu	metal/water
OX (earth)	Feb 15, 1961 - Feb 4, 1962	Sin Chou	metal/earth
TIGER (wood)	Feb 5, 1962 - Jan 24, 1963	Zen Yin	water/wood
RABBIT (wood)	Jan 25, 1963 - Feb 12, 1964	Kway Mao	water/wood
DRAGON (earth)	Feb 13, 1964 - Feb 1, 1965	Chia/Ch'en	wood/earth
SNAKE (fire)	Feb 2, 1965 - Jan 20, 1966	Yi Szu	wood/fire
HORSE (fire)	Jan 21 1966 - Feb 8, 1967	Ping Wu	fire/fire
SHEEP (earth)	Feb 9 1967 - Jan 29, 1968	Ting Wei	fire/earth
MONKEY (metal)	Jan 30, 1968 - Feb 16, 1969	Mou Shen	earth/metal
ROOSTER (metal)	Feb 17, 1969 - Feb 5, 1970	Chi Yu	earth/metal
DOG (earth)	Feb 6 1970 - Jan 26, 1971	Ken Hsu	metal/earth
BOAR (water)	Jan 27, 1971 - Feb 14 1972	Sin Hai	metal/water
RAT (water)	Feb 15, 1972 - Feb 2, 1973	Zen Tzu	water/water
OX (earth)	Feb 3, 1973 - Jan 22, 1974	Kway Chou	water/earth
TIGER (wood)	Jan 23, 1974 - Feb 10, 1975	Chia Yin	wood/wood
RABBIT (wood)	Feb 11, 1975 - Jan 30, 1976	Yi Mao	wood/wood
DRAGON (earth)	Jan 31, 1976 - Feb 17, 1977	Ping Ch'en	fire/earth
SNAKE (fire)	Feb 18, 1977 - Feb 6, 1978	Ting Szu	fire/fire
HORSE (fire)	Feb 7, 1978 - Jan 27, 1979	Mou Wu	earth/fire
SHEEP (earth)	Jan 28, 1979 - Feb 15, 1980	Chi Wei	earth/earth
MONKEY (metal)	Feb 16, 1980 - Feb 4, 1981	Ken Shen	metal/metal
ROOSTER (metal)	Feb 5. 1981 - Jan 24, 1982	Sin Yu	metal/metal
DOG (earth)	Jan 25, 1982 - Feb 12, 1983	Zen Hsu	water/earth
BOAR (water)	Feb 13, 1983 - Feb 1, 1984	Kway Hai	water/water

LUNAR BIRTH YEAR TABLES 1984 to 2007

ANIMAL	WESTERN CALENDAR DATES	YEAR NAME	HS/EB ELEMENT
✪ Start of 60 year Cycle			
RAT (water)	Feb 2, 1984 - Feb 19, 1985	Chia Tzu	wood/water
OX (earth)	Feb 20, 1985 - Feb 8, 1986	Yi Chou	wood/earth
TIGER (wood)	Feb 9, 1986 - Jan 28, 1987	Ping Yin	fire/wood
RABBIT (wood)	Jan 29, 1987 - Feb 16, 1988	Ting Mao	fire/wood
DRAGON (earth)	Feb 17, 1988 - Feb 5, 1989	Mou Ch'en	earth/earth
SNAKE (fire)	Feb 6, 1989 - Jan 26, 1990	Chi Szu	earth/fire
HORSE (fire)	Jan 27, 1990 - Feb 14, 1991	Ken Wu	metal/fire
SHEEP (earth)	Feb 15, 1991 - Feb 3, 1992	Sin Wei	metal/earth
MONKEY (metal)	Feb 4, 1992 - Jan 22, 1993	Zen Shen	water/metal
ROOSTER metal)	Jan 23, 1993 - Feb 9, 1994	Kway Yu	water/metal
DOG (earth)	Feb 10, 1994 - Jan 30, 1995	Chia Hsu	wood/earth
BOAR (water)	Jan 31, 1995 - Feb 18, 1996	Yi Hai	wood/water

RAT (water)	Feb 19, 1996 - Feb 6, 1997	Ping Tzu	fire/water
OX (earth)	Feb 7, 1997 - Jan 27, 1998	Ting Chou	fire/earth
TIGER (wood)	Jan 28, 1998 - Feb 15, 1999	Mou Yin	earth/wood
RABBIT (wood)	Feb 16, 1999 - Feb 4, 2000	Chi Mao	earth/wood
DRAGON (earth)	Feb 5, 2000 - Jan 23, 2001,	Ken Ch'en	metal/earth
SNAKE (fire)	Jan 24, 2001 - Feb 11, 2002	Sin Szu	metal/fire
HORSE (fire)	Feb 12, 2002 - Jan 31, 2003	Zen Wu	water/fire
SHEEP (earth)	Feb 1, 2003 - Jan 21, 2004	Kway Wei	water/earth
MONKEY (metal)	Jan 22, 2004 - Feb 8, 2005	Chia Shen	wood/metal
ROOSTER (metal)	Feb 9, 2005 - Jan 28, 2006	Yi Yu	wood/metal
DOG (earth)	Jan 29, 2006 - Feb 17, 2007	Ping Hsu	fire/earth
BOAR (water)	Feb 18, 2007 - Feb 6, 2008	Ting Hai	fire/water

The lunar birth year tables above and in the preceding two pages will enable anyone to determine their respective ruling animal or earthly branch. The cut off annual dates for year beginnings and year ends enable conversion from western dates of birth. Please note these cut off dates carefully, so as to ensure that animal signs are determined correctly. For instance a person may be born in 1945, but if the date of birth is before 13th February 1945, the person is a Monkey and NOT a Rooster ! The tables also contain the HS/EB element. This refers to the heavenly stem and earthly branch elements and are by themselves, already very useful information, since these element combinations offer immediate clues on compatibility and luck, based on cyclical element analysis.

LUNAR BIRTH YEAR TABLES
How to use them ....

The best way to use the tables is to use them to initially determine the ANIMAL sign which rules a person's year of birth. These animal signs represent the earthly branches of an individual's horoscope and offer wonderful insights into character and personality. After determining the relevant animal, refer to the pages which offer descriptions of the men and women born under the respective animal signs. This is the first step in relationship analysis ⁻ the generalized reading. You will be surprised at how uncannily accurate the behavioral tendencies and personality types are !

Notice also that each of the animals has a ruling element which does not change. Thus the Rat is considered to represent the element water, the Dragon is considered to be of the earth element, the Horse is fire, the Monkey is metal and so forth. By themselves the elements do not mean very much. However, when matched with the element represented by the particular heavenly stem of the year of birth, the elements, or rather, the *combination of elements*, become potent additional indicators of characteristic tendencies, both positive and negative. Thus the next stage in the analysis is to delve a little deeper by investigating for example what kind of sheep you may be dealing with, a water sheep, or a metal sheep, or a fire sheep ... and so forth. We have seen that in a sixty cycle, the five elements appear only once per animal year. At this stage of the analysis there are already sixty different *types* of personalities !

First therefore you use the tables to determine compatibility of the animal symbols i.e. yours with the person you are investigating ! But you cannot stop there. You should also investigate the compatibility of the elements that are represented by the heavenly stem of the year of birth.

EXAMPLE: You will discover from the affinity tables that the dragon and the dog are natural enemies. They generally have no time for each other and a match between a dragon and a dog is usually not good. However, if you dig a little deeper and discover that one is a *wood* dragon and the other is a *fire* dog, the pairing of the two individuals might just well work, since *wood produces fire*. Thus, the heavenly stem might well prevail over the earthly branch (and it usually does, since the influence of heaven is often more potent than that of the earth.) By the same token if we are assessing the combination of a *wood* dragon and a *metal* dog, the incompatibility would be further compounded by the clashing of the elements (since *metal destroys wood*). Such a match would be extremely inauspicious at best, and disastrous at worst, and thus, best avoided.

# GOING DEEPER: THE MONTH TABLES

If you wish, you can go deeper into the analysis by further examining and comparing the month of birth as well. This does not require intensive examination of the heavenly stems and earthly branches of the exact lunar month. What is required is merely to determine in which season a person was born and then analyze the suitability of the match from there. To undertake this analysis, first determine the heavenly stem element of YOUR year of birth. Next, determine whether YOU were born in a summer, autumn, winter or spring month. You will then be able to see from the chart reproduced here whether you are a strong or a weak representation of your element. The earth element has been excluded since earth is regarded as being equally strong or weak throughout the year, and this part of the analysis does not apply to those born in earth years.

SEASON	METAL	WOOD	WATER	FIRE
SPRING	dying	thrives/strong	weakening	born
SUMMER	born	in bloom	dies	thrives/strong
AUTUMN	thrives/strong	dying/weak	born	weakening
WINTER	weakening	born	thrives/strong	dying

The above chart gives an indication of the seasonal strength of the elements. The way to conduct the analysis is best shown via examples. Thus, if you are a wood person i.e. the heavenly stem element of your year of birth is *wood*, and you were born during the autumn months e.g. in the month of November or December, when it is cold, and when plants usually wither, then it can be said that you are a a very weak *wood*. If however you had some *fire* to warm you, bring you some sunlight, you will start to flourish, grow strong and thrive ! Thus for someone like you, a *fire* person would be wonderful, ie someone born in a year when the heavenly stem element is *fire*, since that person would make you strong, look after you and nurture you. The elements in this case will be exceedingly compatible for you, and work in YOUR favour ! Meanwhile YOU will also be good for that person since *wood* produces *fire* in the cycle of element relationships.

Another example : If you are a *fire* person born in a summer month e.g. June, you can be regarded as a *strong fire* person. YOU do not need more fire. Neither do you need more wood to feed your fire. But a *water* person might be good for you since the *water* will temper your fire and ensure it does not grow too strong. The *water* person could also benefit from you since *fire* will transform the *water* into steam which represents energy and power ! You would thus find a water person could be good for you. Note that because you are a strong *fire*, the *water* cannot destroy you !

 EXAMINING THE HOUR TABLES

One useful analysis to undertake is to determine a person's hour of birth since this provides additional clues to character and personality. Chinese Astrology divides a 24 hour day into twelve two hour time slots, and assigns each of the Animals to these time slots. Depending therefore on whether one is born in the hour of the Rat, or Boar or any of the other animals, some of the characteristics of these animals will overlap onto a personality reading. The hour tables are reproduced here for ease of analysis. Make a note of the Animal represented by the hour of birth and read the relevant sections accordingly although in terms of weighting, do note that the hour influence merely complements the year readings.

RAT HOUR:	11.00 p.m. to 1.00 am
OX HOUR	1.00 am to 3.00 am
TIGER HOUR	3.00 am to 5.00 am
RABBIT HOUR	5.00 am to 7.00 am
DRAGON HOUR	7.00 am to 9.00 am
SNAKE HOUR	9.00 am to 11.00 am
HORSE HOUR	11.00 am to 1.00 p.m.
SHEEP HOUR	1.00 p.m. to 3.00 p.m.
MONKEY HOUR	3.00 p.m. to 5.00 p.m.
ROOSTER HOUR	5.00 p.m. to 7.00 p.m.
DOG HOUR	7.00 p.m. to 9.00 p.m.
BOAR HOUR	9.00 p.m. to 11.00 p.m.

Another perspective of the hour analysis is to use the hour to detect nuances to personality characteristics. Thus, the night time RAT is more curious, brave and alert than his daytime sibling. The OX which sleeps at night and works hard during daylight hours similarly demonstrates this trait. The TIGER hunts and prowls in the dark, and the night TIGER is therefore more dangerous and ferocious. The RABBIT is most alert when born in the early hours of the morning. The DRAGON is believed to come into his own during the mornings, while the SNAKE slithers most effectively into your heart and boudoir during the early evenings. The HORSE is a daytime animal, while the SHEEP is believed to think best during the early evening hours. The MONKEY is at his most cunning during the afternoon hours. The ROOSTER reigns supreme when born in the early hours of dawn when his singing sounds the wake up bell and calls successfully for the sun. The DOG's faithfulness shines forth during the nights, while the BOAR just goes to sleep at nights !

PUTTING THINGS TOGETHER

You are now in a position to begin your analysis of the relationships in your life. Once you understand how the heavenly stems and the earthly branches translate into elements, and using the basic personality descriptions contained in the following sections of the book, you can draw up comprehensive compatibility readings for yourself and any of the people in your love life or working life. Also undertake a complete investigation of the way your ruling elements interact with those of the people around you.

Study the section on elements thoroughly since knowledge of the way elements interact according to their relationship cycles, provide much of the explanations behind who you get along with, and who you don't; who is good for you, and who is not, can all be explained in terms of the interactions of the elements that dominate your birthcharts.

If there is someone special you wish to investigate, you can also consult the *I Ching* . Use this wonderful divination tool to provide insights about the future potential of any relationship.

If your relationships always seem to go nowhere, or if you just have a hard time getting your love life together, you might want to seriously activate the relationship sector of your home by using the *feng shui* tips included for just this purpose !

This is a book about compatibilites and about using the Chinese astrological sciences to find your perfect partner. Much of the information contained in this book also represent extremely useful inputs for destiny analysis. The basis of interpretations hinge much on the interaction of the stems and branches of a birthchart. Thus if you should one day have your Chinese *Paht Chee* drawn up, you can use the information contained in this book to supplement whatever the fortune teller tells you, particularly since much of Chinese divinition depend on superior element analysis to provide indications of life's turning points.

Finally, remember that to a large extent, although destiny as such, cannot be changed, it can nevertheless be vastly improved. The Chinese believe in the concept of *Tien, Ti,* and *Ren Chai* or Heaven, Earth and Man luck. While you cannot control heaven luck, your earth and man luck is in your hands. Use the information in this book to load the dice in your favour when it comes to choosing your partners. The right choice brings great happiness. The wrong choice, on the other hand could well be disastrous !

15 THE CHINESE HOROSCOPE

CHARACTERISTICS OF THE TWELVE ANIMAL SIGNS

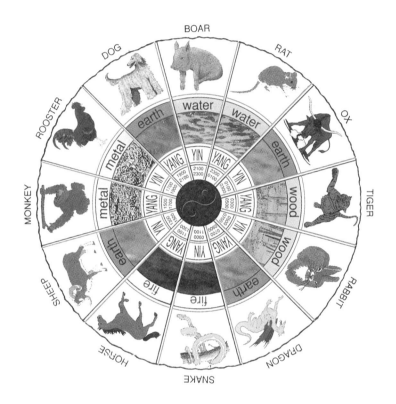

The twelve animal signs are featured here according to their gender as well as their (heavenly stem) elements. Differences between males and females show up in the aspects and degrees in which certain key characteristics manifest themselves. In addition, these characteristics are either magnified or modified according to the elements that influence a person's year of birth. Thus a Wood Rat may be similiar to an Earth Rat in some ways, and different in others. For instance feelings of insecurity, which are a dominant Rat characteristic, may be more strongly evident in an earth Rat than in a Wood Rat. These differences should be taken into account of when comparing your compatibility with the people who make up your world.

The spirited RAT lady

Magnetic, vivacious and dynamic - these are the visible give-aways of a RAT lady. They are rarely beautiful in the classical sense, but they exude outward sophistication, a certain hauteur and an aplomb which effectively hide an insecure but bossy, sometimes dogmatic nature. They love and seek pleasure but more than anything in the world, they crave security.

RAT women are not for flirting around with. They are seldom coy in their love relationships. Not for them the one night stand, nor the loose relationships that pass for platonic friendships. RAT women crave and need security - the kind that comes with social acceptance, with being part of a club, a family. Solid and firm protection from being left out is, and always will be, her first priority. RAT women take their relationships seriously, and marriage is never far from their minds when they date a guy !

RAT women have few close friends as they tend to be quite rigid and judgmental. Keeping up appearances is important to them, and their view of life is coloured by their own preconceived ideas about their role in the context of their specific environment. They tend to be fundamentally honest in an old fashioned sort of way, and at their worst can be quite opinionated, although this often hides a raging insecurity and a terrible lack of confidence.

To get along with her, demonstrate an understanding of this underlying and overpowering insecurity and give her plenty of reassurance. To win her, promise her material and emotional security and she will devote her many talents to making you exquisitely happy !

RAT women need men in their lives. They do not like being single and secretly fear being left on the shelf. She wants marriage, babies and a family ... more than she craves a career ! And even if your particular RAT lady friend is a seemingly successful, apparently independent careerwomen, she will give it up for marriage, love et al ... if you can give her the material security she wants.

As a boss, she is fiercely protective. As a subordinate she is loyal. And as a wife, she would be totally supportive, placing the husband's needs, wants and ambitions above her own. But she is not necessarily easy to live with. She constantly requires reassurance. She can be moody and she has a tendency to impose her will on how things should be done. And unless you are able to cope with her social and other ambitions (for you), the RAT wife could drown you with her devious and unending store of good intentions !

The WOOD FEMALE RAT

is intensely aware of her image. But she is also more confident and more enchanting than her sister Rats. She is also more attractive and her air of confidence borders on a certain hauteur and pomposity. She will not hesitate to let you know what she cannot and will not tolerate ! To win her love, you must be prepared to adore her and massage her ego. You must also be prepared to accept that she can be a nag ... most of the time !

The FIRE FEMALE RAT

is clever and devious. She knows what she wants and pursues it with ferocious determination. She is aggressive and forward in the way she goes about acquiring what she wants. If she wants you badly enough, it will be tough to resist her ... if you seriously want her, be direct. Appeal to her intense need for a serious commitment ... it will almost always work !

The EARTH FEMALE RAT

tends to be self centered but disciplined in her approach towards life. She is sociable and easy to get along with ... but she cannot completely hide her smudginess and feelings of superiority if she is higher up the social hierarchy than you are. She is very family oriented, and to win her, smother her with hints about how much you love family life ... hint at sexual adventursm because she is impressed with a small show of passion ...

The METAL FEMALE RAT

is the social worker type. She massages her ego and her need for public approval by working hard at feel good causes. But she is genuinely meticulous and hardworking, and can be relied upon to see things to completion. If you love such a Rat lady, the easiest way to her heart is to share her ambitions at being recognized socially. Accept that she will be a little lacking in a sense of humour ... and understand that she takes pride in being a serious member of society !

The WATER FEMALE RAT

is feminine and soft. She is also wiser and kinder than many of her sister Rats. But she is very aware of who she is and where she is placed on the social ladder. The most easily satisfied of all the Rat ladies, all she wants is to live a comfortable life. Offer her a home in the country where she can bring up her children, and good prospects for a cozy life, and she could be yours ! Your chances will be even better if you can also offer her some status to go with being your wife ... because the Female Water Rat often harbour secret ambitions to bask in the reflected glory of a successful husband.

The distinguished gentleman RAT

Handsome and charming, witty and eloquent, the gentleman RAT has a most engaging personality. The key to winning the approval, and love of a RAT male is to do what you can to boost his ego. At their best, they are wonderfully interesting, full of creativity and oozing with confidence. But criticize them, shake their confidence or disagree with them too much, and you will see the negative side. When cornered, the RAT male becomes extremely dangerous, even violent ! In short, if you are able to bring out their best side, RAT men make great partners and lovers. If on the other hand you cannot provide endorsement, support and respect, on a continuos basis, or you are the sort who is too critical, you want to think twice before getting entangled with a RAT man !

RAT gentlemen are not generous by nature - in fact they can be quite stingy and tight fisted with money. They are not great risk takers. And they are restless and impulsive. Their need for approval is sometimes so strong, they could, in the initial stages of a serious relationship endeavor to cultivate a splashy nonchalance when it comes to conspicuous spending. But in the long run, understand that they are not naturally generous souls.

Deep down, RAT men are insecure. They thrive on praise, and are happiest when basking in the glow of perceived popularity & recognition. Outwardly, they appear cool and dignified. They carry themselves really well and have a genuine talent for hiding any nervousness, fear or feelings of insecurity. But although they can be stubborn and dogmatic, they are also relentless and are not easily discouraged. When riled, the RAT male reacts with determined and devious ferocity. They hate being ordered around or be made to feel small. Remember, whether you are dealing with a boss, a subordinate or a boyfriend, the RAT is won over by praise and flattery, not by criticism. Diplomacy is always required when dealing with the RAT man ! This is because they are terribly sensitive to censure of any kind, whether it be implied or direct ! They need tender loving care, and it is easy to bring out their loving side. Just love them and love them and adore them !!

RAT men make excellent husbands. They are romantic and sentimental to those they love, and they make caring and enjoyable lovers. If you win their hearts, RAT men are generally honorable in their intentions. They take marriage seriously and you can also rest assured that they will stay faithful. Anything extra marital will stay that way. Their marriage will always be more important than their love affairs ! They are also seldom jealous to the extent that it crams your style. To the right person, they make great mates.

The WOOD MALE RAT

is steadier, calmer and more confident than the other Rats. He is more confident of his abilities and his place in society, and is thus, not as susceptible to flattery as the others. As a result he will show more courage, and could be a lot more fun. But that does not mean he does not also have a gigantic ego. His greater tolerance for disapproval or criticism or disagreement merely takes second place to his fierce determination to be accepted in the company of those he wishes to identify with ! Pander to this side of his social ambitions and you would have increased your chances of winning him !

The FIRE MALE RAT

demonstrates greater intensity and brilliance than the other Rats. He is also energetic, sharp, impatient and highly strung. Outwardly, they tend to be louder and appear more composed. Inwardly, their insecurity and nervous lack of confidence is more acute.. Fire male rats fear being alone. They fear rejection and they are very *kiasu* (afraid to lose) in their attitudes. If your boyfriend or boss is a Fire Rat, do not be fooled by his charm and outward show of confidence. Re assure him constantly; encourage him; and shower him with praise and approval. He will respond by *liking* and *loving* you with the most heart warming intensity.

The EARTH MALE RAT

has enormous determination, being the most focused, in terms of his ambitions and goals in life, of all the Rats. His will power and strength is quite phenomenal, but he is also judgmental and has tendencies towards being self righteous. Yet he is also soft spoken and congenial, and is the most romantic and passionate of all the Rats.

The METAL MALE RAT

is unashamedly ambitious socially. To win his heart, drop some names. It will appeal to the social climber in him ... he loves being part of the beautiful crowd, and he is a great believer in networking skills. He uses his charm and good looks to cultivate influential friends. But beware ... metal male rats can be very possessive. They are certainly dogmatic and stubborn.

The WATER MALE RAT

is probably the most relaxed and laid back of all the Rats. He is not as intense, nor as determined than some of the other Rats. He is also not madly ambitious, being easily satisfied with his lot. To win him, share his love of good food and good wine. Wear elegant clothes, and listen adoringly each time he pontificates on some favourite topic ... and be prepared to party with him ! Do not challenge him ... and do drop the occasional piece of flattery !

The steely female OX

Quiet, conservative, and strong, describes the Ox lady. They are seldom sentimental and rarely romantic. Possessed of an iron will and a vivid sense of responsibility, Ox women are also self disciplined and high principled. Think of women like Maggie Thatcher who achieved success in her own right as Britain's Prime Minister, and Barbara Bush the immensely popular wife of the former US president, and you will get a good idea of their persona. In public, they come across stoic and possessed of a steely determination, taking their life, their work and even their hobbies very seriously. In their work, they face all challenges with characteristic resolve. In their roles as wife and mother, they place family needs above their own. Virtuousness and righteousness are important to them - often to the extent of becoming judgmental and intolerant of what to them is silly behavior ... like idle gossip, mindless chatter and stooping to low class cheating and dishonesty. OX women hold on to their high ground with great resilience !

Do not expect great passion from the OX woman. Nor expect them to be fashionable and glamourous. Well dressed and well groomed, yes, but they are not the seductresses of the horoscope. They are uncomfortable in clingy sexy clothes, preferring sensible dressing instead. Nor are they comfortable with make up, perfumes and other cosmetic trimmings. Their charm and attraction comes from their aura of strength and reliability. They are great at soothing and reassuring those around them and are perfect mates for those in need of stability or strength. They can be domineering although this is usually viewed as *being for your own good* ! OX women make good, down to earth wives, and their homes are usually well set up and filled with sturdy exquisite furnishings that reflect their love of elegant surroundings.

To win the love of the OX lady, understand that flattery seldom gets you anywhere. Appeal instead to her practical and sensible nature. Impress her by being dependable, punctual and reliable. Talk about your ambitions, and hold out the promise of a secure and solid future. Rather than send flowers and perfumes for her birthday, buy her presents she can find a use for. At all costs do not try to dominate her. She is not impressed with the macho types. For her, actions speak louder than words. Appear to be action oriented. Demonstrate your feelings for her rather than write poetry or send her frivolous cards. Her sense of humour is limited. And she has little time for that kind of romantic nonsense ! Finally, do not criticize her, especially when she is in the wrong. She can be unforgiving when made to lose face. Let her deal with any of her so called shortcomings herself ... in return she will make you very happy with her quite outstanding brand of initiative and leadership. She is someone you can definitely rely on !!

The WOOD FEMALE OX

Probably the most formidable of the OX women, the wood element relentlessly compounds all the attributes of the OX character. Here is a female who is tough, strong and domineering, capable of brushing aside weaker mates and taking full control. Both Maggie Thatcher and Barbara Bush are wood OX ! This OX is also usually very capable and quite brilliant. Think carefully before challenging or engaging them in combat. Far better to go with the flow and gracefully let them take charge !

The FIRE FEMALE OX

She is probably less understated, and definitely more impatient than the rest of her OX sisters. But she is less formidable. The fire element introduces an element of passion and excitement to an otherwise subdued and heavy duty character. She also plays her cards close to her chest, but she is less restrained, and occasionally, could even be enticed to be more forthcoming and demonstrative of her feelings. But remember she is nevertheless an OX and therefore *has* to be in charge !

The EARTH FEMALE OX

Here is a female who is self possessed and very confident of herself. The earth OX is more glamourous and a touch more flamboyant than other Ox females. Think of Paloma Picasso, Ivana Trump and Whoopi Goldberg. They pursue their goals with characteristic determination and intense hard work, and they are resilient in the face of adversity and difficulties. Earth Ox women seldom give in without a fight. They can be relentless and are possessed of great patience. They are also clever. Don't mess with them !

The METAL FEMALE OX

She comes across warmer and more charismatic than her Ox sisters (e.g. think of Princess Diana) but she is just as steely and can be just as tough. Prone to bouts of depression, she nevertheless has the ability to rise above it, and work horrendously hard at overcoming setbacks and tribulations. The metal OX can be generous to a fault but wrong her, and she will never let up. Forgiveness is not part of her make up, so tread warily with her.

The WATER FEMALE OX

She is strong and fearless and has a long fuse. Water Ox females are more gentle and probably kinder than her Ox sisters, but she is equally tough underneath. She is also more understated and patient, exuding an outward calm that can be reassuring. She hides her thoughts superbly, and is usually reserved and secretly sentimental. But cross her, or in any way betray her trust, and even if it takes years, she will get her revenge one day, plotting and scheming behind the scenes. A water Ox seldom forgets.

 The understated OX gentleman

He is the strong silent type, the sort of man who plans and plots his moves carefully; who thinks things through before speaking his mind, and who is hard and tough under the skin ! He is very sure of himself and is clear about his ambitions and what he wants from life. At his worse he could be quite ruthless as he works his way through life, and even at his best, his sense of superiority will show through. OX men are clever, often brilliant at what they do, and they usually rise to positions of leadership quite easily. OX men are never to be trifled with, or under estimated, although their calm, quiet and understated exterior often encourage people to do so. Some of this century's most feared men are OX ... think of Saddam Hussein and Adolf Hitler, and you will get a feel for the kind of toughness and ruthlessness that is part of the latent character of the OX male.

OX men are seldom obvious or showy. They are also not great conversationalists, preferring to observe from a distance and merge into the background, but engage them in conversation and you will find them enormously interesting and full of substance. This is because OX men read widely and have quite brilliant intellects. They are not particularly warm or loving. Neither are they especially sentimental. They dislike frivolity carried to excess, and are averse to obvious shows of grandeur. What they respect and respond to is genuine knowledge and a matching intellectual capability. They like people who are sure of themselves and they identify with those who express themselves with clarity. There is nothing vague about the OX gentlemen, yet he is generally a man of few words. For him actions speak louder than words.

Like his female counterpart, he is not especially romantic, but he can be passionate and is capable of quite extraordinary loyalty and great love. With those he loves, he is extremely generous. But he seldom gives diamonds or furs. His gifts of love are far more tangible and practical, a house, a car, a piece of real estate ! To win him, you do not need to play the coy temptress. Nor is it necessary to flatter him or stroke his male ego. He will only suspect you of being false. Much better to meet him head on; let him know how much you respect and admire his intellect, and do be very genuine about it. And refrain from being too obvious. OX men do not find aggressive females attractive. They are also too macho and too clever to succumb to cheap seductive tricks. They also dislike possessiveness in a mate, since OX men do indulge in quite profuse sexual activity outside a relationship. To them, sex is not necessarily the same thing as love ! Thus they can be physically unfaithful, yet be convinced of their fidelity. And they are fiercely loyal and protective of their wife and family. Their declarations of love are often genuine., and their strength can be utterly spellbinding.

The WOOD MALE OX

Ruthless to a fault the wood OX man is crafty, wily and brilliant ! He is ambitious and unrelenting in the pursuit of his ambition. Let no one stand in his way ! He is also exceedingly eloquent and is a gifted politician but the wood OX does tend to bring out passionate hatred in those who get stamped on by them. Often authoritative and domineering, here is a man who does not suffer fools gladly. Nor can he stomach disagreement or criticism. If you want him, be prepared to bend to his will !

The FIRE MALE OX

This OX is supposed to be less ruthless than his other OX brothers; yet Saddam Hussein is a fire OX ! Perhaps the passion of the fire element does ignite the vigorous toughness of the OX character ... nevertheless, he is impatient, more so than OX of other elements. And he has strong endurance and resilience. To those he loves however, he can be exceedingly generous and protective.

The EARTH MALE OX

This *very down to earth* OX tends to be a perfectionist. The earth OX male is unrelentingly ambitious, completely confident, and quite impossibly autocratic. He could be tender and soft inside but it takes a fair bit of digging to find these aspects of him ! Earth OX have strong endurance. They are meticulous to a fault, and highly disciplined, pursuing their goals with almost single minded resolve. Fiercely protective of those he loves, he can be rough on those who cross him. The Prime Minister of Malaysia, Dr Mahathir, is an earth OX.

The METAL MALE OX

This OX has great staying power and quite tremendous dogmatism in his approach to life and living. He tends to be stubborn and uncompromising in his attitudes, and is quite impossibly difficult to live with, being also critical and quite unimaginative. He is also monstrously hardworking and expects all who work with him to demonstrate similiar industry and determination. Steer clear unless you are of a like mind.

The WATER MALE OX

He can seem dull at first meeting, coming across slow and ponderous. But the water element does imbue this OX with a certain amount of lightness that can be attractive.. Like his OX brothers, he works hard and relentlessly pursues grand ambitions, but perhaps with less single-minded vigour. He is thus laid back and more relaxed, and certainly more realistic and more sensitive to alternative viewpoints. This is perhaps the most attractive of the OX men, simply because he does respond to simple affection, and is even capable of demonstrating a certain amount of tenderness !

 The mesmerizing lady TIGER

Desirable, adventurous and brave, the tiger lady oozes sex appeal. Often brazen and impulsive, they dash through life with fervent zeal, constantly on the lookout for new thrills and spills. Tiger women are ferociously exciting creatures, unshackled by rules and fiercely independent. Theirs is a passionate existence, and everything they do is lavishly heaped with emotion and enthusiasm. Their attitudes are often extreme. For them there are no half measures. It is almost always a *do or die* situation with them; an *all or nothing* approach which endears them madly to some and totally puts off others. Thus there will be tiger females who appear twice as dramatic as the dragon, or three times as obstinate as the ox. They can also be extremely crafty and wily, especially when it concerns a pet project or sweetheart of the moment. But TIGER females are also highly vulnerable, and often become victims of their own flamboyant passions. Because they are easily bored, they move from one relationship to another, desperately seeking love. Plus, their innate honesty can blind them to potential dangers. As a result they often fall victim to unscrupulous and manipulative men. And when confronted with rejection, they stay crushed and broken ... until the next great love comes along ! Think of the tragic lives of Christina Onassis and Marilyn Monroe.

Relatively speaking, Tiger women usually have few financial worries. They are good at making money, being both creative and imaginative. But they are also fun loving and adore the good life so that they often squander away hard earned cash without a second thought !

To win the heart of the Tiger woman, appeal to her sense of excitement. Think up creative ways to spend the time of day. Be flamboyant. Wine and dine her. And be as passionate and as ardent as you wish. Tiger females do not understand subtlety, so do be direct. Don't waste time hinting or sending signals or playing games. Be straight, be frank and be obvious about your intentions, whether or not they are honourable. Tiger women are not necessarily out to land a husband. For her *le grand passion* sounds as enticing as a marriage proposal. But Tiger women can and do make devoted and responsible wives and mothers. They may be unconventional but they are protective and capable of making great sacrifice for loved ones. Just do not expect great tenderness or huge warm hugs from them !

Traditional Chinese parents generally do not approve of sons marrying Tiger females, believing them to be unlucky ! They also believe that the ferocity of the Tiger spirit could well cause untimely deaths for their sons. Personally I think this is pure superstition !

The WOOD FEMALE TIGER

For sheer excitement and activity, very little can match the company of this hyper energetic lady ! In her company, you will never be bored. Indeed you could be mesmerized by waves of mad behaviour that send ripples of anticipation down your spine ! She is totally unconventional and full of fun ideas. She is charming, temperamental and flamboyant, and unless you can keep up with her mood swings and impulsive propositions, better to stay clear. But if you want her, be manipulative. Flatter her, cajole her, appeal to her passionate nature, and she'll lap it all up !

The FIRE FEMALE TIGER

Women born of the fire element are no less vibrant or charismatic as her other Tiger sisters, but she tends to mellow as she grows older. Ruled by her heart rather than her head during adolescence and teenage years, she matures gracefully although her sensual and passionate nature never quite cools. Fire element tigers are probably the most resilient of all, and for sheer guts and staying power, they are hard to beat. They are excellent to have beside you in times of adversity.

The EARTH FEMALE TIGER

The calming influence of the earth element makes this Tiger less headstrong and impetuous than her Tiger sisters. She is definitely less impulsive, using her head as much as her heart when making decisions. But she is wildly passionate and adores the excitement of a love affair, although she is less carried away by the pleasures of the boudoir than her more gullible sisters !

The METAL FEMALE TIGER

Probably the most conservative of the Tiger ladies, here is a woman whose principles and convictions translate into meaningful action. She is more of a strategist than the rest. She is also an optimist and she has a compassionate nature, but to causes rather than to people. She can also be cold and chilly once love flies out the window. But she is magnetic and once under her spell, it is hard to pull away. If you love her be prepared to work alongside her harmoniously. Do not fan the flames too intently.

The WATER FEMALE TIGER

Probably the most appealing of the Tiger women because the water element adds great charm to her nature, transforming this passionate creature into someone loving and worthy of admiration and respect. Water Tigers are stable and serene and hence more powerful. They are neither as vain nor as vulgarly ambitious as other Tigers and are hence much nicer and charming. But beware the explosive temper that lies underneath calm waters. Bask in her love and friendship but play fair with her !

 The dazzling TIGER man

Noble, action oriented and possessed of a magical aura of excitement, the Tiger man is hard to resist ! Here is an energetic human dynamo who could well sweep you off your feet with his tempestuous, gutsy and passionate nature. You can almost feel the tingle of excitement each time he sweeps into your presence, because his charm is legendary, and his eloquent gestures of love quite irresistible.

Tiger guys mesmerize with their unpredictability. They are hard to pin down, and are full of tantalizing grand plans to conquer the world ! It is easy to get carried away by their sense of adventure, their obvious ambitions and their super social graces. You sense they are the sort to get things done, to achieve great things; and you find their easy disdain for social snobbery both refreshing and even enticing. And then of course, there is their air of hidden passion and sensuality ... truly the Tiger man is quite dazzling !

But Tigers have claws that can be lethal; and fangs whose bite can be quite fatal ! They can be fierce and dramatic, and they can be stubborn and vengeful as well. Think carefully and long before you fall for the Tiger ! Why ? Because, in dealing with him you will need tons of emotional resilience. Tigers need constant and lavish attention to stay close by your side. They get bored easily when not the object of your adoration. And because they are very intense dramatic people. A Tiger boyfriend or husband could leave you totally drained ! Vigorous in protecting his space, his deals, his ideas and his domain, (yes even from you) he could well wear you down with his demands. And don't expect understanding from him. It is not in his nature to be understanding.

Dealing with a male Tiger requires acres of energy. Unless yours is a sign of strength and equal vitality, he could literally kill you with his demonstrations of explosive recklessness. Remember that engaging in a superficial friendship with a Tiger is easy, and even fun ... but up close, it's another story. Just dealing with him could burn you out ! Plus ... the Tiger man will not think twice about walking out on a relationship or a marriage.. They love change, and often crave the excitement of new conquests and new homes ! And while pressure and unhappiness could cause you to lose strength, the Tiger male thrives on it. It is thus foolish to trifle with him unless you are certain you can, and want to cope. If you are, by all means go for it. Be as adventurous, as dramatic and as courageous as he is. Be sensitive to his *all or nothing* attitude. Share his majestic passion for the world class project. Participate in his grand plans to transform the world, to make a billion dollars, to reshape society ! And be hugely passionate !

The WOOD MALE TIGER

This is a man addicted to change. Vital and energetic, he is full of grand plans and seems to be always on the move. Whether planning, plotting or strategising, he craves the excitement of testing out new and innovative ideas. In his company, you will never be bored, but he could wear you out if you lack the energy to keep up. Remember that the wood element is his natural habitat. His full nature shines forth. Be an adoring and supportive mate if you want to win and keep him.

The FIRE MALE TIGER

Ah, such charisma, such passion ... and so irresistible ! Here is the ultimate male chauvinist, someone dripping with macho sensuality, and with the conviction of his revolutionary ideas. Think of Hugh Hefner who changed an entire generation's attitude towards sexuality, and John Derek, the svengali of some of the world's most beautiful women, and Edourd Leclerc, the French billionaire who built a business empire by undercutting and underselling everyone else ! If you can stay mesmerized by his zeal and his passion, woo him by being traditionally feminine. Let him be king !

The EARTH MALE TIGER

Here is a man who is wildly, madly passionate. He is an expert at seduction so beware you do not get caught prematurely. For he also loses interest fast. He loves the chase and savours the hunt, and once successful thinks nothing about walking away - often without a shred of regret or remorse. Yet once snared, he is loyal and loving, though seldom faithful. But he demands total love, and to keep him by your side, you will have to understand this. Even if you stray, constantly and loudly declare your love !

The METAL TIGER MALE

More somber and conservative than the rest of his Tiger siblings, here is a less energetic, and more thought oriented Tiger male. Although he is as energetic, and as impatient as all Tigers are, the metal element seems to lend an air of thoughtfulness which sits well on him, making him quite impossibly attractive ! To win him, recall his Tiger nature. He loves the chase, and when he has caught you he expects total submission !

The WATER TIGER MALE

Think of the delicious Tom Cruise and you see the water Tiger. He is lovable and loving; he is easily successful and just as easily admired and respected by his peers. Certainly he enjoys the kind of popularity his Tiger brothers find hard to come by. This is because he is more stable; certainly more diligent and disciplined. He keeps his passionate Tiger nature in tight rein; and hence comes across totally magnetic. To win him, you have to be beautiful and talented; sexy and passionate ! Growl your way into his heart !

 The virtuous female RABBIT

The lady Rabbit is diplomatic, tactful, and impossibly virtuous ! Hers is a life of order and security. She works at being liked, and friendships are important to her, although the rabbit woman rarely, if ever sticks her neck out for anyone. She is seldom the bearer of bad news, and she colours her interactions with one and all with well meaning optimism. But she is sensitive and considerate and very eager to please. She can also be depended upon to keep up appearances. One never finds the rabbit lady spilling the beans on family scandals or being in any way indiscreet. Indeed she will not hesitate to tell the odd white lie to preserve the status quo.

Social acceptance is vitally important to her well ordered existence, and indeed, she can and often is an inveterate social climber. She is at her snobbish best as the wife of a successful man. Appearing feminine, unassuming and modest is her forte, and she also comes across shy and sentimental. Her dressing is understated and sedate, her manners impeccable, and she has the knack for saying just the right thing at the right time. She is motivated by strong instincts of self preservation, is seldom outrageous and never blatant or aggressive..

This popular lady has a superb sense of prudence and intuition and is blessed with uncanny abilities to conform and accommodate. She is also an excellent listener and in her company you feel calm and restful. She is indeed the epitome of female modesty. But she is also probably the most materialistic of all the signs, and quite one of the most cautious.

It is no easy thing winning the heart and hand of a Rabbit woman. Indeed if anything, she will be the one to choose her mate. She is the hunter and a very clever, subtle strategist at that. Men usually adore her and see her, quite rightly as having the potential of being the ultimate supportive wife. But the Rabbit lady has quite stringent and well thought out ideas of the perfect mate. Not for her the mad passionate fling or the unstable love affair. What she wants is a good marriage, a grand home, a successful husband and a picture perfect family ... to which she will bring her considerable organizational and home making skills. She will not expect to work after marriage and even if she does, it will only be to pass her time or lend prestige to her existence. She will rarely marry anyone who has no prospects. Rabbit women are rarely ambitious for themselves. Rather it will be her husband and her sons who are the lucky beneficiaries of her very considerable networking and social advancement skills. If you are presently wooing this paragon of virtue you would do well to come across serious and clever. Take her to nice places. Be well groomed and well mannered. Do not frighten her off with mad schemes or wild ideas. And never surprise her.

The WOOD FEMALE RABBIT

She is truly the solid citizen type. Generous, altruistic and immensely diplomatic, this lady is also shrewd and exceedingly clever, especially at camouflaging her true feelings. You would never realize how self centered she can be because she is just so good at keeping her private ambitions and opinions private. The wood element intensifies her sense of tradition. Appeal to her *feel good* sensibilities if you want to get anywhere with her.

The FIRE FEMALE RABBIT

The fire element adds a bit of dash and verve to the Rabbit character. More outgoing than the rest of the Rabbits, she will seem more aloof, more reserved and even more arrogant than other Rabbit females; but she is also brilliant at stage managing relationships and her own image. If you want to get along with·her, don't fence with her. And don't play games. She is the expert at subterfuge, and will probably be far more skillful than you in ultimately getting her way. She could smilingly demolish you, and you would not even know it !

The EARTH FEMALE RABBIT

Perhaps the sexiest of all female Rabbits, here is a lady who could love you and leave you ! Candid in speech and possessed of an outstandingly keen mind, the earth lady uses her skills to huge personal advantage, without at anytime appearing to do so ! The influence of the earth element also safeguards her from ever being overambitious, overoptimistic or overenthusiastic in the pursuit of self interest. There is always the veneer of understated and virtuous elegance in everything she does. Quite a lady !

The METAL FEMALE RABBIT

The metal element adds a steely strength of purpose to this lady's otherwise easy going nature. She could have hidden agendas which stay cautiously closeted, using her considerable Rabbit like skills to create a veneer of studied modesty and diplomacy. This lady seldom acts on impulse, deliberating her actions and words carefully. Don't try to pry her secrets from her. Accept her the way she is and you will get along famously. When she decides to, she will confide in you. Not before !

The WATER FEMALE RABBIT

So proper and calm on the surface, yet so fearful inside ! This water lady has a more delicate disposition than the rest of her Rabbit sisters. Her sense of style and her good taste is more evident but she is also less devious and clever. She is totally averse to taking risks, and will do nothing to upset her well ordered existence. For her the symbols of security ... a fine home, a steady job, creature comforts et al are exceedingly important. She wants and needs looking after. Give her that and she will love you ...

# The amiable RABBIT man

Low profile, tactful and accommodating - these are some of the words that accurately describe this easy going and very nice man ! Always correct, always well groomed and always well mannered, the Rabbit gentleman will almost never offend you. He has honed the art of diplomacy to perfection, and you will never hear him utter anything negative about anyone. He is seldom confrontational, preferring to walk away from arguments or at the slightest hint of trouble.

Rabbit males often have excellent judgments, and they are very shrewd about people. They really are very good at networking. And because he is so aware of how others come across, he works at making certain his own image is impeccable. For him, impressions count for much more than substance, and this reflects his carefully hidden social climbing ambitions. He is much taken up with the trimmings of success ... the right address, the right clothes, the right friends ... all these outward shows of social success impress him, and are important to him. Thus he carefully cultivates his image, and comes across very polished and amiable. Indeed, the Rabbit male knows how to accommodate and to conform in the nicest possible way. He also knows how to lavish attention on anyone who is important to him. He is the ultimate survivor ... smooth and suave and oozing charm. But always, in a nice, inoffensive way.

But he is also clever and can be quite self centered. He is also vastly materialistic and is a genuine snob. He will not hesitate to manipulate situations and people to his advantage, although in doing so he is always extremely cautious, making certain his image is never tarnished, and always wearing a mask of amiability to hide his true intentions. See this as a masterful skill, for this is what it is ... the ability to hide one's feelings and to hold one's peace, to always come across reasonable and rationale. And never to offend. This is a man who plans his moves and charts his course very carefully. There is little room for spontaneity. But this is the way he likes it. And it is very much evident in his relationship with people.

In love, he is careful to go only for women that are deemed *suitable*, and suitability is equated with all the material trimmings. Family background, pedigree, manners, appearance and conformist behavior are vital pre requisites in his search for a wife. For him the chase must be dignified, and he is meticulous in checking out these things before committing to a marriage proposal ! If you are a sexy siren, or love fooling around with other men (no matter how innocent) you can forget about winning his hand. He abhors improper behavior. His approach to love and sex is both pristine and correct. If you find this attitude tedious and boring, let him go !

The WOOD MALE RABBIT

A real gentleman ! Here is a man who represents all that is stable and correct and rationale ... He is easy to get along with, he is kind and he provides more than adequately for those near and dear to him. Perfect husband material ! But he needs to be in control. His is a traditional view. He will work at maintaining peace and harmony in the home. But he expects support and good behaviour. Give him tranquillity and obedience and things are fine. Shame him, or make him lose face and he will walk away without a trace of remorse !

The FIRE MALE RABBIT

The fire element imbues a caustic sense of humour to an otherwise serious and staid disposition ! The fire Rabbit is less shy, and more forthcoming than other Rabbits. But although he is just as affable as the rest, he is also self centered to the point of arrogance. He can also be aloof and very reserved. When successful, he could even become quite a snob and have little time for those he deems are beneath him, yet all the while continuing to be smoothly amiable to those important to him. This guy truly is great at practicing the virtues of hypocrisy. But of course he is a survivor !

The EARTH MALE RABBIT

More stylish than the rest, this man's keen intellect is often camouflaged beneath a seemingly laid back approach to life that can be deceptive. Do not be fooled by his easy going manner. Underneath that smooth and pleasant exterior lurks a crafty mind that is both sharp and knowledgeable. The earth male makes a good mate for those who cherish conformity and outward compliance of the traditions. Behave outside the norms of social decorum, and he will treat you with disdain. Expect little sympathy from him.

The METAL MALE RABBIT

Honourable, strong and perceptive describes this metal man. He possesses steely determination and systematically implements meticulously thought out plans that map out his life and career. This is a man who will be quite madly successful. He also has good taste and an air of dignified good breeding that can be quite overpowering. Stay loyal and true to him; be scrupulously honest ... and he will pull you up with him.

The WATER MALE RABBIT

He is faithful, charming and always dignified, carrying himself with an air of refinement. This water gentleman has it all. Usually well educated and widely read, he is also an interesting conversationalist. He will work at getting ahead, and will have much to offer. But keeping up appearances is important to him. Support him in this and he will stay true to you.

 The charismatic DRAGON lady

She is so captivating and vibrant, so imperious and stunningly sexy, you cannot ignore her ! The dragon lady makes an entrance as only she knows how. Her arresting looks and haughty classiness sets her far apart from lesser mortals, and she exudes the kind of sexuality that often make mincemeat of the men who pursue her. This is the conventional true dragon woman ... and as if that was not enough she also possesses tremendous personal magnetism and a brilliant intellect. Heady stuff !

There is an irresistible air of superiority about her. Hate or love her. You cannot ignore her. Her leadership qualities are universally acknowledged. Her creativity and flair for making money are legendary. Success, good living and wealth seem to come to her easily and effortlessly. She is intimidating.

And she carries it all off with easy nonchalance. Dragon women are neither modest nor unassuming. She is not shy. She is seldom understated. And she is never self effacing. Hers is almost a fantasy biosphere where *she* is the center of attraction. She views the world as revolving around her. Yet she is rarely boastful ... yes she drops names and surrounds herself with loud and lavish luxuries ... but they seem to sit easily on her shoulders. She has class, good taste and is supremely confident. She can also be generous, and is scrupulously fair. Seldom is she tortured by insecurities.

She loves publicity. She loves to be recognized. She loves attention. She is vocal, tough, strong and independent. She will never play second fiddle to a man. Not for her a whimpering, mousy relationship where the man is completely in charge. No, she demands and often gets equal billing.

Men are mesmerized by her and many pursue her. If you fall for a dragon lady be prepared to face massive competition. She will flirt with you and entice you. She could even seduce you and make mad passionate love with you, but don't mistake it for love ... To win her, you will need to match her fiery dynamism. Massage her ego shamelessly. Never hurt her pride or burst her bubble. She does not take kindly to criticisms, no matter how well intentioned. And don't talk drivel to her. Don't gossip, don't whine. Don't try to be subtle. Laugh with her. Play with her. Party with her. Take her to smart bashes and cocktails. Hob nob with the beautiful people and invite her along. She adores the good life ... champagne and caviar are her thing ! And most of all refrain from being possessive. Dragon women cannot be shackled ... curtail her independence and she will drop you like a lead balloon. If you are the sort who likes privacy and the quiet intimacy of romantic candlelight dinners, she is not for you. Get out before you get hurt.

The WOOD FEMALE DRAGON

The wood element modifies the Dragon obsession with self, and the lady comes across warm, kind and full of goodwill. She is also clever and uses her innate wisdom to help those around her. Her counsel is valid and wise. The lady is nevertheless dramatic and extravagant. Encourage her exhibitionism tendencies and she will lavish all her attention on you. But help her when things go wrong. She cannot handle crisis very well at all.

The FIRE FEMALE DRAGON

She is the most charismatic lady of the Chinese Zodiac ! And she is also brilliant, being endowed with a powerful intellect. She is rampantly attractive and totally mesmerizing. Yet she is also vulnerable and easily hurt, presenting in effect a contradictory persona. She comes across strong, yet can be enticingly weak. She makes grand gestures and initiates massive projects, yet can get steered off course because of a fragile ego. She wants and needs support, but whoever provides it must stay behind the scenes.

The EARTH FEMALE DRAGON

She is the most charming, but also the most vindictive and dangerous of the Dragons ! Ego driven and in constant need of praise and flattery, this lady wants power and recognition. She needs to be acknowledged, acclaimed and applauded. She also demands complete and utter loyalty. Cross her at your peril for she is feisty and unforgiving !

The METAL FEMALE DRAGON

This lady is supremely, achingly ambitious ! She will let nothing stand in her way, and will go to great lengths to get what she wants. Tough, steely and ruthless, she is the epitome of the corporate big shot. She will often make tons of money. She wants power. She wants a lavish lifestyle with everyone deferring to her, and adoring her ... and she will get it all, by fair means or foul, either through her own wiles and ability or by sleeping her way there !

The WATER FEMALE DRAGON

This lady is extremely talented and creative, and often achieve remarkable success in the performing arts. She is less bombastic, and less of a show off compared with other dragon types, but she can be imperious and spoilt in her expectations. Nevertheless the water element does cool much of her ardour, and she is less impulsive and less prone to the sweeping extravagant gesture. This water lady is also intuitive and is less disdainful of love and romance. Woo her with compliments. She loves being flattered.

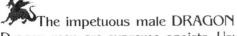The impetuous male DRAGON

Dragon men are supreme egoists. Usually charismatic and dashing, they run through life, armed with massive doses of impetuous self confidence. They have huge ambitions, and their dreams of success are usually larger than life. In their minds failure is never a possibility, so they implement plans and ideas, schemes and things with enthusiasm and great fervor. And because they are convinced that they will succeed, they usually do. Many formidable projects and deals of the Dragon man take root, grow and flourish ! Dragon men are wonderful performers and great exhibitionists. They face challenges head on, often with courage and vigour, and even when situations sour, they rise to the occasion with great fortitude. Dragons are thus described as born winners, achievers and tough guys. To the Chinese, a Dragon son is cause for celebration because he is believed to be blessed with massive doses of luck. Because of this, Dragon sons are often forgiven their brattish behaviour when young.

The confidence of the Dragon manifests itself in varying degrees of pompous and arrogant behavior, which can be exceedingly obnoxious when demonstrated in large doses ! Yet for the most part Dragon men breeze through their relationships quite oblivious to the fact that their superior attitudes may be causing negative impressions all round. Even when they behave as perfect cads, they seem totally unaware of it ! Dragon men can also be tyrannical and despotic, although oftentimes, their innate kindliness peeps through. But they demand acknowledgment of their positions of authority, being great snobs and hence terribly conscious of their job titles and social status. Sometimes the self centered arrogance of the Dragon male can become quite tiresome, but because he almost always delivers on everything promised, his monstrous ego is easily forgiven !

In love this guy is notoriously unfaithful. A relationship with him is also fraught with fights and arguments. Everything becomes an issue especially if any of his intentions are thwarted. To cope with Dragons, understand his king size ego and it will be easy. Flatter him, constantly and regularly ! Feed his need for recognition, and for an audience. Listen adoringly as he pontificates and lectures you on his multitude of talents. To be fair, he is not just hot air. There IS substance in most of what he says ... and never try to mother him. He will feel crowded by any show of maternal caring. He does not need that kind of nurturing. It only makes him feel inadequate, and he will feel hemmed in, smothered. Just sit and listen with an attentive ear to all that he is saying. And dress magnificently when he takes you out. Remember, he loves to party, and to make spellbinding impressions. He sees his mate as some kind of trophy, so play the part if you want to keep him.

The WOOD MALE DRAGON

This is the deep thinking Dragon who directs his massive intellect towards creative and artistic pursuits with great success. Flamboyant and unconventional, he is the master of the grand gesture. Salvador Dali, the spectacular Spanish artist whose sweeping canvases stunned the art world was a Wood dragon. So was the singer Bing Crosby. Applaud him loudly if your man is also a wood dragon. He needs it !

The FIRE MALE DRAGON

The fire element brings huge doses of energy to an already energetic character and the result is a dragon that is feisty, magnetic and hugely impressive. The fire Dragon's ardour and vigour drives him into schemes so grandoise and vast, it will take your breath away ! Yet his enthusiasm is also matched by an almost instinctive skill at bringing his schemes to fruition. Go for him if you have the energy to match his. He will not disappoint you. But make certain you do not also get burnt in the process.

The EARTH MALE DRAGON

His ego is massive. His passion almost frightening. This guy has an intensity that is hard to match. The earth element gives him resilience, and tons of charm. He will never lack for friends and supporters. Flatter him and he comes alive. Withdraw your support and he degenerates into depression, and he might not forgive you ! Be smart, feed his ego, because he will be loyal to those close to him, and his success will ultimately be yours too. Despite his many admirers, he needs the stability of family. Let him have it.

The METAL MALE DRAGON

This highly ambitious dragon lets nothing stand in his way. He is tough and he is rough, and could even be ruthless. He also has a huge temper, which could get out of control when thwarted. Yet he can also be affable, gentle and kind when the occasion suits him. Beware the metal dragon for he can sometimes take a perverse pleasure in playing cat and mouse with those he loves. Unless you are prepared to put up with his tantrums and dark moods, and have the strength to do so, far better to not to trifle with him.

The WATER MALE DRAGON

This dragon is gentler, kinder and more loving than the others. The water element adds a softer touch to his fiery temperament so that friends and lovers benefit from his generosity. He is however less single minded, and perhaps less confident than his other Dragon siblings. Nevertheless it would be unwise to underestimate him for he is massively talented. To win him, appeal to his innate nature. Actively boost his confidence and he will be forever indebted to you.

The tantalizing SNAKE woman

Endowed with exceptional beauty, the Snake lady is cool, alluring and dignified Her excellent manners and sensitivity often endear her to many, and her impeccable good dress sense make her exceptionally attractive.. She also has the good fortune of being unintentionally and innocently seductive, and is seldom short of admirers, often inspiring great love. Men fall madly, passionately and irrevocably in love with her. She also evokes uncontrolled jealousy and friendships with other women could be hard to come by.

The Snake slithers through life, blissfully unaware of her considerable charms, casting her serpentine spell with neither forethought nor malice. With her, it is never a case of trying to score ... the Snake is simply the Chinese Zodiac's symbol of feminine sexuality. Snake women are also exceedingly clever, and are capable of deep intellectual and philosophical thought. If they pursue academic careers they will be extremely successful. And they are wily as well. If they sometimes seem vague, it is done on purpose. This is because Snakes are really good at evading and omitting inconvenient truths. Telling white lies come easily to them. They also often skillfully colour facts with tiny embellishments. The Snake temptress knows how to mislead and misrepresent in the nicest possible way.

They are meticulous in everything they do and this gets reflected in the way they work, the way they organize their space and their social life, and most of all in the way they dress. They have expensive tastes. Not for them plastic or fakes. They want the real thing ... furs, jewellery, designer clothes, fine mansions and jet set holidays. They are often narcissistic, loving themselves shamelessly and spending hours on their appearance. Their love of luxury and langour is legendary. They adore opulence and are greedy for the good things in life ... and they are often lucky, usually marrying above their own class so that money and wealth are seldom hard to come by.

Winning the heart of a Snake woman requires patience and a genuine understanding of their nature. They should be wooed with expensive gifts and offered the prospect of a genuinely good time. They are predictable and respond favourably to being protected and cosseted. They have no great urge for independence or to fly the roost. They are neither rebellious nor do they have strong feelings about any issue. They love tradition and routine. They value security. They need the mod cons. They do not like roughing it out. Not for them the African safari, or a hike up the Himalayas. They prefer the QE2 or a luxury ski holiday. Wrap them in a warm cocoon of love and they will slither happily into your heart.

The WOOD FEMALE SNAKE

This is the dreamer of the Snake pantheon, but she is also pragmatic when it has to do with her work and career. The wood lady's burning urge to attain fame and fortune is fueled by her ambition to win universal approval ... part of the narcissism that is so much a part of her nature. But the wood element makes her vulnerable to rejection and irrational jealousies. She suffers from an acute fear of loneliness and craves popularity. To bring out her sparkle, love her and adore her, and make her feel secure.

The FIRE FEMALE SNAKE

She is the brilliant one, being deep thinking and quite masterful as she slithers her way into boudoirs and boardrooms. This lady means business ! She has strong willpower, makes friends and allies easily and glides in and out of parties and social occasions with panache. Fire Snakes can be ruthless and are definitely glamourous and clever ... a heady combination of beauty and brains. She is elusive and tough to pin down, and she will stay devoted to you only if you stay true to her. Waver, and she could quietly and coolly slither out of your life.

The EARTH FEMALE SNAKE

She is the power hungry one, a Snake whose head is full of glamourous dreams of power and wealth, fame and fortune. Think of Jackie Kennedy Onnasis and Imelda Marcos, two of this century's most outstanding earth Snakes. Amazingly intelligent and persevering, the earth snake has the uncanny ability to seek out rich and powerful mates who provide them with the power and luxury lifestyle they crave. But they can also be resilient and courageous, fighting back in times of adversity. Never underestimate them.

The METAL FEMALE SNAKE

A more powerful and resilient lady it will be hard to find. Here is a mighty talented lady whose life often gets hit by major reversals of fortune, caused by the lost of either loved ones or family fortunes but they often rise again and go on to better things. The metal snake is vulnerable to heartbreak, caused by an uncharacteristic naiveté. There is also a tendency to be a loner ... Assuage her insecurities if you wish to win her.

The WATER FEMALE SNAKE

She is a force to be reckoned with. Possessed of a huge intellect, terrific determination and the ability to plan and plot meticulously to achieve everything she sets out to achieve, the water element Snake often becomes outstandingly successful in her chosen field. Usually despite great odds. Think of Oprah Winfrey ... vanity features strongly in her nature, which can sometimes sink into paranoia, but she also has huge doses of common sense and often pulls through when wallowing in self pity.

The seductive gentleman SNAKE

Strong, silent and seductive, the male of the species is as irresistible as the female. His special appeal for women comes from his sunny disposition and pleasant manner. He is never offensive or confrontational. He seldom raises his voice or lose his temper and is sensitive to the feelings of others.

Snake gentlemen are always careful not to make waves. His approach to life is largely coloured by his instinctive philandering ways, and his success with women tend to encourage this side of his personality. He is inclined to be lazy, although he also has the ability to pursue intellectual and other pursuits with great success ... that is, if he can discipline himself to be focused and stay resolute. Indeed, if he does master the ability to stay on course and concentrate on what he does, his success potential is quite exceptional. Snakes make smashing and attractive mates, especially when they also succeed in their work and careers.

He is cautious and quite prudent, and rarely makes a good entrepreneur because he lacks the courage to take risks. Most of the time he adopts the line of least resistance, preferring to compromise and prevaricate, to hedge his bets, rather than come right out with firm and definitive decisions. He also lacks the streak of ruthlessness required in managing large businesses. In the face of aggression, he will turn away from a fight rather than stand his course. He does not see this as weakness. That is just the way he is. Indeed, most of the time he stays oblivious to acts of aggression, and even when riled, he prefers to turn a blind eye; and will not do anything that will upset his tranquil and peaceful existence.

He is a thinker more than a doer, and to those addicted to the fast lane ... to quick action and speedy decision making, the snake's sedate pace may not be for you. He cannot abide chaos and dislikes the frenzy of fast paced activities, valuing predictability and routine. He hates surprises, especially nasty ones. Plus he is not very good at handling rejection or setbacks, and his way round this is to maintain a beguilingly cool exterior. Inside, he could be hurting like crazy, but on the surface he will stay cool.

Where entanglements of the heart are concerned, emotional traffic jams and jealousies resulting from too many relationships going on at the same time can sometimes occur, and here the Snake gentleman is no gentleman at all. He deals with the situation by taking off, and seeking greener pastures elsewhere ! Women who fall for his charms should be prepared to mother him, and take the initiative in fending off the competition. If you can shield him from his own indiscretions, he will happily let you do it ...

The WOOD MALE SNAKE

He is such a skillful communicator, and so exquisite in the art of public speaking, this charming man is quite irresistible ! Especially with his special brand of understated humour. The wood element makes him resilient and pragmatic, and although he fears rejection and the prospect of being alone, his gregarious nature makes him a great social success.

The FIRE MALE SNAKE

John F Kennedy was a fire Snake, and the world knows what a charming and capable cad he was ! Fire snakes are brilliant and power hungry. Possessed of strong willpower and surrounded by adoring cohorts, this guy makes and keeps friends easily. He is also highly principled and has the courage to stand up for his convictions. He thinks deeply and makes full use of his intellectual prowess, usually to good cause, and though he finds it tough to be faithful, he nevertheless regards his wife and family with deep respect. Turn a blind eye to his infidelities if you want to keep him.

The EARTH MALE SNAKE

Here is a gentle, delicate charmer whose dreams and fantasies protect his fragile ego from the harsh glare of reality. Earth Snakes are always full of grand plans, although they lack the perseverance and determination to transform ideas into reality. But he is usually blessed with the luck to attract, and wily enough to manipulate, capable women who fall at his feet and happily give him the support and stability to see things through. If you are prepared to do the dirty work for him, and to take charge, he will present you with every opportunity to play out your maternal instincts !

The METAL MALE SNAKE

He is such a braggart ! The metal snake yearns for fame and widespread recognition, suffering delusions of grandeur and believing himself a creative genius. His *modus operandi* is built around his not inconsiderable charms, and though he is slow to trust those around him, they usually love him enough to play along, doing all the work, yet allowing him to wallow in his own self importance, and to take the credit ! Lucky lucky snake !

The WATER MALE SNAKE

Vanity, combined with a huge dose of common sense and an almost genius like ability at self promotion separates the water snake from the rest. Think of Mao Tse Tung, who made himself into a living god to millions of Chinese ! Water snakes are so clever, and so focused on attaining the heights they set themselves, they usually succeed. Stay with him. He is generous and quite prepared to share all that he has with those he loves !

The warmhearted HORSE lady

Proud, individualistic and restless, she has a natural self assurance and a unique confidence that comes from a genuine belief in her own self worth. Hers is the ultimate free spirit that should neither be broken or confined. In any case, this woman born of the Horse year can never be shackled either by conventions or any man made rules she deems stupid or unjust. Anything which seem to threaten her independence is regarded with deep suspicion. She has a mind of her own and courageously speaks out, loudly and clearly. She is nobody's fool but she is amazingly warmhearted.

And she is generous, and quite fantastically courageous. Usually the Horse woman breaks free of the family at a very young age. Pursuing her independent nature she will either indulge her thirst for adventure by exploring far away places, or she will travel to distant lands in search of new experiences. She will be restless if not allowed to pursue this wanderlust. She also needs to be surrounded by activity, and enjoys championing causes, although she often loses interest after a short time.

The Horse lady is usually highly principled. Lying and dishonesty are anathema to her. She is neither a fraud nor is she boastful, going about her life with little fanfare. But she will never compromise, always standing up for what she believes in. She can thus be idealistic. She does not require the trimmings and outward shows of success, and is disdainful of lesser mortals who seem to derive their self worth from material accessories. More than being liked, she prefers respect. She is bossy, insisting on always doing things her way but she is seldom autocratic. Nor is she intolerant of other people's viewpoints. There is always room for discussion.

But once decided, she rarely changes her mind, and can thus be dogmatic. Yet her unusual strength; her perseverance in any given situation; and her interest when confronted with challenge, often allows her to get her way.

The Horse lady is difficult to love, and hard to satisfy. Her emotional make up is complex and unstable. She tends to be hyper sensitive, being easily offended. Any threat to her independence causes her to bristle. She also lacks a sense of fun, and is intolerant of those deemed weak or superficial. Plus she can be outspoken and argumentative.. Be prepared to let her talk while you listen. Make her respect you and your views and she will quiet down. Once she respects and loves you; and sees you as someone strong and indomitable, she will buckle down and be a great wife !

The WOOD FEMALE HORSE
She is opinionated and judgmental. Highly sociable, she is a born over achiever, and she can be self centered. Because she is often blessed with a multitude of talents, and her Horse nature makes her headstrong, she runs riot in a million different directions, unfocused and quite without a real target ... hence she tends to suffer from burn out. Her boldness often skirts on foolhardiness, and because she continually chaffs at the bit, and is insensitive with people, this lady has problems finding and keeping friends.

The FIRE FEMALE HORSE
Oh dear ... She is like a volcano about to erupt. This is a rebellious and headstrong female. Everything in the horse nature gets magnified in this lady. She is a mass of contradictions, being naive and sophisticated, forthcoming and irrationally wild, greedy and generous, at the same time. But there will be those who find her stimulating and exciting. Unless you are confident you can tame her spirit without breaking it, leave her.

The EARTH FEMALE HORSE
She is far more good natured and easy going than her fire sister. She is also less impetuous, less hotheaded, less selfish, less excitable ... and definitely far more stable. The earth element adds a dose of pragmatism and she knows how to accept authority and play the game according to the rules. She is sensible and faithful and will make those who love the country and traditional family life, a very good mate indeed. But don't forget she's still a horse and if you want her, appeal to her sense of adventure.

The METAL FEMALE HORSE
She too is a tame horse. She is law abiding and serious. She does everything right, is careful about hiding her true feelings and seems to prefer a more ordered existence, although in her young days she could have been quite an adventurous filly ! Emotionally she is dignified and stable. If you love a metal horse allow for the occasional bursts of energy. Give her a long rein, and she will give you a well balanced ride.

The WATER FEMALE HORSE.
Here is a winner of a woman ! Generous, gregarious, confident, competent, adaptable and usually successful in everything she undertakes. But she can seem aloof and reserved. This is because she often opts for the cool correct behaviour which is reflected in the carriage of her head. She will not allow just anyone to get intimate with her, and true to her nature she abhors frauds and phonies. She is not easy to win over. Patience is needed to understand her complex nature. Hang in there if you love her.

The headstrong male HORSE

Independent, outspoken and eloquent, the male of the Horse species is the sporty type. He loves the outdoors and delights in fitness exercises and athletic pursuits. There is always an air of suppressed restlessness about him because he is by nature headstrong and restless, yet in public he maintains an almost elegant image of seriousness. But the non conformist underneath creates an ambivalence of behavior and he continually needs to find outlets for his impatient spirit. He is also pragmatic, respecting the traditions and paying, at least lip service to social conventions in order to find acceptance and build a sterling reputation for responsibility and hard work. Yet he cannot deny his innate honest nature, eschewing subtlety and behind the scenes diplomacy. The Horse is not a politician. He speaks his mind, maintains a healthy ego and rejects dishonest behaviour. Male horses seldom lie, being direct and straightforward in all his dealings. He does have courage of conviction, and though he lacks finesse and polish, he is nevertheless reliable. Once he gives his word, you can depend on him to stay loyal to the work on hand.

He is also a man of few words. He is neither aggressive nor does he come on strong. Indeed Horse men sometimes appear shy and even modest. But he is attracted to glamour and finds sophisticated women with painted fingernails and long hair quite irresistible. The sporty types also turn him on, and once hooked, he can be quite the fast worker ! Horse males are attractive because they can come across quite macho and strong. When in love, they are capable of doing crazy things and going all the way. They do not just like the women in their lives. They fall madly in love and often carry a torch for the same woman for years. Faithfulness comes easily to them, and when occasionally they succumb to the excitement of the one night affair, they are ridden with guilt often confess to their infidelities.

Horse men make good providers and excellent husbands. Just never try to lock them in or corner them, they need to be free and to be allowed to be in charge. They must stay the master in any love relationship. They must always have something to do. They must be kept busy. Understand all these things, and you will find it easy to keep him. To win him, use all the standard womanly wiles. Do not be *mousy* in either your dress or your behaviour. Remember the Horse is wildly attracted to glamourous women. Woo him directly. Do not come across weak and *wishy washy.* Have the patience to listen to him pontificate ... he needs a good listener. And never lie to him. He hates dishonesty and subterfuge. Be genuine and sincere and trust his capacity for understanding. Take a rational approach in all your dealings with him. He will not fail you.

The WOOD MALE HORSE

Here is a horse who has a pretty high opinion of himself, and indeed, his special brand of self centered-ness could seem quite obnoxious. Yet he is a man of substance, usually demonstrating great talent in a variety of fields; but he is also bold and foolhardy. Intolerant of fools, he cannot work well with just anybody. Often his uncompromising attitude cause him to self destruct and his insensitivity could sabourtage his chances of success.

The FIRE MALE HORSE

He is probably the most difficult Horse to get along with. Fiery, touchy and temperamental he is a mass of wound up energy. Extremely proud and opinionated, he is hard to understand and seems easily upset. This is a free spirit that spins out of control at the slightest hint of disagreement. Personal relationships often suffer as a result. Yet they are exciting and seem wildly attractive. With him, you will never be bored. But take care !

The EARTH MALE HORSE

This Horse is much more good natured and easy going. Though he can be just as skittish and impetuous, this is a Horse who seems in better control of his nerves. He is thus less excitable and certainly a lot less selfish. Often clever, he is also a survivor and holds his won counsel, even when cornered. The earth element seems to give him the ability to tone down the excesses of his Horse nature. He is the sort who will give in, in order to live and fight another day. He also makes a great mate and is most easy to love.

The METAL MALE HORSE

This Horse walks tall and dignified. He is emotionally stable, a bit of a snob, and ambitious. He conforms to society s norms and is very good at hiding his feelings. Even when riled he keeps his temper under wraps. Indeed the metal Horse wants to make it and be someone special in life. So he works at it ... but because he keeps things bottled up inside him, he could explode and suffer from nervous collapse. He needs a supportive mate who can give his pent up nature some release ...

The WATER MALE HORSE

He is confident and adaptable, and the water element soothes his restless spirit making him more relaxed and laid back. As a result he finds success in his pursuits, and enjoys the material fruits of his success. The water horse makes a wonderfully warm and fun loving mate. He is reliable, honest, highly principled and quite the best kind of friend. If he appears at first aloof and seems uncomfortable with tenderness or intimacy, don't let it fool you because, really, he has a heart of gold.

The gentle SHEEP female.

Here is a lady who comes across, gentle and dreamy. And seemingly pliable. She is always willing to please and will be the first to sympathize and commiserate when any of your plans go awry. Sheep ladies almost always avoid confrontations, preferring to let everyone win and have their way rather than get into an argument. They display this same attitude in other areas of their life. Not for them heavy decision making or the taking of sides. They prefer to let others lead, decide and take the responsibility.

Thus sheep women are rarely madly ambitious for the corporate career. But don't run away with the impression that sheep women are weak. They kill, they overcome and they overpower with their special brand of passive non resistance. They never directly humiliate or annihilate their enemies. Their way is to manipulate totally behind the scenes and they are subtle and patient. Because of this, sheep women make very dangerous enemies. Because they will confound even their worst adversaries by being so seemingly innocent and nice. Think of the concubines of the Chinese Imperial courts ... it is said the most successful in worming their way into the hearts and minds of the emperors, were those born of the sheep year. Such ingenues ! Think of Julia Roberts and Leslie Caron, all wide eyed and innocent looking !

A sheep lady is long suffering and there is no limit to what they can endure. Such inner fortitude sets them miles apart from those who give in to fatigue and obstacles. On the surface they go about their well organized lives, following dull routines and demonstrating the highest form of self discipline. And yet they can also be infuriatingly spontaneous, giving in to whims, succumbing to the catalyst of the moment, and seemingly easily distracted. When they put you out of sync by standing you up, rather than apologize directly, they will shower you instead with gifts galore ... it is all part of their charm; they break your heart with not the slightest intention in the world of doing so ... and they often appear surprised even when they let you down because of course they never intended to hurt you at all !
There is something ethereal and very beautiful about the sheep lady. They are always serene and feminine. And they never come across threatening. Sweet natured to a fault, always ready to oblige ... to win her, promise her a secure and substantial future. Show her you can and will look after her always. Marriage is important to her, but more than anything she wants material security and a life of comfort and ease. Forgive her, her flirtatious nature; she cannot help being the gentle manipulative creature she is; and do not betray her for she seldom forgets a wrong done to her. And remember, she responds to gentle persuasion, not heavy handed and abrasive behaviour.

The WOOD FEMALE SHEEP

Think of Bo Derek, this stunning beauty who openly allows her husband to make her a sex object ! Here is a whimsical, seemingly dumb blonde whose gentle smile hides a tough interior. Wood ladies are simply exquisite at using people; they are expert at worming their way into the affections of those that will be useful to them. They do not mind living off the generosity of others, and indeed will go all the way to achieve material security.

The FIRE FEMALE SHEEP

The fire element adds passion and excitement to an otherwise controlled nature. The fire lady is also excitable and exceedingly dramatic, especially when things go wrong. She needs the solid and dependable support of a strong mate to bring out her innate refined nature. She needs security, yet can be annoyingly careless with money, squandering her resources, and that of her mate without a second thought.

The EARTH FEMALE SHEEP

Here is the ultimate *femme fatale*, a lady who works (often successfully) at being the favoured love of a rich and successful man. She is often more vocal than other sheep females; gliding happily into an entire series of dependent relationships. She is able to completely rely on the support and largesse on others, yet is often able to also keep her self respect intact. This earth female's femininity is quite legendary. Think of Zsa Zsa Gabor !

The METAL FEMALE SHEEP

It is oh so easy to underestimate the metal sheep. She comes across a total pushover, innocent, simple and apparently bird-brained. On the surface this lady is all a sheep is reputed to be ... gentle, non confrontational and easy going. But the element lends a toughness of spirit, and a hard heart. She is expert at subterfuge, and is a master puller of strings behind the scenes ! She is proud and sensitive. Be wary. Don't hurt her.

The WATER FEMALE SHEEP

Here is the sex siren of the Sheep species ! This is a powerfully attractive lady, whose irresistible charm and intuitive skills in the art of flattery gets her, literary, everywhere. She is often a great social success, moving gracefully amongst high society with great ease. Nevertheless she maintains her reserve, and it will not be easy getting close to her. She prefers the company of important people; and she has her own agenda. Unless you are somebody, forget her ... she has no time for you.

The romantic male SHEEP

Cunning, manipulative and unpredictable, the male Sheep is probably the Chinese Zodiac's most crafty and insidious politician. Not for him the obvious show of strength, or the dramatic display of resources. He plays his game with the cards close to the chest, cultivating an image of dignified rectitude. He comes across placid, unruffled and seemingly vague.

But inside, he will be hatching one great scheme after another. He is extremely ambitious and in his head are great and fabulous dreams. He wants power and influence and wealth, but he is careful never to let the world know of his ambitious schemes. His strategy is almost always subterranean. He is never obvious. In business, he builds layers of protective structures that shield him from having to deal directly with anyone, and he stalks the competition patiently, cautiously. As a boss, he is never patently autocratic but he will not tolerate insubordination or criticism. Unless you have already won his respect, don't try to influence him. Far better to enjoy his benevolence .... in politics, he can be ruthless and quite devoid of scruples. For the male sheep there is no such thing as friendship or goodwill. He is ultimately relentless.

When crossed, he will not forgive or forget ... and he makes a terribly fearful adversary. But his methods are never brash or foolhardy. Instead he relies on the unexpected attack and on the art of seeming non resistance. He is insidious and totally unpredictable. He will never allow his guard down.

But in love, he is adventurous and imaginative ... and quite the romantic. If he wants you, he will get you, annihilating the competition with his characteristic and quiet perseverance.

If you want to get along with him, you must bow to his wishes. Never use emotional blackmail on this man ... it doesn't work. Instead, admire him. Tell him how much you respect him. Encourage him to share his schemes and dreams with you, and yours will be a fun and fulfilling relationship.

Don't confront him.. Don't belittle or in any way ignore him. Don't blackmail him. Don't challenge him. Instead cajole and persuade him. He will despise any obvious effort to manipulate him. Being a master at this game, he sees through subterfuge easily. But he is consistent in his feelings and is seldom a philanderer. This gallant gentleman is worth fighting for, and life with him will be peaceful and graceful !

The WOOD MALE SHEEP

Here is a less serious, more amenable sheep. He is not as ambitious as his sheep siblings, nor does he have the same steely determination. But he can be just as wily and clever. The nature of the sheep is to be cunning and manipulative, and the wood variety is no exception. His forte' lies in his immense social success. Using a combination of charm and affability he lives off his friends quite shamelessly. And they continue to love him for it !

The FIRE MALE SHEEP

Such a sensitive and romantic gentleman ! This fire specimen is quite irresistible. He has an air of quiet dignity and calm refinement which sets him apart from others. He is also blessed with a persuasive countenance that makes him extremely influential ... men and women respond positively to his style and show of substance. The fire sheep is thus easily successful. He has charisma and is often incredibly lucky. Stick with him.

The EARTH MALE SHEEP

He may not be as eloquent, or as hardworking as the others, but this Earth sheep has the uncanny ability of attracting the most wonderful coterie of friends and acquaintances, all of whom chip in and help him along. His success comes from a vivid imagination as well as a brilliant ability to get along with just about anyone. In human relations there is none more effective as him. Unless you are as people oriented as he is, think twice before entangling with this man.

The METAL MALE SHEEP

Casual and easy going, here is a gentleman who will charm you with his bohemian outlook and often disheveled appearance. This is a kind and thoughtful gentleman who is always eager to please. But don't be fooled. The metal element has given him a steely outlook. He can also be temperamental and moody. And he is definitely not a pushover, being capable of quite uncharacteristic combative behaviour. He can also be quite a show off. Be firm with him, but take it slow. He will not be hurried.

The WATER MALE SHEEP

This is the most outstanding of the sheep men ! Clever, intuitive, and intensely charming, he is the master of all that is best and outstanding of the sheep nature. He is a survivor and will rise to great heights, no matter what his background circumstances. He looks innocent and simple, almost childishly lovable but he is a ruthless manipulator. Think of John Major, the British Prime Minister who survived so many attempts to unseat him, and you will get a feel for his brand of understated politicking !

The delightful MONKEY lady

Unconventional, gracious and hospitable, the Monkey lady is a delightful and entertaining friend.. Extremely generous (almost to a fault) and a great hostess, she tends to be a sweet busy body, always busy solving everyone's problems. She is seldom boring, always full of gossip and anecdotes ... yet she is never intentionally malicious. Monkey ladies have opinions about everything and everyone, but hers is a fun filled attitude where everyone is viewed as an ally and a chum. She is tolerant of other people's shortcomings, is rarely over critical or judgmental. No matter how you offend her, she will not hold a grudge against you.

Plus she has a beautiful sense of humour and has the ability to laugh at herself. She is a very good sport indeed. As well as a most loyal friend. She will never bad mouth anyone she knows. Her spirited approach to life stops short of sarcasm or biting retorts. Her jokes are seldom at anyone else's expense; she is just a most delightfully nice person.

But she is hard to pin down. Often unconventional and quite undisciplined she tends to be disorganized and is not very good at keeping to schedules and things like that. She is not a great planner or a plotter, and yet she does have a most natural flair for cunning. She can be slippery, and is hugely quick-witted. Like a will o wisp, she will slip through your fingers if ever she feels threatened. And any attempt to confine her, or lock her into an untenable situation will make her take off. The Monkey lady cannot abide by anything which constrains her independence or her freedom. But instead of letting you know directly, she will perform a disappearing act

This lady also has a fantastic memory for details. Though not the most efficient of people she is nevertheless meticulous in her work, and is excellent as an editor or accountant. Very little escapes her eagle eye and small things going awry can occupy her attention to the extent of seeming petty. She can also be penny wise and pound foolish, expending enormous energy on the small amounts and the small things around her.

Appeal to her sense of fun and her love of excitement and glamour. Woo her with pretty gifts, candlelight dinners and small romantic touches. She loves being loved. If she seems at times eccentric, don't mind her. Let her own nimble brain sort out her own little foibles.
And when her facts get a little crossed, causing her to feel frustrated, and a little depressed, leave her be as well. She can cope, and will almost always come to her senses. The Monkey knows how to pick herself up each time she stumbles.

The WOOD FEMALE MONKEY

The gorgeous and supremely talented Diana Ross is a wood Monkey. She epitomizes all that is stunning about the species. Much of her hectic schedule and jetsetting lifestyle reflects the busy wood Monkey's many commitments to friends and business associates. Here is a social creature who is enormously entertaining and a good natured, social climbing phenomenon who will always be surrounded by people. If you like partying and socializing, stick with her ! You'll have a ball !

The FIRE FEMALE MONKEY

Such a glamourous and stunning female ! The fire element lends extra drive to an already smouldering character. She is ambitious, dominating and hugely imaginative. Her energy levels are high, and for her, the thrill of the chase is what makes life exciting. Here is a trendsetter *par excellent*, a free spirit consumed by a fierce passion for life and a smouldering need for power and influence. With her your life is both exciting and intense.

The EARTH FEMALE MONKEY

This is definitely a sentimental and more serious female who is loved and consulted for her wisdom and insights. It is easy to like and respect her enormously, for she has a view of the world that is both jolly and inspirational. She is achingly romantic, and adores the intrigues of a love affair. Her heart is as big as anything and she lavishes a great deal of tenderness and affection for those she loves. But she is a perfectionist, and is much too intense. Get her to relax a let down her guard.

The METAL FEMALE MONKEY

She is the tough one; being feisty and hostile. She is also cunning and crafty when put on the defensive. Like their siblings they are sociable and gregarious, and they love travel, but they tend to melancholia. There is an air of tragedy about them, and when despair sets in, which is not uncommon, they often get caught in a spiral of depression. The metal element seems to compound the dark negative side of the Monkey nature.

The WATER FEMALE MONKEY

Elizabeth Taylor is a water Monkey ... beautiful and talented, a star who never played the role of prima donna. Unselfish, and totally supportive of her man, here is a witty, clever and resourceful Monkey ... a glorious survivor who meets with disappointment yet picks herself up again and again, each time getting stronger. She epitomizes ultimate femininity, the type who is strong yet gentle; seductive yet vulnerable. If you love a water Monkey, woo her with diamonds and a great passion, and she will swoon at your feet. Make certain she is never bored however, for she will leave you if she finds herself with nothing to do. She needs to be busy. Challenge her !

 The impudent male MONKEY

Here is the most extravagant suitor of the Chinese Zodiac ! He will woo you with diamonds and sapphires,; serve you the best champagnes; buy you the best furs; take you to the most expensive dining rooms of the world and fly you first class everywhere ! He is the master of the extravagant gesture. Monkey men are so generous they will give you everything they own; but they will never give themselves, or their freedom. Monkey men guard their independence jealously. It is easier being his girlfriend than his wife. Legal commitments and marriage contracts scare him half to death, so that the best way to *catch* him is to be really good at pretending that you don't want to !

The Monkey gentleman is generous, outrageous and loud ! He loves the sound of his own voice and is happiest when he has an attentive audience. Prone to spending sprees and impulsive binges, he will happily lend money to a friend in need, but will balk at extending his palm out for help. He would rather suffer in silence than lose face by admitting to any financial difficulty. He is warmhearted and gives of himself with no ulterior motives. Indeed, the Monkey is often unrelentingly obvious. He wants only to be well thought of and to be liked. He may be crafty as hell, but never to get the better of you ... only to get himself out of scrapes !

He is also quite funny, never taking himself too seriously. In business he is a fantastic risk taker, often getting himself into a bind as a result. But being a Monkey he also has the supreme ability to wriggle out of difficult situations and tight spots. Indeed he is crafty and wily; and he survives as much by his wit as by his unerring charm which never fails him. The Monkey male often has a boyish appeal that attracts the maternal instinct of women, and the paternal instinct of men ... saying much for his immense social skills. People like him enormously because at face value he almost always comes across trustworthy and seemingly deserving of help.

If you are in love with a Monkey gentleman, you will have to understand his enormous appeal for one and all. But he is not a jealous lover, and is quite undemanding. He neither needs nor craves flattery. And he does not lean overly much on his mate for support, being quite independent and perfectly capable of looking after his own well being.
But curb any instinct you may have to smother him with too much loving. If he even suspects for a minute you are out to snare him, he will take off. Be subtle when wooing a Monkey. Let him take the initiative, and give him the opportunity of planning your outings and your times together. He does not like aggressive and domineering females !

The WOOD MALE MONKEY
Here is a man literally oozing with charm and good intentions. He is the ultimate social climber with the consummate skill of moving gracefully through a roomful of strangers with total ease. He comes across superficial mainly because most of the time he is. The wood Monkey is not one for deep friendships. Intimate relationships make him uncomfortable. There are traces of insecurity in his behaviour, but he knows it and accepts it; so he seldom takes offense, even when teased by those who laugh at his name dropping and transparent efforts to cultivate socially prominent people.

The FIRE MALE MONKEY
He has drive and ambition and a more focused outlook. Here is a self starter whose enormous energy and fertile imagination could well propel him into the stratospheres. He is an achiever, he wants to have a good time. And he craves excitement. This is not an innocent guile-less socialite. Here is a man of substance, who will be driven to excesses even as he climbs the ladder of opportunity. He can be ruthless; is deeply passionate and go to great lengths to achieve his ends. Be wary of this one.

The EARTH MALE MONKEY
He is a more perceptive, calmer personality. The Earth element makes him scholarly and thoughtful, and indeed he makes an excellent teacher being both ingenious and creative in the way he presents things. He is often popular and has an attractive sense of humour. His sentimental view of the world makes his approach to love and romance attractive to the opposite sex. And in this his Monkey nature makes him something of a Don Juan. You could well get sleepless nights if you shack up with an earth monkey !

The METAL MALE MONKEY
Macauley Culkin is a metal monkey. Cute, totally adorable and quite impossibly sweet, this man can sweet talk his way into anything. Though argumentative, he has a winning demeanour, and this often hides dark motives and even darker thoughts. The metal male can be resentful of other people's success, and sibling rivalry could bring out the fighter in his nature.. If and when this happens, he can be a formidable adversary.

The WATER MALE MONKEY
Such a swell guy ! The water Monkey is delightfully clever and witty. He is just so wonderful to have around ... being fun, gregarious, spirited and affable. This man is highly popular, being generous both in spirit and in kind. The water Monkey is helpful and supportive, and unlike his darker metal sibling, rarely hostile or vindictive. He tends to be wildly sexy, and often gets attracted to temperamental fiery females.

 The purposeful ROOSTER lady

This is a resourceful, extremely practical woman whose organizational talents are legendary; who is forthright and frank, and who literary struts through life, supremely confident, unbowed convention and comfortable with both prestige or power. The rooster lady is loyal , devoted to those she loves ⁻ friends or family ⁻ and is the sort who will go to great lengths to protect her roost. But she rules this same roost with a heavy hand, expecting her attitudes and her feelings to be reciprocated, or else ... ! Roosters love deeply, and when disappointed develops a veneer of protective shield against those who have hurt her. She rarely wears her heart on her sleeve, preferring to suffer in silence and carry on as if nothing has occurred. Rooster women take life seriously; and they are terrifyingly efficient and purposeful. They have little patience for those who prevaricate, give excuses and otherwise appear purposeless and lazy. They are equally disdainful of impressive rhetoric that is not backed with solid substance, dismissing such people as frauds. They also hate snobs and are distinctly unimpressed by social climbers.

When challenged, she responds head⁻on, often adopting a confrontational approach, plainly taking the tiger by the tail and rarely, if ever, mincing her words. In short she comes across forbidding and hard .... as a result of which she is very often misunderstood and even disliked. The truth is, neither her words, actions or intentions are malicious. She is not a vindictive person. She merely lacks the diplomatic skills which seem to come so easy to others. She makes insufficient effort to control her temperamental outbursts, often showing annoyance in the most intimidating fashion. But don't corner her. When her back is to the wall she will lash out, and she can be crushingly cruel. The Rooster is one powerful lady !

Inside however, she is as kind as can be, seldom holding grudges or scheming to get even. Plus she is one person who seldom suffers from imagined wrongs, and indeed can be quite forgiving. She can also be sentimental, and when touched by love, or when she meets someone she vastly respects, her toughness gets mellowed and she becomes a lot nicer, and also a lot more diplomatic. Professionally, the Rooster woman is multi talented. There is nothing she cannot do well, hardly a career she cannot succeed in. She pursues self sufficiency and independence resolutely, often placing work above family. She appreciates things that are tangible. Not for her empty declarations of love and romantic poetry. She likes cars and yachts and real estate. She tends to attract weaker men, but it is the strong she will die for ! Win her respect if you really want to forage deep into her heart. Stand up to her. Impress her with the substance of your intellect and your bank account.

The WOOD FEMALE ROOSTER

She is a strong persevering female. Think of Dolly Parton, Goldie Hawn and Bianca Jagger, hardworking women who demonstrate vigour and enthusiasm in the pursuit of their careers. They are efficiency experts who are great at expressing social niceties, and also quite adept at diplomacy. But they seldom reveal their true feelings. They are rarely original, but give them something to improve on and their brilliance shows forth. Make her relax and hang loose. When she does unwind she is lovely !

The FIRE FEMALE ROOSTER

Complex and passionate, the fire element lights up the Rooster's temperamental nature. This is a lady raring for a fight She thrives on arguments, taking joy in demolishing lesser mortals. She is also impulsive and headstrong and is often her own worse enemy. Yet she can be emotionally fragile. She needs and wants close friends. And she is a great pal to have on your side. Like the phoenix, this lady rises from the ashes repeatedly. Nothing will keep her down for long. She is a survivor ...

The EARTH FEMALE ROOSTER

She is an elegant fowl indeed. Quick-witted and clever, hers is a penetrating mind that effectively sifts out the chaff to find the substance. Nothing fools her. Her powerful memory is awesome and her knowledge of all things quite intimidating. Here is a female who will shine and shine in a structured corporate environment where all the support systems are in place. In love she avoids anything sentimental. She resolutely wants to stay down to earth.

The METAL FEMALE ROOSTER

Here is the ultimate performer. She thinks she is always on show, and has to somehow come across impressive. She blows her own trumpet a lot, not because she is egotistical or needs to impress others, but only because of her naturally boastful nature. There are those who love to be entertained by her flamboyance, and enjoy her company. You either like her a lot or you cannot tolerate her ! Go for her if extrovert behaviour appeals to you.

The WATER FEMALE ROOSTER

Probably the most attractive and substantial of all the Roosters, this water lady is multi talented, adaptable and terrifically attractive. She pampers her appearance, works hard at everything she takes on and surrounds herself with beautiful people. She makes a fabulous boss, a true benevolent despot; and often makes it to great heights of success late in life. She has secret ambitions to be as rich as Croesus, though wealth almost seldom comes easy. She needs to work for it. Water roosters have a seductive streak that make them quite irresistible.

 The resilient male ROOSTER

This very macho and masterful male is the epitome of *the outward appearance person* ! Like the Rooster that he is, he truly does enjoy strutting his stuff for all to see and admire ! There is a studied elegance in the way he stands and carries himself, and the way he reacts to situations. Yet he is no empty Beau Brummel and he most certainly is not a clothes horse. There is substance to this man !

The Rooster male is frightfully clever; very productive and even quite surprisingly creative. They think deeply, are capable of superb analysis and often have tremendous organizational and management skills. Indeed they make great CEO's of large corporations. Rooster bosses are methodical, highly responsible and play closely by the rules of the game. They are just and fair, but tend to have favourites. Power sits easily on them, as does the odd subterfuge, although they are not, by nature the scheming type. Rooster males are not very good at playing political games, being too direct and too transparent. Honesty is one of their more obvious traits and this is often also their greatest weakness, because they tend to be loudly righteous about it. Most of the time, they keep their thoughts under wraps, but in dealings with people they often express their opinions in no uncertain terms. This tendency for being outspoken and blunt sometimes get them into serious situation conflicts; but they are resilient when they get steered off course or when things go wrong. In most cases they successfully pick themselves up again, even though bruised and in difficulty.

In love, this man tends towards infidelity. He can love several women at a time without a twinge of conscience. If you love such a man, your emotional stability could get quite seriously injured. The Rooster male is unrelenting when it comes to breaking hearts; indeed there are those who take a perverse pleasure in doing so. He is a passionate and skillful lover, but with this man it is mainly physical. Do not expect him to whisper sweet nothings into your ear. Don't expect sympathy and mostly do not expect him to hug you when you need it most, His needs will often take precedence over yours. It has nothing to do with the depth of his love; this is his nature. When you are ill or unavailable, you can expect him to fly the roost in search of gratification elsewhere. Unless you are clever enough, and sufficiently strong emotionally, think twice before hitching yourself to him. Having said that Rooster men will seldom permanently desert their family. While you cannot expect any emotional support from him, he is nevertheless a good provider. Keep him by your side by playing along with him. Accept the complexities of his emotional makeup.

Be patient and loving. In time he might respond.

The WOOD MALE ROOSTER

Wood Roosters are singularly *image* oriented. *Face* is extremely vital to this man's make up and he will go to great lengths to maintain appearances, especially as it applies to his physical countenance. He is an outspoken man, but will rarely reveal his true feelings. He will often keep his own counsel, preferring to remain silent even when he may be riled. But he is sociable and amiable, and makes a sincere friend.

The FIRE MALE ROOSTER

This is a bad tempered fellow indeed. The fire element lends friction and explosiveness to the Rooster character, and this manifests itself in a tyrannical and despotic rage when crossed. He lacks the stability of the other element Roosters, and is often emotionally irrational as well. His ego is inflated and needs a lot of stroking. If he can settle down however, this Rooster can be a great friend and a most amusing companion.

The EARTH MALE ROOSTER

This gentleman has a penetrating wit, a great intellect and a gift of the gab. He is direct and very focused. He also makes a great team player, and can usually be found working with people in large corporations or in committees, planning, organizing, and implementing. The earth element seems to be good for the Rooster. Neither too impulsive nor over enthusiastic, this male is also less showy than his more flamboyant siblings.

The METAL MALE ROOSTER

He has such tremendous charm and so much bottled up vigour, being in his company is a genuine experience. Women find him intensely attractive; men seek out his company. The metal Rooster is often the elegant soul of the party, holding forth eloquently, and with great style. He is extremely suited to the theatre where his skill at giving dramatic and impressive performances will hold him in good stead. A great guy !

The WATER MALE ROOSTER

Conservative and often old fashioned, the water Rooster is less rigid and forthright than the others. He is gregarious, eager for companionship and full of good intentions. The water element seems to make this Rooster suffer from feelings of inferiority, and this could prevent his innate self confidence from showing through, thereby seriously impairing his chances of success, either at work or in love. If he can overcome this serious defect, the water Rooster is a joy to know and love. If you want this truly delicious man, understand his basic insecurities; encourage him vigorously and you will bring out all that is strong and productive in him.

The generous DOG lady

Agreeable, self effacing and shy, the Dog female comes across quiet and introspective. Often a loner, always low profile and not terribly sociable, she drowns herself in work and is most comfortable when engaged in some charitable and noble purpose. She is generous, happily giving her time to those around her and dutifully fulfilling her chores, meticulously and with great fortitude. The Dog woman is often naive and innocent. Her world is wrapped around *feel good* causes. To her everything in life is serious, and there is little room for frivolous pursuits. She is neither materialistic nor very ambitious, being profoundly convinced that it is always advisable to be sober and careful, punctilious and correct. As a result she seldom takes risks, and could even be said to be dull and frightfully boring. Most of the time she appears nervous. especially when her in bred pessimism makes her expect things to go wrong.

Despite the tendency at negativism however the Dog lady is genuinely nice and touchingly candid and sincere. She makes the dearest friend possible., and it would be difficult to find a more loyal or helpful ally. It is just that she can be so righteous in her view of the world. She takes great pride in being honest, faithful and proper, sometimes to the extent of being *holier than thou* in her attitude, all of which can come across quite tiresome.

This lady is always worrying. She is always fearful and panicky. As a result her whole attitude is one of anxiety. In any given situation, you can depend on her to list out all the things that can go wrong. In the company of courageous and foolhardy people she will tend to come across as that dreadful *wet blanket*. Yet she really cannot help herself.

She requires a great deal of emotional support and loads of tender loving care. Her heart is fragile and like marshmallow. On top of which she is often naive in matters of love and romance. It is really quite easy to take advantage of her easy trusting nature. Often she knows it and will find herself a powerful mate to protect her from the big bad world. Think of the lovely Sophia Loren who lived under the protection of her powerful husband, Emotionally, the Dog woman develops maturity late in life. And when she does, she might well devote herself to a cause that means a lot to her. Think of Brigitte Bardot and her animal foundation.

But the pessimism is all pervasive and most Dog women cannot shake it off. As a result many end up alone, as spinsters or favourite aunts ! Unless she can find a mate who is prepared to invest massive doses of nurturing to strengthen her emotional make up.

The WOOD FEMALE DOG

She is profoundly affectionate, a real sweetheart, warm and caring and totally reliable. In fact she is so meticulously dependable you tend to think she is a pushover. But she truly is not. She is basically a giver, but she gives only to those she cares for, and to causes she believes in. Hers is a strong conviction but she is never motivated by material gain, nor by the promise of recognition. She has to believe in what she is doing and when she does, she brings to it, all her formidable doggedness to see things through.

The FIRE FEMALE DOG

Here is a modest and idealistic lady whose sincerity and earnestness endear her to many. The fire element imbues her with an eloquence that is persuasive and even influential, and when blessed with good luck this brilliance makes her a compelling spokeperson for her favourite causes. But when success eludes her, she can spiral into a dangerous vortex of addictive behaviour and suppressed rage. She feels things much too deeply and needs to lighten up. Otherwise she could veer off course.

The EARTH FEMALE DOG

She is reserved and secretive and uncomfortable with crowds. She avoids parties and heavy social occasions where she feels decidedly out of place and awkward. The earth lady is hypersensitive, and her view of the world is coloured by a deep seated conviction that everything will always go wrong and because she believes it so strongly, things usually do go wrong for her. She does try to be adaptable and will usually respond positively to someone strong and loving.

The METAL FEMALE DOG

This lady has a bark and a bite ! She is the dame with the confidence to accomplish great things .. climb Mount Fuji, find a cure for Aids, revolutionize the education system ... the metal element adds sparkle to her idealism and spurs her to action. She is choosy but loyal, and will growl her way into your heart ... but take care, she is not to be trifled with.

The WATER FEMALE DOG

She is quite terrifically beautiful, with a slight air of aloofness that says it all. She is the hardest of the Dogs to know and is more aware of her pedigree than the other element dogs. She can be aggressive, but not vicious or malevolent. Her bark is worse than her bite. As a friend she is as loyal as all dogs, but it is not easy getting close to her. She has an instinctive internalized spirit of self preservation which she rarely lets down, and unless she has researched you, chances are she will keep you at arms length. But break through and she will overwhelm you with affection.

The faithful male DOG

Affectionate, faithful and loyal, the male of the Dog clan wears a sober, droopy countenance that reflects his pessimistic view of life. Here is a man who is cynical of the world. He whines and growls a lot, often about the multitude of wrongs, injustices and tragedies that befall mankind. Yet unless he is possessed of a strong dose of energy, he seldom does much about it. He prefers to pontificate rather than do something to change the world, unless of course his element gives him the sorely needed courage and determination to do so. For of course the dog gentleman does lack courage. Indeed, he is usually very risk averse. He is fearful and nervous, sometimes verging on a paranoia. There is also a defeated look about him, as if the burdens of the world are just too much to bear.

But the dog male is fastidious and industrious. He does work well, and he can rise to great heights when sufficiently motivated. But this is often the exception rather than the rule. This is because he is seldom ambitious, and he has no great yearning for that pot of gold at the end of the rainbow. He prefers to stay cocooned in his own self righteousness rather than join the hot pursuit for material success. Once he reaches a plateau in his career he is quite content to spend his days researching, analyzing and criticizing the ills of mankind.

What is important to him ? Justice ! The environment ! Human rights ! Global warming ! The rain forests of the world ! All the lofty and noble causes of today's world. Yet he is no visionary. He supports all of these causes from the armchair. And he will pontificate, loudly and with a certain eloquence to all who will listen. But will he stick his neck out, take risks for the cause, or die for his principles ... most certainly not. The dog is not martyr material.

But he is loyal and a great chum. He makes a devoted friend and a most affectionate companion. At a personal level he is the ultimate giver. In his personal relationships he goes for the overkill and could quite easily overwhelm you with his acts of benevolence.. He is appreciative of every little kindness; meticulously indebted for every small favour; and profuse in his gratitude. He fears rejection with a passion and works at all his friendships. In any relationship he is comfortable only when he is the giver and you the taker. But he needs loads of re assurance. If you are his girlfriend he expects daily doses of tenderness, love and care. And you better keep every promise you make, because he is a hypersensitive soul, and will read unintended slights into it, if you don't.

The WOOD MALE DOG

He is your best friend, your complete ally ... the loyal chum ... the faithful subordinate ... the trustworthy partner. He can be relied upon absolutely. But the wood dog abhors all things underhand. Play fair and straight with him and he will reward you with long term service and loyalty. This wood man often becomes a great success in later life. Theirs is a self made success and the climb to the top will have been achieved through industry and conviction. But he is sensitive and fragile so treat him with TLC.

The FIRE MALE DOG

He is an uncompromising champion of the underdog. Well meaning and feisty this fire male's idealism is often naive and quixotic. Yet he plods along, unfazed by any cynicism or opposition he may encounter. When and if he does give up, he could be a broken man. The fire element's influence on the idealism of the Dog species can be that deadly. Cool his passions by redirecting his energies to other causes. Alter his pessimism with down to earth positive behavior. Soothe his nerves by teasing him.

The EARTH MALE DOG

Michael Jackson is an earth dog. Note how he makes brilliant music and gives stunning performances ... and then goes back to his California sanctuary to recoup. Look at his well meaning attempts to take on causes, to love children ... and then see how he gets physically sick at the way his good intentions have been transformed into court suits against him ! A typical dog tale indeed. This earth man needs solitude and peace. He lacks the bite of his other Dog siblings.

The METAL MALE DOG

This is the dog who has the bite, as well as the bark, and both can be equally painful. He is also the cleverest and most likely to succeed amongst his Dog siblings. The earth element gives him the confidence and strength and perseverance to marry his idealism with action. This dog does not just talk. He also delivers. He does not whine. He growls. Plus he is a great conversationalist and a superb mixer. Do some research if you want him. Find out what he believes in strongly ... there will surely be something ... then go with the flow.

The WATER MALE DOG

He is affable and amiable, a real good friend. But his good intentions often border on being meddlesome and he is frequently taken advantage of. He is extremely handsome but often lacks courage and self esteem. Water dogs tend to be impetuous. Theirs is a false bravado. They need strong mates. Motivate him with a sense of self worth and he could well start to sparkle. Otherwise he could sink into a well of pessimism.

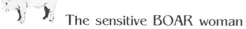 The sensitive BOAR woman

These lovely compliant ladies make the best girlfriends! They are delightfully compassionate, devoted to your well being, affectionate and supportive of all your hair brained schemes, and instantly forgiving when you wrong them. Little wonder they are well liked and popular. According to the Chinese, Boars are born to receive and yet in truth they are always giving ... of their time and their friendship, and often of their money as well.

The Boar lady almost always nurtures her friends, piling them with gifts, obliging them with favours; and running little errands for them, even at some sacrifice. And everything done graciously and with a smile. It is little wonder that the Chinese of olden days almost always welcomed the Boar girl as wives into their household. It seems like it is part of their nature to be good, to be caring and to serve. They tend however to be naive and gullible and often fall prey to unscrupulous cads. As a result they are frequently misused.

Particularly in matters of the heart, boars tend to take a fantasy view of romance, dreaming of the dashing prince in shining armour, and often being stubbornly naive and refusing to see anything but goodness in the men they love. They appear to be in love with love, and this artlessness cause them to fall for just the wrong sorts of guys. When wronged however, they are seldom vengeful. Yes they might rant and rave for the first couple of days but it is not in their nature to aggressively hit back. And when they are taken advantage of, boars merely shrug it off to experience.

Boars have a passion for food, and are often gourmet cooks. They also love opulence and luxury, and because they are frequently blessed with a good deal of money luck (they either inherit or marry into money) most boars have the wherewithal to indulge their sumptuous tastes. Boars are comfortable at dinner parties either as guests or as the hostess. They adore hotshot famous names and will often go to great lengths to have the titled and the famous invited to their homes ... if only to be able to talk about it afterwards. Boar women are incurable name droppers. They love being able to indulge in this sort of social pastime. But boars guard their friends and lovers jealously. They are possessive and will not share. Theirs is an exclusive right and if there is one thing they take umbrage with it is if you try to *steal* their friends. Or boyfriends. They can then become quite petty and competitive. Yet even then, they are guileless, and will seldom demonstrate any vindictive or bitchy behaviour. Boars really do shy away from confrontation and quarrels. At worse they will drop you from their guest list and quite literally cease being your friend. Be very aware of the boar's sensitivity if you want to woo her.

The WOOD FEMALE BOAR

She is the most considerate and compassionate of the Boars. Kind hearted and sweet natured, she gives of herself to friends and colleagues with an outpouring of kindness which can sometimes go to extremes. She can also be excruciatingly shy and extremely self effacing. She is home based and oriented, and in love is timid, requiring loads of encouragement. She will seldom take the initiative. If you want to woo this lady make your intentions clear. Don't be put off by her seeming non response. She is merely being shy and reserved and this is her intrinsic nature.

The FIRE FEMALE BOAR

She is the more aggressive boar. She is energetic, obstinate and has fixed and rigid ideas about how she wants things done. Fire boars tend to be fervent idealists and they love taking up arms on behalf of some seeming social injustice. She also loves being the silent but powerful one in a successful partnership. You can depend on her full and whole hearted support in all your endeavours if she is married to you. She doesn't want or need the limelight. She just needs to believe in you. But she can be a nag !

The EARTH FEMALE BOAR

Here is a female who can be really hard to live with. She always starts with the best of intentions, and with an idealistic view of how relationships (and the state of their world) ought to be ,,, but when the reality of situations upset her view of things, she will stomp and rave and make your life quite miserable. She can be coarse in her speech and quite pointed in her attacks ... but she is often lucky as well. She does attract doormat types who accept her for what she is, sulks, grumbles and all !

The METAL FEMALE BOAR

She is honest and forthright and has impressive personal integrity. Unlike some of her boar sisters, she is always rational and unemotional, and it is easy discussing things with her because she always allows for the alternative point of view. She strenuously avoids confrontations and prefer to reach quiet consensus rather than argue things through. In a stalemate she will give in and back off gracefully. She is not ambitious, either for herself or her mate. She prefers to live a life of quiet contentment.

The WATER FEMALE BOAR

The water element makes an already sweet-tempered female even more amiable and calm. She is seldom headstrong and never gets carried away by strong feelings. She is level headed, sane and has quite excellent manners. But she is neither sophisticated nor does she yearn for the materialistic life style. Water boars need to have friends, and though she is seldom gushing about those she cares for, she is always loyal.

 The perceptive male BOAR

This beautifully opulent gentleman truly inspires confidence. Everyone likes him, and thats because he is so perceptive, so sensitive to the feelings of those around him, and so willing and eager to make everyone feel comfortable. They are also delightfully self effacing, always giving way and never ever being at all aggressive. At its most extreme boar men appear meek and always seem slightly apologetic And there is nothing sinister or sarcastic about their good nature, they are sincerely and genuinely nice guys !

And like his female counterpart, the male boar loves opulence. When he is thus surrounded by the security which luxury represents, the boar man's confidence soars, and it is this sense of well being that brings out the best in him. He will then perform wonders and even surprise one and all with some quite surprising outcomes.

But when things don't work out his way, the boar male finds it hard to cope. His tendency is for him to turn on himself. He will blame and flagellate himself, feeling guilty and depressed at his own stupidity. Yet if his downfall is caused by any mistake on his part ... like trusting the wrong people, or backing a bad investment ... seldom will the boar have learnt his lessons. He will repeat his mistakes ... again and again.

The boar male is not very trusting of all and sundry, and in love he is slow to enter into a relationship. In other words he is neither impulsive nor does he succumb easily to the wiles of women. But he is successful with the opposite sex, and he plays his game slow and steady.

To win this amiable character, mother him mercilessly. He just adores being smothered, being treated like a child again. Cling close to him, and tell him again and again how you absolutely cannot live without him. His underlying lack of self esteem requires daily doses of reassurance.

Professionally, the boar is very industrious and productive. Contrary to popular view the boar is not lazy. He works hard and is capable of serious commitment to the work at hand. In business he tends to be lucky, and though his naiveté sometimes makes him vulnerable to unscrupulous types he usually pulls through and has little difficulty making money. He also has good taste in personal grooming as well as in the design of his work and living spaces. This is a man worth going for !

The WOOD MALE BOAR

This gentleman is both bashful and shy, and he needs loads of practice and much encouragement to take the initiative in friendships and relationships. He is no social butterfly, and indeed strenuously avoids occasions where he may be required to make idle conversation and introduce himself. He is distinctly uncomfortable with emotional outbursts and scenes. Be gentle with him. He cannot cope with aggressive behaviour.

The FIRE MALE BOAR

This boar is more forthcoming and energetic than the others. The fire element imbues him with spirit and courage. As such he does tend to be more self centered and opinionated, and can be stubborn and recalcitrant. Fire boars make excellent powers behind the throne, and can be counted upon for loyal and faithful support. He prefers to bask in someone else's glory rather than be in the limelight himself.

The EARTH MALE BOAR.

This gentleman tends to be obvious in his interface with people. He doesn't know the meaning of subtlety. Sometimes his lack of sophistication makes him come across as something of a country bumpkin, but he plods on, quite oblivious to criticism. He is the sort who can take nasty jokes directed at him ... but he usually has the last laugh, because success does come easily to him. And he is so refreshingly guileless.

The METAL MALE BOAR

This is a really nice rational sort of man. His life is well ordered and he follows the traditions and the conventional way of doing things. He is definitely unadventurous and much prefers the well trodden path. His is a practical and pragmatic view of life and he can also be dogmatic. Usually reserved and retiring, he shuns the spotlight, and will prefer being an anonymous nobody. Accept his low profile ways ! Don't try to change him. Mother him if you want to ... he will respond to the homebody act, but don't try to push him to do what he doesn't want to do. He will resist.

The WATER MALE BOAR

A diplomat if ever there was one, and a clever diplomat at that, This boar is ambitious and quite power hungry, but he works from behind the scenes, and he moves with little fanfare. The water boar is a born *big picture* man. He is idealistic and a visionary. His ambitions have nothing to do with materialistic gain. He literally wants a better world ! Think of Henry Kissinger and you get a feel for what this man is like. Not every water boar can achieve what Kissinger has, but at any level, this gentleman has the same noble aspirations and also the same kind of drive.

64 HOROSCOPE COMPATABILITIES
THE AFFINITY TRIANGLES

In the Chinese Zodiac of earthly branches, there are four major groupings of compatibilities, where people born under each of three animal signs are believed to exhibit generally similiar characteristics, and therefore tend to think alike. They may not necessarily do things the same way, nor have the same energy patterns, the same courage, or the same kind of self confidence; but because their thought processes are similiar they will tend to get along, and are said to be supportive and good for each other. They may also have vastly different natures but their actions will tend to complement and bring out the best in each other. Pairings, partnerships and marriages between any two animal signs within any of these triangle of affinities have a better than even chance of success.

These triangles of affinities are summarized below.

THE COMPETITORS The RAT, The MONKEY and The DRAGON

They are all action oriented, highly competitive, positive and determined individuals. But the RAT is massively insecure requiring the DRAGON's courage and supreme self confidence. The DRAGON is headstrong, and needs the craftiness of the MONKEY or the RAT's astute eye for opportunity. The MONKEY is fueled by the DRAGON's enthusiasm and buoyed by the RAT's intelligence.

THE INDEPENDENTS The HORSE, The DOG and The TIGER

These are the free spirits of the Zodiac, emotional, subjective, highly principled, impetuous and restless. The HORSE is the strategist but he needs the TIGER's impulse to get started or the DOG's determination to see things through. The TIGER's ferocity needs to be tempered by the DOG's good nature, while the HORSE's restless spirit requires an outlet which the TIGER provides or the calming influence which the DOG can give.

THE INTELLECTUALS The SNAKE, The ROOSTER and The OX

These are the thinkers, the visionaries and the pragmatists of the Zodiac. They are purposeful, confident, resolute, and generally have formidable capabilities, as well as tenacious, unwavering and strong personalities. The OX is rock solid and stable but will benefit equally from the SNAKE's charm and smooth diplomacy or the ROOSTER's flamboyance. The SNAKE is crafty and ambitious but will go further if helped along by the OX or the ROOSTER, and the ROOSTER's forthrightness will be tempered by the seductive Snake temperament or the OX's stable approach

THE DIPLOMATS The RABBIT, The SHEEP and The BOAR

These are the cooperative, soft sell, low profile types. They are sensitive, sympathetic, sociable and eager to please. These are not risk takers, nor are they madly intellectual or crafty. They provide each other with tender, loving care. The RABBIT's astuteness safeguards the SHEEP's generosity, while the SHEEP benefits from the RABBIT's sense of priorities. The BOAR's strength complements the RABBIT'S strategic thinking and the SHEEP'S more gentle approach.

 RAT/DRAGON

An absolutely delicious marriage

This union brings together the vital energy of the dragon and the resourcefulness of the Rat, each efficiently enhancing the other's strengths and capabilities. The Rat will admire and be drawn to the Dragon's dynamism, and will happily draw both inspiration and strength from the Dragon's exuberance and enthusiasm, in the process assuaging his or her own sense of insecurity. There will be trust and belief in each other, and neither will be jealous of the other. The Dragon is the *big picture* person, content to leaving all the tedious details in the hands of the capable and ingenious Rat. At the same time, the Dragon's lack of guile will be more than made up for by the Rat's more crafty ways. Together they will make a handsome and magnificent pair and go very far indeed.

The influence of the Elements

The Rat's natural element is water while the Dragon's natural element is earth. In the cycle of element relationships, earth is said to destroy water, yet together, earth and water provide the ingredients for plants to grow. In this relationship therefore it is the Dragon that will have the upper hand, and indeed should be the dominant partner. It is the rat that must look up to the Dragon and cheer him/her own. Because they have a natural affinity to each other, the Rat will be willing to play this role, and there will be no fear of things going wrong.

If the Dragon is an earth dragon i.e. the year of birth is 1928 or 1988 the earth element could be too strong. A pairing with a water rat (i.e. born in 1972) could be difficult but as the years of birth signify, this is unlikely since there is a sixteen year gap.

Dragons of marriageable age are those born in 1964 (wood dragons 32 years old in 1996) or 1976 (fire dragons 20 years old in 1996)
Rats of marriageable age are those born in 1960 (metal rats 36 years of age in 1996) or in 1972 (water rats 24 years old in 1996)

In any cycle, the rats will be older than the dragons, and it is conceivable that the rat will be the male and the dragon will be the female ... in this relationship the male must be prepared to give way to the female ! Meanwhile a pairing between a fire dragon and a water rat introduces the additional elements of extra water for the rat and fire for the dragon. This pairing is not ideal since the double water of the rat could exhaust the dragon. However it could still work because the fire creates earth hence strengthening the dragon. It is thus still a workable match !

RAT/MONKEY
Fun and games on a roller coaster ride

These two highly compatible individuals will have a roaring good time. The Rat's shrewd nature will find ready sympathy and acceptance with the Monkey's equally audacious sense of fun. Wrapped in their own materialistic world, they share the same values and pursue the same ambitions. They will be mutually admiring of each other's guile and methods, and will enthusiastically applaud each other's accomplishments. Equally clever and similarly ingenious, they will work well together furthering a match quite literally made in heaven. One will tolerate the other's foibles. They will share the same jokes, strive for the same goals and boost each other's confidence. Together they will accomplish much !

The influence of the Elements

The Rat's natural element is water while the Monkey's natural element is metal. In the cycle of element relationships, metal is said to produce water. One therefore supports the other. In this relationship it is the Monkey that supports the Rat. Indeed, the Rat will more likely exhaust the Monkey ! But because they have a natural affinity to each other, the Monkey will be willing to play this role, and he/she will do much to bolster the rat's flagging confidence and insecurities. In other words the Monkey will give strength to the Rat In this pairing, either party can be of either sex for things to work.

Monkeys of marriageable age are those born in 1968 (earth monkeys 28 years old in 1996) or 1980 (metal monkeys 16 years old in 1996)

Rats of marriageable age are those born in 1960 (metal rats 36 years of age in 1996) or in 1972 (water rats 24 years old in 1996)

In any cycle, the rats will be older than the monkeys, and it is conceivable that the rat will be the male and the monkey will be the female ... in this relationship the female must be prepared to support the male, and she most definitely will ! Meanwhile a pairing between a metal rat and an earth monkey introduces the additional elements of metal for the rat (excellent) and earth for the monkey (not so good) . This combination causes the additional metal of the rat to boost his intrinsic nature, while the additional earth for the monkey could create some problems for the rat. This is because earth is said to destroy water.

A metal monkey and a water rat union is excellent. Both the heavenly stem and the earthly branch of the two horoscopes match perfectly !

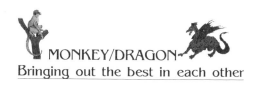

MONKEY/DRAGON
Bringing out the best in each other

These are two high performers whose combined energy and resolute determination will be hard to beat. The Dragon's grand plans find ready acceptance and support from the ambitious Monkey; and when things go wrong as they invariably will, the Monkey's guile and shrewdness will invent solutions for getting them both out of their tight spot. The Dragon admires the Monkey's ingenuity ... nay, is mesmerized by it, while the Monkey ardently admires the Dragon's courage and strength. Together, this formidable pair is not to be trifled with especially since their natural affinity make them natural allies. In business, their teamwork and cooperation brings out the best in each other. In love, they will inspire and excite each other. This is potentially an unbeatable match.

The influence of the Elements
The Dragon's natural element is earth while the Monkey's natural element is metal. In the cycle of element relationships, earth produces metal. One therefore supports the other. In this relationship it is the Dragon that supports the Monkey. Indeed, the Monkey could well exhaust the Dragon, unless he gets extra doses of earth, or is helped along by fire ! Their natural affinity to each other makes the Dragon quite willing to play second fiddle to the Monkey. It will not be at all surprising for the Dragon to quite adore the Monkey in this union !

Monkeys of marriageable age are those born in 1968 (earth monkeys 28 years old in 1996) or 1980 (metal monkeys 16 years old in 1996)

Dragons of marriageable age are those born in 1964 (wood dragons 32 years of age in 1996) or in 1976 (fire dragons 20 years old in 1996)

In any cycle, the dragons will be older than the monkeys, and it is conceivable that the dragon will be the male and the monkey will be the female ... in this relationship the male must be prepared to support the female, and he most definitely will ! A pairing between a wood dragon and an earth monkey introduces the additional elements of wood for the dragon and earth for the monkey. This combination causes the additional wood of the dragon to cause him some problems (because wood destroys earth); but the additional earth for the monkey will reinforce the dragon.

A marriage between the fire Dragon and the metal Monkey strengthens both equally, and this is deemed auspicious. The elements are well balanced, and both sides benefit.

SNAKE/OX
A deeply abiding love match

Theirs will be a mutually enhancing relationship. The powerful and dependable OX is irresistibly drawn to the seductive and ambitious Snake who in turn finds the Ox's strength comforting and attractive. Both are able to see and appreciate the synergy inherent in a pairing, and the support they give to each other will intensify the relationship as years go by. In terms of control the wily Snake exerts a greater influence over the Ox but it will be the Ox who will be the one to publicly accomplish great things, although he/she will forever stay under the spell of the Snake. Theirs is a relationship that will be immune to outside interference and the commitment they give to each will be strong and abiding. This will be a love match that grows healthier with the years.

The influence of the Elements
The Snake's natural element is fire while the Ox's natural element is earth. In the cycle of element relationships, fire produces earth. One therefore feeds the other. In this relationship it is the Snake that supports the Ox. Indeed, the Ox could well exhaust the Snake unless he/she gets an extra dose of fire, or is helped along by wood ! Their natural affinity to each other makes the Snake quite willing to play second fiddle to the Ox. It will not be at all surprising for the Ox to totally adore the Snake in this union !

Snakes of marriageable age are those born in 1965 (wood snakes 31 years old in 1996) or 1977 (fire snakes 19 years old in 1996)

Ox of marriageable age are those born in 1961 (metal Ox 35 years of age in 1996) or in 1973 (water Ox 23 years old in 1996)

In any cycle, the Ox will be older than the Snake, and it is highly probable that the Ox will be the male and the Snake will be the female ... in this relationship the female must be prepared to support the male, and she most definitely will ! A pairing between a water Ox and a fire Snake introduces the additional elements of water for the Ox and enhances the fire of the snake. Here the Snake will have a lot of fire indeed, but luckily the Ox (being earth) will exhaust the Snake's fire, and water will cool down the flames. There is thus good balance of the elements in this match. If the Snake in question is born in the summer months, this Ox will be even more suitable to counter the effects of the additional fire influence, but if the Ox is also born in the summer months, the pairing could be fiery !

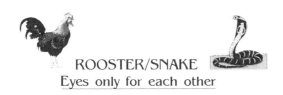

ROOSTER/SNAKE
Eyes only for each other

These two think alike, have similiar tastes, and simply adore each other. In this relationship, the Snake is the planner, the strategist and the one with the eye for the main chance. But it will be the Rooster who has the tenacity, the decisiveness and the skills to take productive action. Together however they make a powerful pair. The Rooster will listen to, and admire the Snake's ingenious schemes, and with characteristic efficiency and hard work will transform all their grand plans into reality. Both individuals have formidable intellects, and while the Snake is intuitive, the Rooster is practical. In business, they are hard to beat. In love they stay devoted and true to each other. A very passionate pair indeed !

The influence of the Elements
The Snake's natural element is fire while the Rooster's natural element is metal. In the cycle of element relationships, fire destroys metal. One party is therefore clearly dominant. In this case it is the Snake that dominates the Rooster. Their natural affinity to each other however makes the Rooster more than willing to bow to the Snake's clearly more superior role. It will not be at all surprising for the Rooster to totally succumb to the Snake's considerable charms !

Snakes of marriageable age are those born in 1965 (wood snake 31 years old in 1996) or 1977 (fire snakes 19 years old in 1996)

Roosters of marriageable age are those born in 1969 (earth Rooster 27 years of age in 1996) or in 1981 (metal Rooster 15 years old in 1996)

In any cycle, the Snake will be older than the Rooster, and it is highly probable that the Snake will be the male and the Rooster will be the female ... in this relationship the female must be prepared to support the male, and it will be the male who will be clearly dominant !
A pairing between a wood Snake and an earth Rooster introduces the additional elements of wood for the Snake and earth for the Rooster. In this example the additional wood feeds the Snake's fire enhancing the energy of the Snake. At the same time, the earth element also enhances the Rooster's metal. Both parties therefore become stronger. The pairing becomes more volatile. All the good and all the bad between the two will get enhanced. This will be a match that will either be explosively successful or they could exhaust each other to death !

ROOSTER/OX
A match made in heaven

Such a sensible and supportive pair ! Both individuals are practical, stoic, prepared to sacrifice for the greater good ... and both so ambitious and so determined to make their partnership, and/or their marriage work ! There's will be a home or a business where everything runs like clockwork; where the efficient hand of the Rooster is clearly in evidence and where the influence of the Ox's down to earth taste in furnishings and decor are everywhere in sight. The patient Ox puts up with the Rooster's tendency to take control and dominate, and the Rooster's pragmatic attitude appreciates the Ox's seemingly tedious prevarication. The Rooster understands the way the Ox's mind works and accepts that the Ox cannot be rushed. Theirs is a long term and successful commitment to each other.

The influence of the Elements
The Ox's natural element is earth while the Rooster's natural element is metal. In the cycle of element relationships, earth produces metal. One party is therefore clearly supportive of the other, and in this case it is the Ox that supports and provides for the Rooster. Their natural affinity to each other however makes the Ox more than happy to do so, and the Rooster clearly enjoys the role of the taker in this relationship. Indeed, the Ox is likely to quite hero worship the high flying Rooster !

Ox of marriageable age are those born in 1961 (metal Ox 35 years old in 1996) or 1973 (water Ox 23 old in 1996)

Roosters of marriageable age are those born in 1969 (earth Rooster 27 years of age in 1996) or in 1981 (metal Rooster 15 years old in 1996)

In any cycle, the Ox will be a lot older than the Rooster, and it is highly probable that the Ox will be the male and the Rooster will be the female ... in this relationship the male must be prepared to support the female, and it will be the male who will have to be the more patient, being older and more important because the elements dictate so !
A pairing between a metal Ox and an earth Rooster introduces the additional elements of metal for the Ox and earth for the Rooster. Here the metal enhances the Rooster, and at the same time, the earth element also enhances the Rooster's metal. The Rooster clearly rules. The match works purely because the OX is delighted to let the Rooster dominate !

 DOG/TIGER

Quite adorably perfect ?

Here we are talking about a totally darling Dog and an equally engaging Tiger ! Both have volatile tempers and can get quite angry, but their natural affinity becomes evident when together, and although they may get annoyed with each other, they never stay so for long. The Dog understands the Tiger's impetuous nature completely, and is quite happy to stay indulgent. The Tiger meanwhile comprehends the Dog's altruistic and cautious nature and does not resent being reined in occasionally. Indeed there is a great deal of mutual respect in this relationship and the ferocious Tiger becomes a pussycat with the Dog ! It is an adorable match !

The influence of the Elements
The Dog's natural element is earth while the Tiger's natural element is wood. In the cycle of element relationships, <u>wood destroys earth.</u> One party is therefore clearly dominant of the other, and in this case it is the Tiger that dominates and is in control. But here the Dog does not mind. Their natural affinity softens the Tiger's touch and the Dog is content to let the Tiger be in charge.!

<u>Dogs</u> of marriageable age are those born in 1970 (metal Dog 26 years old in 1996) or 1958 (earth Dog 38 years old in 1996)

<u>Tigers</u> of marriageable age are those born in 1974 (wood Tiger 22 years of age in 1996) or in 1962 (water Tiger 34 years old in 1996)

In the cycle, the Dog will usually be older than the Tiger. In a match between the <u>metal Dog</u> and the <u>wood Tiger</u> it is likely that the Tiger will be the female. In this case the elements have given the male Dog the metal element which controls the wood of the Tiger. This strengthens the Dog considerably (note that metal destroys wood), and enhances the match between the two.

A match between the <u>earth Dog</u> and <u>water Tiger</u> is excellent and balanced. This is because wood destroys earth and earth destroys water, so there is balance between the two. A match between the <u>metal Dog</u> and a <u>water Tiger</u> is not as balanced because the additional elements cause the Tiger to be hurt. The Dog's metal wounds the Tiger's wood while the Dog's earth damages the Tiger's water.

DOG/HORSE
Durable and solid but a trite dull ?

Such an endearing couple. These two individuals have perfectly compatible temperaments. Theirs is a peaceful home where there will be a noticeable absence of fireworks and bad tempers. They give in to each other most of the time, both being sensible and rational human beings. There is cooperation and communication between the two, and even when the Horse occasionally gets restive, it does not affect the relationship since the Dog is able to understand and is prepared to listen. Neither will attempt to dominate or compete with the other and their natural affinity makes them trust each other implicitly. At work, the Horse will be the more aggressive but the Dog is happy to let the Horse take the lead. In love, the two will be devoted to each other, being neither possessive nor interfering of each other's space.

The influence of the Elements
The Dog's natural element is earth while the Horse's natural element is fire. In the cycle of element relationships, fire produces earth. One party is therefore clearly supportive of the other, and in this case it is the Horse that supports and provides for the Dog. Their natural affinity to each other however makes the restless and headstrong Horse more than happy to do so, and the Dog sits back and enjoys the Horse's loving generosity !

Dogs of marriageable age are those born in 1970 (metal Dog 26 years old in 1996) or 1958 (earth Dog 38 years old in 1996)
Horses of marriageable age are those born in 1966 (fire Horse 30 years of age in 1996) or in 1978 (earth Horse 18 years old in 1996)

In the cycle, marriages between the Horse and the Dog can have either party being the male or the female. Thus a female metal Dog (26yrs) could marry a male fire Horse (30yrs) or vice versa. This pairing is quite auspicious because the elements tend to work for both parties. The metal exhausts the Dog to some extent but the double fire of the Horse produces more earth thereby strengthening the Dog ! The Horse is the more aggressive but the Dog happily copes with and accepts it. The elements are in favour of the match working.

A match between an earth Dog (male 38 years) and a fire horse (female 30 years) is excellent for the Dog, since fire produces earth. In this match the wife born of the Horse year is extremely lucky for the Dog husband !

Note: These two might not appear to get along at first, but as they get to know each other, they will develop a genuine relationship.

 TIGER/HORSE

An auspicious and volcanic passion ?

These two are kindred spirits ! Their impulsive, restless, and energetic nature gel perfectly, and they have a deep and perfect understanding of each other's temperament. They will fight and argue and then make up with intense good humour. These are two fiery and volatile temperaments ! They are equally happy travelling through the Sahara desert or climbing the mountains of Nepal. Both are free spirits, unshackled by anything unconventional, and their individual courage complement each other.

They will share great adventures together. In business they are both magnificent risk takers, and in love they share a passion only they can understand. This is a high voltage relationship.

The influence of the Elements

The Horse's natural element is fire while the Tiger's natural element is wood. In the cycle of element relationships, <u>wood produces fire.</u> One party clearly supports the other, and in this case it is the Tiger that supports the Horse, and who will bring substance and sustenance to the relationship. But the natural affinity between the two fuel the Tiger's enthusiasm, thereby increasing his productivity and strengthening his resolve.

<u>Tigers</u> of marriageable age are those born in 1974 (wood Tiger 22 years of age in 1996) or in 1962 (water Tiger 34 years old in 1996)

<u>Horses</u> of marriageable age are those born in 1978 (earth Horse 18years old in 1996) or 1966 (fire Horse 30 years old in 1996) .

In the cycle, the Tiger will usually be older than the Horse. In a match between the <u>wood Tiger</u> and the <u>earth Horse</u> it is likely that the Horse will be the female. In this case the elements have given the male Tiger additional wood which supports the fire of the Horse. But the Horse's new earth element exhausts its fire thereby making it easier for the Tiger ! It is indeed an auspicious pairing !

A match between the <u>fire Horse</u> and <u>water Tiger</u> is strengthens the fire element in the Horse and also strengthens the wood element of the Tiger. This is because water produces wood. The elements are thus balanced and the match is equally auspicious.

<u>Note:</u> Friendships between these two might not appear at first to be feasible, but as they get to know each other, a solid relationship could well emerge.

 SHEEP/BOAR

Happy, mellow and smooth together

This has to be one of the sweetest pairings of the Chinese Horoscope. The natural affinity of the Sheep and the Boar is reflected in their genuine concern and patience for each other. The sensitive Sheep nature finds sustenance, comfort and love from the Boar whose broad shoulders willingly enfold the Sheep in a warm cocoon of love. Nor is the Sheep merely a love object; indeed the two find pleasure in working and planning their life together. The earthy Boar admires the Sheep's gentle and classy disposition. They both have healthy appetites and are equally generous. In love they enjoy simple pleasures with neither going off on a tangent or succumbing to outside distractions. Loyalty features prominently in this relationship and it is one of the most compatible of the horoscope pairings.

The influence of the Elements
The Sheep's natural element is earth while the Boar's natural element is water. In the cycle of element relationships, earth destroys water. One party is clearly in control, and in this case it is the Sheep who dominates the relationship. But the natural affinity between the two smoothes the interactions between them, and the more aggressive Boar gives in easily to the subtle and understated Sheep. That it is the Sheep who will dominate this relationship is not surprising, since the Boar is neither as clever nor as worldly wise as the Sheep. Indeed in this union it will be the Sheep that steers the Boar out of dangerous waters, and the latter accepts it with a smile and with good grace !

Sheep of marriageable age are those born in 1979 (earth Sheep 17 years of age in 1996) or in 1967 (fire Sheep 29 years old in 1996)

Boar of marriageable age are those born in 1972 (metal Boar 24 years old in 1996) or 1959 (earth Boar 37 years old in 1996) .

In a marriage between the Boar and the Sheep, the chances of either party being male or female are about even. In a pairing between metal Boar and the fire Sheep, where the male is likely to be the Sheep, he is strengthened by the fire element while the female Boar too is equally strengthened by the water element. The pairing is thus auspicious for this match.

Similiarly, in a match between the earth Sheep and metal Boar, both parties are also strengthened equally and the match is likewise auspicious.

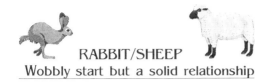

RABBIT/SHEEP
Wobbly start but a solid relationship

This is a partnership between two beautifully matched individuals who will make fantastic music together. The normally secretive Sheep will open his or her heart to the astute and diplomatic Rabbit.; and the Rabbit will skillfully draw out all of the Sheep's latent and hidden talents via a combination of tender care and genuine loving. A hazy combination of encouragement coupled with outstanding motivational skills on the Rabbit's part, draws out all that is best in the Sheep. As a team therefore this two work well together and they achieve much, whether it be in constructing and growing a business or in building a comfortable and loving home. In terms of temperament also, the Rabbit is able to soothe and comfort the Sheep's tendencies towards despondency and depression, in the process injecting tremendous zeal and confidence to his/her mate. Truly a great match.

The influence of the Elements
The Sheep's natural element is earth while the Rabbit's natural element is wood. In the cycle of element relationships, wood destroys earth. One party is clearly in control, and in this case it is the Rabbit who dominates and controls the relationship. This augurs well for the alliance because it is the Rabbit who brings out the best in the Sheep, and though he/she is in control, it is a control that is couched in subtlety and is self effacing. The Rabbit is happy to stay behind the scenes.

Sheep of marriageable age are those born in 1979 (earth Sheep 17 years of age in 1996) or in 1967 (fire Sheep 29 years old in 1996)

Rabbit of marriageable age are those born in 1975 (wood Rabbit 21 years old in 1996) or 1963 (water Rabbit 33 years old in 1996) .

In a marriage between the Rabbit and the Sheep, any combination of gender is possible and analysis of compatibility and workability over the long term is always strengthened by element analysis.

Hence if we look at a marriage between the fire Sheep and a water Rabbit, with the Rabbit being older and in all likelihood, the man ... we see that the elements strengthen the Sheep (fire produces earth) and equally strengthens the Rabbit as well (water produces wood). The match is thus balanced and will be auspicious; and the Rabbit i.e. the man will be dominant.

Note: At the start, these two might not hit it off, but as they get to know each other, a firm affinity could well come forth.

RABBIT/BOAR
Almost custom made for each other

In many ways this is a case of opposites attracting; the Boar being loud and somewhat aggressive while the rabbit is quieter and more subtle. And then again the Boar has a tendency to use strength and stamina while the Rabbit depends on his/her innate intelligence and careful thinking through of problems ..... and yet, the two also seem to think alike; and they want the same things in life. Where they differ is the way they each go about achieving their goals. When the two come together it is like a blending of two complementary halves. Their natural affinity make them like each otherfrom the beginning, and when they start discovering each other's talents, the two get along like a house on fire. Plus they make a great team because while the Rabbit is happy to manipulate things from behind the scenes, the Boar does not mind being in the spotlight. Each brings out the best in the other, and where either one should stumble, one will always be around to give the other a helping hand, and a broad strong shoulder.

The influence of the Elements
The Boar's natural element is water while the Rabbit's natural element is wood. In the cycle of element relationships, water produces wood. One party clearly provides the sustenance and support here, and it is the Boar, who is thus deemed to be excellent good fortune for the Rabbit ! This augurs well for the alliance.

Rabbit of marriageable age are those born in 1975 (wood Rabbit 21 years of age in 1996) or in 1963 (water Rabbit 33 years old in 1996)

Boar of marriageable age are those born in 1972 (metal Boar 24 years old in 1996) or 1959 (earth Boar 37 years old in 1996) .

A marriage between the water Rabbit and the metal Boar, where the Rabbit is, in all likelihood, the male has the elements on their side. The rabbit is strengthened by the water element while the Boar too is considerably strengthened by the metal element. Since the Boar/Rabbit combination of elements is also productive (which is water/wood, reflecting the earthly branch elements for these two animals), this is deemed to be an extremely good match. A match between the wood Rabbit and the metal Boar is equally auspicious as demonstrated by the elements also strengthening both parties. Except in this case, the Rabbit will most likely be the female, and she will marry a rich Boar who will provide for her.

OTHER COMPATIBLE PAIRINGS
AFFINITIES EXTEND BEYOND THE TRIANGLES

While partnerships between individuals belonging to animal signs that form part of the Affinity Triangles usually enjoy great compatibility, the Chinese Zodiac does not restrict compatibility only to these Triangles. Indeed, outside of it, there are other quite outstanding pairings as well.

The degree of suitable matches between one animal sign and another is often coloured by other considerations, and these need to be inputted into any analysis of compatibility. Thus for example, the influence of element relationships plays a large part in determining whether a pairing will or will not generally be successful; and auspicious and productive element relationships depend not merely on the element of the earthly branch, but also that of the heavenly stem, of the years of birth being investigated.

To refine the investigation, the relevant element of the month and hour of birth can also be examined, and there are tables contained elsewhere in this book for the reader to do so. But because the effect of the year elements have the largest influence, any investigation of compatibility must start with the earthly branch i.e. the animal signs. Thus we continue our examination of compatible matches !

The RAT can often find happiness with another RAT or with the OX, the TIGER or the BOAR. The OX can happily cuddle another OX, marry a RABBIT, a MONKEY, a DOG or a BOAR. The TIGER and the MONKEY make great pals and also find love with the BOAR. The RABBIT is suited to another RABBIT, but also with the SNAKE, the MONKEY and the DOG. The DRAGON and the SNAKE make a brilliant couple, but is also suited to the HORSE, the SHEEP, the ROOSTER, the MONKEY and the BOAR. The SNAKE can love the HORSE, the SHEEP or the MONKEY. The HORSE can also be paired with the SHEEP, the MONKEY or the BOAR. The SHEEP can marry another SHEEP or a MONKEY. The MONKEY finds another MONKEY attractive, and also likes the BOAR. The ROOSTER can find some happiness with the BOAR who in turn will make a perfect couple with another BOAR

Observe therefore that some animal signs get along with more people than others. The BOAR for instance can find a soul mate from amongst more of the other signs than, for instance the ROOSTER, and the SNAKE has more to choose from than say, the DRAGON ... this does not necessarily mean that all these matches will work to an equal extent There will be nuances and degrees of compatibility, some will match better than others. Be sensitive to these nuances when you make your investigation.

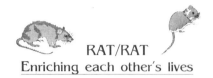

RAT/RAT
Enriching each other's lives

There will be a great deal of sympathetico between these two. Plus a lot of plotting and planning as well. These are individuals with huge insecurities, and also large egos and even larger ambitions, especially in attaining recognition and achieving social status. Because of their instinctive understanding of each other, theirs will be an enriching union. They will have much in common as they direct their energies towards building a comfortable and secure life together; there will also be some harmless and friendly rivalry between them. As a team they can be quite formidable, but only if they can curb their over impulsive natures and refrain from over exposure of limited resources. The man in this pair will tend to be more aggressive and ruthless while the wife will be fastidious and strictly meticulous. Rats are great hoarders. With two of them, this aspect of their personalities will be magnified. This penchant for collecting things will be one of the things that bring them cosily together.

The influence of the Elements
The Rat 's natural element is water. A pairing of two waters could make for too much water, and it will be useful to examine their years of birth so that the ruling element of the year heavenly stem can be examined to see if the productive or destructive cycle prevails. Which party clearly dominates the relationship will be determined by these element relationships.

Rats of marriageable age are those born in:
1960 (metal Rat 36 years of age in 1996)
1972 (water Rat 24 years old in 1996)

Marriages between metal Rats will be happily successful. Metal produces water in the cycle, and this imbues the metal Rat with more than his fair share of luck. With things going their way the Rat husband and wife will have a greater than even chance of being contented with their lot, and of assuaging their basic feelings of insecurity. The only problem is that when there is too much water, it can cause one to drown ... this couple must thus ensure that they *do not get too carried away* with too many grand ideas. A marriage between a metal Rat and a water Rat will also have more than their fair share of water, and the same analysis applies. Likewise a marriage between two water Rats. In these instances, to counter the effect of too much water, it might help if either one or both partners are born during the earth hours, or during the earth months. This is because earth destroys water and will create a better balance.

RAT/OX
Guarantee of marital stability

This is a very good match as it brings the solid dependable Ox together with the enterprising Rat personality. The Ox has the capacity to listen without interruption, which suits the Rat's need to chatter on and engage in long discourses about his views, his opinions ... and his feelings. The Ox's devotion will also do much to reduce the Rat's feelings of insecurity. Both will complement each other. The Rat will accept the slower and more methodical style of the Ox while the Ox will look up to the Rat's innovative and resourceful approach to solving problems and dealing with the world at large. Their goals will also converge since both appreciate and want material and financial success. Where problems occur is when the Ox's leadership abilities are unleashed and if she/he attains greater success ... this will be when the Rat's insecurities could cause tension between the two. But because of the Ox's patient nature, any difficulty will likely get worked out ... this pairing is thus potentially fruitful and workable.

The influence of the Elements
The Rat 's natural element is water. The Ox's natural element is earth. In the cycle, earth destroys water. The Ox will thus be the real boss in this partnership, and will dominate the relationship. The Rat will clearly defer to the Ox because in terms of strength, the Ox will be the stronger.

Rats of marriageable age are those born in 1960 (metal Rat 36 years of age in 1996) or 1972 (water Rat 24 years old in 1996)

Ox of marriageable age are those born in 1961 (metal Ox 35 years of age in 1996) or in 1973 (water Ox 23 years of age in 1996)

Marriages between a metal Rat and a metal Ox will be happily successful, but will favour the Rat, in that his energy level will match that of the dominant Ox. The relative strength of the couple will thus be more evenly balanced since the metal element will exhaust the Ox's earth. Just as well if the Rat is the male in this pairing.

A marriage between a water Rat and a water Ox tips the balance in favour of the Ox since earth destroys water. If the Ox is the female the male Rat could suffer from feelings of insecurity that cause him anxiety, and even a certain amount of resentment at his wife's greater success. Nevertheless the Rat will not be totally bereft of opportunity since the elements also favour him. He has more than enough of his own element !

TIGER/RAT
Initial enthusiasm could waver

This is a relationship characterized by huge initial enthusiasm which carries the couple aloft, fueled by the Rat's admiration of the Tiger's extravagant exuberance, and the Tiger's excitement at the Rat's eloquence. If both can harness each other's many qualities and direct their energies in a cooperative manner, the union is magical and filled with many happy exciting moments. But the exuberance could vanish when both face up to the harsh realities of living and working together. The Rat could well tire of the Tiger's colourful personality, and the Tiger could get fed up with the Rat's nagging insecurities. Both have quick tempers and strong characters, and where the Tiger is outwardly and loudly ferocious, the Rat is crafty and scheming. They could well end up hurting each other. But in many instances, good sense will prevail and they will find ways to accommodate each other. Their extrovert personalities and similiar goals will very likely ensure that both will direct positive energies to making the union work. But the going is not entirely smooth ... these two will have a bumpy ride indeed.

The influence of the Elements
The Rat 's natural element is water. The Tiger's natural element is wood. In the cycle, water produces wood. The Rat, in this case will sustain and support the Tiger. The relationship gains strength from the Rat's wisdom and willingness to harness the Tiger's energy in a clever and diplomatic manner. The Rat will clearly defer to the Tiger, thereby setting the stage for compromise that will lead to greater happiness.

Rats of marriageable age are those born in 1960 (metal Rat 36 years of age in 1996) or 1972 (water Rat 24 years old in 1996)

Tigers of marriageable age are those born in 1962 (water Tiger 34 years of age in 1996) or in 1974 (wood Tiger 22 years of age in 1996)

Marriage between a metal Rat and a water Tiger could create tiny problems due to minor skirmishes and disagreements. Both parties here are benefiting from their second *year* element, and neither party dominates. This could be problematic in the case of two such strong personalities. The relative strength of the couple is however evenly balanced, and if they succeed in working through their disagreements the union will succeed. A marriage between a water Rat and wood Tiger is similialy evenly balanced, and the same analysis applies.

 RAT/BOAR

These two make marvelous mates

This is a perfectly matched couple whose emotional ties bind them strongly to each other. Their personalities, though different, are nevertheless strongly complementary. Where the Rat is thrifty and careful with money, the Boar is generous, making up for the Rat's stingy nature and outlook. Looked at another way, the Rat's careful husbanding of the family cash saves the Boar from over indulgence and unwarranted extravagance. And where the Rat is resourceful, the Boar is hard working. Highly principled, possessed of lofty ideals and always thinking well of others, the Boar tends to be naive, and is thus easily taken in; but with the clever and well connected Rat at his/her side, the Boar will not fall prey to dishonest or unscrupulous people. The Rat will protect the Boar, but will also often nag and criticize, usually attempting to lecture and educate, but the good natured Boar accepts all of this with a positive attitude. There is thus harmony between these two.

The influence of the Elements
The Rat 's natural element is water. The Boar's natural element is also water. Neither party really dominates this relationship. But the Rat, being Yang and the Boar being Yin ... the Rat will be more comfortable if his or hers is the leadership role. More often than not the Rat will lead in this relationship. But the couple could be affected by having too much water if the other year elements are also water, or if they produce water.

Rats of marriageable age are those born in 1960 (metal Rat 36 years of age in 1996) or 1972 (water Rat 24 years old in 1996)

Boar of marriageable age are those born in 1959 (earth Boar 37years of age in 1996) or in 1971 (metal Boar 25 years of age in 1996)

Marriage between a metal Rat and an earth Boar puts the Rat clearly in charge, and this makes the union a happy and successful one. With the Rat in charge, the Boar will be quite happy allowing the Rat to take care of the family's finances and social interfaces. In this instance the Rat could very likely be the wife

A marriage between a water Rat and a metal Boar creates a more balanced match between the two but there is a surfeit of water which could well cause them both to drown. The excess of water could also create higher energy levels in both parties and this is not always necessarily a good thing. They will have to learn to rein themselves in.

OX/OX
Hugely successful and productive

Oh me oh my ! What a pair ! This is an all work partnership; solid, dependable, and always there for each other. Between these two individuals there is no need for long discussions or too much talking. They just understand each other so well ! Together, they will flow into a routine that both will be comfortable with. They have no need for extravagant displays of affection, or for impulsive action, or for spontaneous change of plans. They communicate quietly and neither party will raise his/her voice to the other.

They do not nag each other at all, they seldom quarrel, and though they may appear outwardly dull and uninteresting, in effect there is a very strong bond of understanding between them. Ox marriages last because both parties do not like change. They are also more comfortable living in the country, and their home will be a showpiece of practical, down to earth basics. Ox people are not showy. Theirs will be a traditional and conventional life, with few surprises. But it will also be hugely successful and very productive.
An Ox marriage usually produces several children since both parties are family oriented.

The influence of the Elements
The Ox's natural element is earth. They could do with some fire which not only enhances their element, but will also add a dash of fiery energy to an otherwise staid existence. But fire could cause there to be too much earth, which does not necessarily make for a good balance.

Ox of marriageable age are those born in 1961 (metal Ox 35 years of age in 1996) or in 1973 (water Ox 23 years of age in 1996)

Marriage between two metal Ox will be successful. The metal serves to exhaust some of the Ox's earth energy because earth produces metal. This could introduce an element of lightness to the union. Or it can be interpreted as draining them of their energy. However with two sets of earth energy at work, this might not be such a bad thing.

Marriage between two water Ox does not cause any problem. The additional element is kept well under control because earth destroys water. The Ox couple will stay on top of things and there will be few problems to disturb their well laid out lives.

OX/RABBIT
A cozy, cuddly pair

The Rabbit's quiet and diplomatic nature appeals enormously to the Ox's sense of decorum, and together they could forge quite a cozy and surprisingly cuddlesome relationship. Intellectually they may not be very well matched but other shared interests hold out the promise of amiable companionship. Neither are quarrelsome types, so differences are usually sorted out with little problem. However where tensions get prolonged, the Rabbit could well curl up in despair, and resentment could grow. The Ox's inflexibility can sometimes stand in the way of a reconciliation, although this is unlikely since the Ox will try to work at breaking through the Rabbit's cold reserve. The Ox does care a great deal ! In this relationship, it will be the Ox who will do most of the work, and he/she will not mind it at all. The Ox understands that the Rabbit has other interests, and is not as ambitious. As long as the home stays peaceful and harmonious, this pairing will be quite successful as the role of husband and wife are indeed very well defined. The success of this union depends a great deal on the Rabbit.

The influence of the Elements
The Ox's natural element is earth. The Rabbit's natural element is wood. In the cycle, wood destroys earth. In this case it is the Rabbit who will be in control of the relationship, and not the Ox, even though it will be the Ox who will be the one who works harder at the relationship.

Ox of marriageable age are those born in 1961 (metal Ox 35 years of age in 1996) or in 1973 (water Ox 23 years of age in 1996)

Rabbits of marriageable age are those born in 1963 (water Rabbit, 33 years of age in 1996) or 1975 (wood Rabbit 21 years of age in 1996)

Marriage between the 35 year old Ox and the 33 year old Rabbit (metal Ox with water Rabbit) will be successful. Here the element favours the Rabbit who is strengthened by the water element since water produces wood. The Ox is exhausted by the metal since his natural element, earth produces metal. The marriage has a good chance of success since it gives the Rabbit extra energy to put up with the Ox's plodding ways.

Marriage between the water Ox and the wood Rabbit likewise favours the Rabbit and once more the relationship will benefit from the elements because it is the rabbit that requires the energy to make this union work.

OX/MONKEY
A promise of much happiness

With these two individuals, it will a be a case of opposites being unrelentingly and irrevocably drawn to each other. There is no other way of understanding how the solid, staid and conventional Ox could ever be remotely attracted to the unconventional, extravagant and flamboyant Monkey. And yet they do get quite caught up in each other. One sees the other as refreshingly different, and becomes the perfect foil for the other. In courtship, these two will be quite besotted with each other, seeing all that is positive in the other's personality and character. The Ox admires the Monkey's imaginative ingenuity while the Monkey admires the Ox's solid and stable demeanour. The Ox will be willing to cooperate and work with the audacious and clever Monkey, and the latter will lend much courage and vigour to all of the Ox's endeavours. They will trust and rely on each other, and there is promise of much happiness. Any problems will be caused by betrayal, which could well blow this marriage apart.

The influence of the Elements
The Ox's natural element is earth. The Monkey's natural element is metal. In the cycle, earth produces metal. In this case it is the Ox who will be in real control of the relationship. The Monkey will bow to the wishes and wisdom of the Ox, and will allow the Ox's more sedate influence to prevail. The Monkey's more impetuous schemes will be seen as such and there will be harmony because of the Ox's strong influence.

Ox of marriageable age are those born in 1961 (metal Ox 35 years of age in 1996) or in 1973 (water Ox 23 years of age in 1996)

Monkeys of marriageable age are those born in 1968 (earth Monkey 28 years of age in 1996) or 1980 (metal Monkey 16 years of age in 1996)

Marriage between the water Ox and earth Monkey will be an equal relationship. Neither party will be very dominant. This is because, while the Ox is not affected by the element of water, the Monkey is enhanced by the element of earth, since earth produces metal. The Monkey's energy will be strengthened as will his influence and nature. In this pairing it is also likely that the Monkey will be the husband, and that being the case, the enhanced energy caused by the elements will surely work in favour of the marriage. The danger here is the temptation for the Monkey to have a wandering eye. He must either resist temptation or be discreet !

OX/DOG
Rocky start deepens into true love

At the beginning these two strong characters could find it hard to even tolerate each other but it is a powerful test of wills that will give way to even stronger attraction. The Dog can be quite savage and unyielding in the face of disagreements; and the Ox can be dogmatic and stubborn. There could be a clash of wills ... but at no time will there be malice ... on the contrary even as they argue and debate the two will be falling desperately in love with each other. A marriage between these two will bring out all that is admirable from each other's viewpoint. The Dog admires the Ox's honesty and reliability. He/she sees in the Ox a kindred spirit because like the Ox, the Dog has lofty principles and is idealistic. He believes in the virtues of fairplay, honesty and integrity all of which qualities he/she sees also in the Ox. Dogmatism and an uncompromising attitude are then seen as strength of conviction, and loyalty to each other is viewed as tangible expressions of love ! This is a powerful pairing indeed.

The influence of the Elements
The Ox's natural element is earth. The Dog's natural element is also earth. There's will be a very down to earth and pragmatic relationship ! It is an equal relationship with neither of them dominating the other.

Ox of marriageable age are those born in 1961 (metal Ox 35 years of age in 1996) or in 1973 (water Ox 23 years of age in 1996)

Dogs of marriageable age are those born in 1970 (metal Dog 26 years of age in 1996) or 1958 (earth Dog 38 years of age in 1996)

Marriage between the water Ox and metal Dog will give the edge to the Ox.. This is because, while the Ox is not affected by the element of water, the Dog is exhausted by the element of metal, since earth produces metal. In this case the Dog is very likely the husband, and he will stay loyal and true to his Ox wife whose influence in the marriage will always prevail.

Marriage between the metal Ox and earth Dog also makes the Dog dominant, since the metal exhausts the Ox, and the earth strengthens the Dog. With the Dog also being older, this is a match that could work very well indeed, and it will not be surprising to see a really loving marriage in this pairing.

Note: In being friends, these two might not seem to get along but as they get to know each other, a real feeling of kinship could well develop.

OX/BOAR
Getting along famously

These two get on famously together. The quiet and domineering Ox is madly attracted to the popular and easy going Boar. They become best friends because they are sympathetic to each other's aspirations. The Boar loves the good things in life and tends to be something of a spendthrift. In the Ox, the Boar sees and appreciates a more sensible attitude to life, and is attracted to Ox's integrity, reliability and stability. The Boar on the other hand brings out the protective instincts of the Ox's dominating nature. He/she is comfortable with the Boar's many social and organizational skills. Between the two there is good communication. At work, they blend their energies together in a harmonious way, while on the homefront, they agree on important issues with respect to children and the way the home is run. The only major difference between them is their view of money. Here while the Boar tends to be careless and relaxed in the management of funds, the Ox is frugal and careful. The relationship will work because the Boar will agree with and respect the Ox's insistence on being responsible. As long as the Ox can prevail and have the upper hand in this relationship, it will work. If there is trouble between the two, it will be caused by money problems.

The influence of the Elements
The Ox's natural element is earth. The Boar's natural element is water. In the cycle, earth destroys water, as a result of which it will be the Ox's will that will prevail, thereby laying the basis for a successful pairing. The Ox will take charge and the Boar will listen and respect his/her wishes. There will thus be few problems.

Ox of marriageable age are those born in 1961 (metal Ox 35 years of age in 1996) or in 1973 (water Ox 23 years of age in 1996)

Boars of marriageable age are those born in 1959 (earth Boar37 years of age in 1996) or 1971 (metal Boar 25 years of age in 1996)

Marriage between the metal Ox and the earth Boar allows the Ox to stay in control, and indeed even gives the Ox the edge. This is because while the Ox is exhausted by the element of metal, the Boar is destroyed by the element of earth, since earth destroys water. In this case the Boar is very likely the husband, and he will likely be henpecked by his domineering Ox wife. Which is not to say that such a marriage will not work or even be unhappy. Because of the intrinsic nature of both individuals, the pairing is conducive to a long and fruitful relationship.

BOAR/BOAR
Not exactly the best match, but should be OK

This is a match between two happy go lucky people, who love indulging themselves with little restraint, but have a problem getting themselves sufficiently disciplined to really get their act together. Not exactly indolent, they nevertheless lack the go getter spirit needed to meet challenges and face up to the difficulties of life and work. They could be the best of friends seeing each other as kindred souls, but if provoked they could well turn on one another and become adversaries. However, because they share the same philosophies and approach to life, they are suited to each other, and if they are fortunate enough not to have work or struggle very hard they will get along. When it comes to fun ventures, and enjoying life these two make the most perfect of mates; they are also exceedingly loyal to their mutual interests and can be quite formidable as a team, if and when challenged. But they cannot motivate or inspire each other to any great heights.

The influence of the Elements
The Boar's natural element is water. This matching of two water signs is reflected in their relatively relaxed and laid back attitudes, although latent aggressive tendencies do occasionally see the light of day. Depending on their respective heavenly stem elements, their characters will indicate greater divergence, but because there is a twelve year gap between Boars of different elements, marriages between them will likely be a match between two very similiar Boars.

Boars of marriageable age are those born in 1959 (earth Boar 37 years of age in 1996) or 1971 (metal Boar 25 years of age in 1996)

Marriage between two earth Boars were probably not the most ideal of pairings. In this instance, the Boar's water is destroyed by the element of earth, since earth destroys water. In this case the two Boars could be plagued by depression and bad luck, causing them to turn on each other, unless they are able to join forces and be brought closer together by adversity. The elements however do weaken their spirit, and it seems unlikely. Marriage between two water Boars on the other hand have a greater chance of succeeding, and in fact could be an excellent match since the elements work in their favour, water being produced by metal. The excess of water in this case could work in their favour due to the intrinsic character of the Boar. As long as they don't both drown in too much indulgence.

 TIGER/BOAR
A loving and romantic pair

These two will party all night ! They love a good time, and are simultaneously generous and gregarious, surrounding themselves with friends and associates. They are loving towards each other, constantly declaring their love, loudly for all to hear ! They are also demonstrative, and have a huge appetite for life and living. It is possible that they will eventually tire of the fast life, and their happiness could be short lived ... but while they're at it, it would seem that nothing can stop them. Unless of course they run out of money and resources. This is a coupling of two fun loving individuals who could have trouble coping with bad times. When the food runs out and the tap gets dry, they could turn against each other, indulging in quite useless recriminations, and causing the once beautiful relationship to collapse. Or they could just as well pull themselves together and combine their energies to rebuild. In such a situation, they can depend on their strong bond to see them through. If they do not take each other for granted, and respect each other's strengths it is likely that the union will last. The Tiger's powerful determination coupled with the Boar's networking skills could be parlayed into a great partnership. But only if the Tiger stays focused, and the Boar starts to do some real work, and takes charge !

The influence of the Elements
The Tiger's natural element is wood. The Boar's natural element is water. In the cycle, water produces wood, as a result of which it will be the Boar who must provide the lead. If the Boar is unable to support the Tiger, the union could well collapse.

Tiger of marriageable age are those born in 1962 (water Tiger 34 years of age in 1996) or in 1974 (wood Tiger 22 years of age in 1996)

Boars of marriageable age are those born in 1959 (earth Boar 37 years of age in 1996) or 1971 (metal Boar 25 years of age in 1996)

Marriage between the wood Tiger and the metal Boar is an excellent pairing. The elements are working in favour of this match. This is because the Tiger benefits hugely from the strengthening provided by the woo element; while the Boar is likewise energized by the metal element, which which produces water ! The favourable element influence gives this marriage a better than even chance of success, bringing greater resilience and strength to both parties. It will however depend on the Boar, who will likely be the husband, and therefore the breadwinner, to make things work.

RABBIT/RABBIT
A mutual admiration society

There is a great deal of mutual respect between these two very congenial and well mannered people. They work and live well together, mindful of each other's need and always sensitive to each other's eccentricities. They think highly of one another, and they do succeed in creating a bond that is quite special. When they have differences of opinion, there is no noisy shouting match; instead, like two ever polite individuals, they sit, discuss, talk things through sensibly, and altogether behave in a most rationale and sane fashion. The Rabbit is basically a diplomatic quiet sort of person. Two of a kind being together does not change their intrinsic nature, Thus, because they tend to turn chilly and sulk when thwarted, this trait could cause tension between them. Both will find it hard to be the first to break any frosty silences between them, and this could cause problems as they mature into married life. Politeness then gives way to coldness, and though nothing directly is said, the relationship could break down. But Rabbits seldom admit to failures and the marriage could continue even if the love may long ago have died !

The influence of the Elements
The Rabbit's natural element is wood, and with an excess of wood in a pairing of two Rabbits, other elements can either heighten or reduce the chances of success.

Rabbit of marriageable age are those born in 1975 (wood Rabbit 21 years old in 1996) or 1963 (water Rabbit 33 years old in 1996).

A marriage between two wood Rabbits will definitely have an excess of wood, which should benefit from the introduction of some fire or metal elements to balance out the excess.

A marriage of two water Rabbits is just as problematic since water produces wood. The effect of this excess wood is to magnify the Rabbit personality. If the union is a happy one where there is genuine love and continued mutual respect, the surplus wood benefits.

But like a double edged sword, the energizing of the two personalities could also work against them.

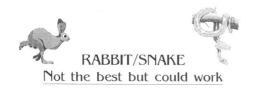

RABBIT/SNAKE
Not the best but could work

These two very refined people share a range of mutual interests ... art, music, theater, the finer things in life, and therein lie their affinity and attraction for each other. The Rabbit is mesmerized by the Snake and will go to great lengths to create togetherness opportunities, and because of the Rabbit's persistence, the Snake could succumb. The match could well work because there is much that pulls these two quite different individuals together ... what could be difficult to resolve would be their basically selfish natures. The Rabbit tends to always put him/herself first, and above everyone else. So does the Snake, unless she/he is involved in a great and passionate love, although, it would be difficult to imagine the Snake viewing the Rabbit in this light. As a result, the match could break down. In a situation, where there is a great deal of resources available, to smooth the way, this match could work, but if both parties have to build from scratch, the chances of success are indeed quite slim. The Snake would slither quietly away ... and the Rabbit would hop elsewhere in search of better pastures. And because both parties are yin, they are equally likely to yield to their own intrinsic natures ...

The influence of the Elements
The Rabbit's natural element is wood, while that of the Snake is fire. In the cycle, wood creates fire. Thus the relationship is dependent upon the Rabbit providing the resources for the relationship. He/she must be the breadwinner, and given a demanding Snake it is possible that the Rabbit would feel too pressured. Plus fire burns wood, indicating the pattern of the relationship between the two. The Rabbit will need to be strong.

Rabbits of marriageable age are those born in 1975 (wood Rabbit 21 years old in 1996) or 1963 (water Rabbit 33 years old in 1996).

Snakes of marriageable age are those born in 1977 (fire Snake 19 years old in 1996) or 1965 (wood Snake 31 years old).

A marriage between the wood Rabbit and the fire Snake can be successful. Here both parties are energized by their respective elements. Wood strengthens the Rabbit just as fire strengthens the Snake. The match could also be auspicious. A marriage of the water Rabbit with the fire Snake would also work since the Rabbit is similiarly strengthened by the water element. A marriage between the water Rabbit and the wood Snake is likewise auspicious, the elements strengthen both people equally.

MONKEY/RABBIT
Intellectually well matched

They are both clever and quick-witted individuals, and they share similiar artistic and intellectual pursuits. There is much they have in common, and they will find each other's company refreshingly enjoyable. But where the Rabbit tends to adhere to the conventions and to observe the norms of accepted behavior, the Monkey tends to be more outrageous, often delighting in making a big splash with his unconventional approach. This could cause problems between them. If there is contention, neither will give in easily, and they could wear each other down with excuses, prevarication and recriminations, and in the end the Monkey could well give up and seek his pleasures elsewhere. Yet these are also two rational human beings, who will be too clever to throw away a good relationship. Their underlying amiable natures and sensible attitudes will generally tilt attitudes in favour of compromise ... and the Rabbit is also tenacious, and will not give in to failure or the breakdown of a relationship without a fight.

The influence of the Elements
The Rabbit's natural element is wood, while that of the Monkey is metal. In the cycle, metal destroys wood Thus, the relationship will see the Monkey having the stronger influence.. He/she will dominate the relationship, and set the pattern of behaviour between them.

Rabbits of marriageable age are those born in 1975 (wood Rabbit 21 years old in 1996) or 1963 (water Rabbit 33 years old in 1996).

Monkeys of marriageable age are those born in 1980 (metal Monkey 16 years old in 1996) or 1968 (earth Monkey 28 years old).

A marriage between the wood Rabbit and the earth Monkey will be very auspicious and successful. Here, both parties are energized and strengthened by their respective elements. Wood strengthens the Rabbit's own element, just as earth strengthens the Monkey. Here the wife will likely be the Rabbit while the husband will be the Monkey, which augurs well for the relationship since the it will be the Monkey who will be the leader in this union. The Rabbit wife will be happy to accept the stronger role taken on by the Monkey husband, accepting his way of doing things and adapting well to his more extrovert and flamboyant approach. One additional aspect in their favour is that the Monkey is yang while the Rabbit is yin, thereby reflecting the balance of the harmonious whole.

RABBIT/DOG
An OK match ... dull but solid

Here, we have two very compatible human beings, who are reasonable, extremely nice to one another, and temperamentally suited. It will be a rare occasion indeed for them ever to fight, or yell. The match is a good one, very solid and stable, but the complete absence of fireworks could make them seem like a really dull and boring couple. This is because neither will ever be unreasonable or irrationally demanding of the other. Theirs is a comfortable and cozy life together, characterized by even tempers and a great deal of supportive and cooperative behaviour. It is also a secure relationship, where problems get dealt with calmly, and where differences of opinion are never allowed to develop into big disagreements. The Rabbit and the Dog are also naturally loyal and faithful people, so any chance of either one doing anything to upset the marriage is very slim. Altogether a quite ideal pairing.

The influence of the Elements
The Rabbit's natural element is wood, while that of the Dog is earth. In the cycle, wood destroys earth. Thus the alliance will be dominated by the Rabbit, who will set the tone and the pace of the relationship. This is because he/she will be the stronger of the two. Since the Rabbit is better natured and has greater control over his feelings than the emotional Dog, this is an additional point in favour of the union succeeding. The yin yang configurations are also harmonious and balanced.

Rabbits of marriageable age are those born in 1975 (wood Rabbit 21 years old in 1996) or 1963 (water Rabbit 33 years old in 1996).

Dogs of marriageable age are those born in 1970 (metal Dog 26 years old in 1996) or 1958 (earth Dog 38 years old).

A marriage between the wood Rabbit and the metal Dog can be quite trying for the Dog, who might find it hard to keep up with the energized Rabbit. This is due to the Rabbit (probably the wife) being strengthened by the wood element, while the Dog(likely the husband) is exhausted by the metal element. A marriage of the water Rabbit with the metal Dog has the same elemental influence. The Rabbit is strengthened and energized while the Dog is weakened. In this match, the Rabbit is likely the male, and the Dog is likely the female, and he will very likely lend strength to his wife. The union will not be badly affected.

Note: These two might not appear to have much in common, but as they get to know each other, a solid friendship could well emerge.

SNAKE/DRAGON
A brilliant scorching pair

Only one year separates these two highly charged individuals, but what a fantastic couple they make ! Both are highly ambitious and hungry for success. Both are tremendously talented, clever and dynamic ... yet both have different skills. The Snake/Dragon union brings together the intellectual with the dynamic. the thinker/strategist with the performance person. These two are formidable because they are not mere dreamers, they are action oriented visionaries. This is a partnership where neither will be dependent on the other. Both have strong wills and an iron clad determination to make it to huge success. Their passionate natures find satisfaction in each other; and power sits comfortably on both shoulders. They will have different sets of friends and supporters, but they will also strongly complement each other. And because there will be inherent respect flowing freely between the two, neither will easily betray the other. This is one of the great matches of the Zodiac, and will be even better if the Dragon is the male (yang) and the Snake is female (yin) although the gender of either will not make a huge difference.

The influence of the Elements
The Dragon's natural element is earth while the Snake's natural element is fire. In the cycle of element relationships, fire produces earth. The clever Snake will bring valuable support to the dynamic Dragon. Their natural affinity to each other makes the Dragon quite willing to listen to the Snake. It will not be at all surprising for the Dragon to quite passionately adore the Snake and vice versa in this union !

Snakes of marriageable age are those born in 1965 (wood Snake 31 years old in 1996) or 1977 (fire Snake 19 years old in 1996)

Dragons of marriageable age are those born in 1964 (wood Dragons 32 years of age in 1996) or in 1976 (fire dragons 20 years old in 1996)

In any cycle, the Dragons will be older than the Snakes and it is conceivable that the Dragon will be the male and the Snake will be the female ... A marriage between a wood Dragon and wood Snake weakens the Dragon and strengthens the Snake, but does not jeopardize the union. A marriage between the fire Dragon and the fire Snake, strengthens both equally and is extremely auspicious ! This pair will make it right to the very top together ! The match is not only balanced in horoscope terms, it is also extremely fortuitious for both.

HORSE/DRAGON
A highly physical, electrifying union

Powerful emotions energize these two people ! The Horse is restless, adventurous, and frisky while the Dragon is impulsive, headstrong and dynamic. Together, they make the sheets burn with passion. Their's will be a highly physical and tempestuous relationship, characterized by many dramatic moments. Both have mercurial temperaments, with the Horse being more agile and the Dragon, more highly charged. And they make a truly headstrong couple. If anything can go wrong with this pair, it will be their two yang natures clashing loudly. Yet precisely because they are both so vocal and so forthright, disagreements are dealt with immediately and cleared up pronto. Misunderstandings are kept to a minimum and there will be little subterfuge or sulks between them. It is just not their style. They have no time for petty drivel, and will seldom be handicapped by being immobilized by inaction or insignificant details. Theirs is a big picture environment and their worlds are coloured by long strokes of the paintbrush. Both relish challenges, and have independent spirits that refuse to be restrained. Thus conventions and traditions never get in their way. And they are strongly supportive and loyal, with never a dull moment. Any infidelities are swept into oblivion by the tide of their own passion for each other.

The influence of the Elements
The Dragon's natural element is earth while the Horse's natural element is fire. In the cycle of element relationships, fire produces earth. The communicative Horse will bring valuable inputs to the charismatic Dragon. Their attachment to each other makes the Dragon inclined to heed the advice of the Horse.

Horses of marriageable age are those born in 1966 (fire Horse 30 years old in 1996) or 1978 (earth Horse 18 years old in 1996)

Dragons of marriageable age are those born in 1964 (wood Dragons 32 years of age in 1996) or in 1976 (fire dragons 20 years old in 1996)

In any cycle, the Dragon will be older than the Horse and it is conceivable that the Dragon will be the male and the Horse will be the female ... A marriage between a wood Dragon and fire Horse weakens the Dragon and strengthens the Horse, but does not jeopardize the union.
A marriage between the fire Dragon and the earth Horse, strengthens the Dragon but weakens the Horse but again does not hurt the union.

Note: In friendships, these two might not appear to get along but as they get to know each other, a solid relationship could well emerge.

 SHEEP/DRAGON

An erotic dream

Two earthy individuals engaged in a vibrant and magnificent relationship where one clearly dominates, and the other willingly submits. This is an ultimate pairing of the yang with the yin. The Dragon is strong and domineering, vibrant and full of energy. The Sheep is docile and yielding, creative and imaginative. Together their relationship is an erotic dream. There is no fight for power here, no tussle for control. The Dragon's magnetism and charisma makes the Sheep accept his/her dominant role, while the Dragon is enamoured by the conquest of this beautifully elegant and graceful creature. There is also good communication between them because the Dragon's impulsive and dynamic opinions find easy acceptance with the good natured Sheep, and there will seldom be heated arguments between the two. Theirs will not be a tempestuous union, because the cool headed Sheep knows how to handle the fiery nature of the Dragon. Where they will face problems is when the impulsive Dragon starts taking the Sheep for granted, and misreading compliance for weakness ... if this happens, the Sheep could freeze the Dragon's passion ...by turning away.

The influence of the Elements
The Dragon's natural element is earth while the Sheep's natural element is also earth. The excess of earth could induce excesses that weaken the union, and work against them, but the similiarity of element could also enhance the communication and understanding between them.

Sheep of marriageable age are those born in 1967 (fire Sheep, 29 years old in 1996) or 1979 (earth Sheep 17 years old in 1996)

Dragons of marriageable age are those born in 1964 (wood Dragons 32 years of age in 1996) or in 1976 (fire Dragons 20 years old in 1996)

A marriage between a wood Dragon and fire Sheep weakens the Dragon and strengthens the Sheep, and this could cause problems, since the Sheep will be less agreeable, and more resistant to the Dragon's tendency to dominate the relationship.

A marriage between the fire Dragon and the earth Sheep, strengthens both equally and is good for the union, but there will be a danger of excesses, there being much too much earth between them both.

ROOSTER/DRAGON
A perfectly balanced relationship

A mutually dependent couple where one depends on the other. There is much ego stroking going on here, that succeeds in bringing out the best in the two of the them This pair personifies the synergy of two complementary and opposite sides of the coin coming together, and since they are both clever enough to see the advantages of their union, there is healthy respect between the two ... all of which sets the stage for a happy union. The Rooster is a clever and ambitious individual, able to see all that is valuable and productive in the headstrong, impulsive but very able and very strong Dragon individual. The Dragon, on the other hand, is mesmerized by the Rooster's outstanding talents and optimistic attitude. The match thus brings together a positive pairing of intelligence with power and talent with courage.. But it could all be too good to be true ... there is danger of surplus power in this relationship. Both sides must not get carried away ... or be over confident. But their yin yang balance works in their favour.

The influence of the Elements
The Dragon's natural element is earth while the Rooster's natural element is metal. The Rooster is yin and the Dragon is yang. In the cycle of element relationships, earth produces metal. The charismatic Dragon inspires and motivates the Rooster, drawing out his/her talents. The relationship is a mutually satisfying and challenging one.

Roosters of marriageable age are those born in 1969 (earth Rooster 27 years old in 1996) or 1981 (metal Rooster 15 years old in 1996)

Dragons of marriageable age are those born in 1964 (wood Dragons 32 years of age in 1996) or in 1976 (fire dragons 20 years old in 1996)

A marriage between a wood Dragon and an earth Rooster weakens the Dragon and strengthens the Rooster. This does not jeopardize the union but it does reduce the influence of the Dragon in the relationship, and increases the Rooster's profile. However both parties stand to gain.

A marriage between the fire Dragon and the metal Rooster strengthens both equally, and this is deemed auspicious. The elements are well balanced, and both sides benefit.

BOAR/DRAGON
This match will last

These two individuals are tremendously well suited to each other in terms of temperament. The easy going and amiable Boar is attracted to the Dragon's flamboyance and enthusiasm for life, and has no difficulty letting the Dragon have his head and take the lead. The Dragon finds the genial Boar very agreeable and admires his/her popularity with all the right people. Neither of them are prone to sulking or taking offense easily, and as such are able to accept and respect each other's foibles. The Boar accepts the Dragon's egoism and displays of superiority, and the Dragon is happy to indulge the Boar's expensive tastes and extravagant lifestyle. Indeed, he/she thrives on it and even encourages it. There are thus few barriers to stand in the way of this couple's happiness. They are also resilient people who have a sense of humour so that setbacks are taken in their stride. Difficulties are handled without one blaming the other. This match will last.

The influence of the Elements
The Dragon's natural element is earth while the Boar's natural element is water. The Boar is yin and the Dragon is yang. In the cycle of element relationships, earth destroys water. The autocratic Dragon takes the lead and dominates the relationship, and the Boar is happy to let him do so.

Boars of marriageable age are those born in 1959 (earth Boar 37 years old in 1996) or 1971 (metal Boar 25 years old in 1996)

Dragons of marriageable age are those born in 1964 (wood Dragons 32 years of age in 1996) or in 1976 (fire dragons 20 years old in 1996)

A marriage between a wood Dragon and an earth Boar weakens both the Dragon and the Boar. This does not jeopardize the union in any way, but it does make things less auspicious for them both. Also in this pairing, the Boar is very likely the husband, and it may not be easy for him to accept the Dragon's domineering role in the relationship.

A marriage between the wood Dragon and the metal Boar has a better chance of success since both are equally affected by the elements. The Dragon here is likely the husband and the yin yang configuration reflects greater harmony. A marriage between a metal Boar and fire Dragon makes the Dragon too powerful in the relationship, and this could hurt the union.

TIGER/DRAGON
A most courageous pair

These are two ambitious and highly motivated individuals, and they make an exciting couple. There's never a dull moment between them. They will always be communicating and sharing big ideas, one bringing positive inputs to the other's ideas. The Dragon is impulsive and courageous and so is the Tiger, but both are action oriented people and their grand schemes are often put to the test with little time lost. But neither will be comfortable playing second fiddle. This will be an equal and full partnership, since both are strong characters, who never back off from a fight or a confrontation. Troubles start if there are regular disagreements, because neither will give in. However, because their thought processes are generally similiar, there should be few serious problems between them. The Dragon also appreciates the Tiger's networking skills, while the Tiger acknowledges the Dragon's positive influence on the relationship.

The influence of the Elements
The Dragon's natural element is earth while the Tiger's natural element is wood. Both the Tiger and Dragon are yang animals. In the cycle of element relationships, wood destroys earth. The autocratic Dragon will take the lead and dominate the relationship, and despite the Tiger's strength and ferocity, this is the way the relationship will develop.

Dragons of marriageable age are those born in 1964 (wood Dragon, 32 years of age in 1996) or in 1976 (fire dragon 20 years old in 1996)

Tigers of marriageable age are those born in 1962 (water Tiger, 34 years old in 1996) or 1974 (wood Tiger, 22 years old in 1996)

A marriage between a wood Dragon and a water Tiger weakens the Dragon and strengthens the Tiger. This provides valuable energy to the Tiger, who will very likely be the male in this relationship, and can thus be interpreted to be good for the union

In a marriage between the fire Dragon and the wood Tiger both are equally affected by the elements. The Dragon's earth benefits from the additional fire (because fire produces earth) while the Tiger benefits from the extra wood (because the Tiger's natural element is also wood). This is an auspicious configuration of elements since there is balance between the two and the elements complement each other. The union will be successful.

SNAKE/SHEEP
An unlikely pair but can work

This is a match between two quite different individuals. While the Sheep is sentimental and compassionate, the Snake is indifferent and detached. While one tends to get involved in the problems of others, the other stays aloof and unmoved. Thus the temperaments of the two differ, as do also their attitudes and their way of getting things done. The Snake is a thinker and uses his/her head. The Sheep is intuitive and is often swayed by emotion. On the surface therefore this looks like an unlikely couple. Yet the attraction between them stems from their secret admiration of each other's attributes. The Sheep admires the Snake's rational approach and appreciates the way the Snake thinks things through. The Snake on the other hand is moved by the Sheep's gracious and gentle demeanour. It is therefore a match that has a good chance of success. As long as one allows the other to behave according to their own respective natures, there should be few problems.

The influence of the Elements
The Snake's natural element is fire while the Sheep's natural element is earth. In the cycle, fire produces earth. The Snake, in this case will support and sustain the Sheep. He/she will take command and steer the relationship accordingly, and the Sheep will accept, and benefit from, the Snake's foresight and direction.

Snake of marriageable age are those born in 1965 (wood Snake 31 years old in 1996) or 1977 (fire Snake 19 years old in 1996)

Sheep of marriageable age are those born in 1967 (fire Sheep 29 years of age in 1996) or in 1979 (earth Sheep 17 years old in 1996)

In any cycle, the Snake will be older than the Sheep, and it is highly probable that the Snake will be the male and the Sheep will be the female. As both are yin signs, they are both yielding and can easily compromise.

Marriage between a fire Snake and an earth Sheep introduces the additional elements of fire for the Snake, (which enhances its fire), and earth for the Sheep which exhausts the energy of the Sheep. In this case the Snake's fire will give strength and patience and will be good for the union. A marriage between a wood Snake and a fire Sheep strengthens both equally, and is also good for the relationship.

SNAKE/HORSE
Attraction, but jealousy lurks

Two intuitive yet vastly different personalities are represented in this pairing. The Snake tends to be something of an introvert, ruled more by the head than by the heart. Deeply thinking and cautious he/she rarely makes a move impulsively. The Horse on the other hand is spontaneous and headstrong, and tends toward seeking immediate gratification. The Horse is emotional, often ruled by the heart, and frequently impetuous as well. The attraction between the two could be a case of opposites attracting. One finds the other beguiling, and spurred on by the Horse's enthusiasm, the Snake could well let down his/her guard and get caught up in an exciting frenzy of courtship and passion. Both are stimulated by their fire nature, but deep suspicion could create obstacles in this relationship. They can build a lasting love together if the Horse settles down, as he/she will surely do as maturity sets in, and then the union would become a gloriously happy one ... but the Snake will have to exercise patience, otherwise jealousy could ruin the trust between them.

The influence of the Elements
The Snake's natural element is fire while the Horse's natural element is also fire. Neither dominates in this relationship, and their respective natures will find free rein in the relationship. How successful the match will be, will depend on the influence of their heavenly stem elements. But the yin and yang configuration bodes well for the union.

Snake of marriageable age are those born in 1965 (wood Snake 31 years old in 1996) or 1977 (fire Snake 19 years old in 1996)

Horse of marriageable age are those born in 1966 (fire Horse 30 years of age in 1996) or in 1978 (earth Horse 18 years old in 1996)

In any cycle, the Snake will be older than the Horse, and it is highly probable that the Snake will be the male and the Horse will be the female ... but it is the Horse that is yang and the Snake who is yin !
A pairing between a fire Snake and an earth Horse introduces the additional elements of fire for the Snake, (which enhances its fire), and earth for the Horse which exhausts the energy of the Horse. In this case the Snake's fire will give strength and patience and will be good for the union. A marriage between a wood Snake and a fire Horse strengthens both equally, and is also good for the relationship.

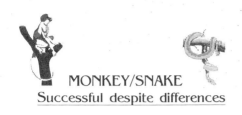

MONKEY/SNAKE
Successful despite differences

Can they trust each other ? Can these two very calculating representatives of the Zodiac forge a successful partnership together. Can they live in the same house, under the same roof ? The answer depends as much on their respective circumstance when they first come together, as on the incidental cooperation of the elements ! If they are individuals from the same social class, the match could well turn out to be brilliant, but where one comes from a family which has a higher social status, there could be difficulties, because there will always be a quiet corner of distrust. Both these people are ambitious and crafty, with independent personalities and a quite different approach to life. The Snake slithers among the bushes, never impulsive, seldom obvious ... the Monkey jumps from branch to branch, frolicking openly and smugly. But both are brilliant strategists, and this alone could be the basis for a solid and workable relationship.

The influence of the Elements
The Snake's natural element is fire while the Monkey's natural element is metal. In the cycle, fire destroys metal. The Snake is in command all the way here. He/she will take control and set the tone of the relationship from the start. The yang Monkey has to follow the yin Snake's lead for there to be happiness in this union ... a not necessarily easy task since the yin/yang indications do not complement the elements.

Snake of marriageable age are those born in 1965 (wood Snake 31 years old in 1996) or 1977 (fire Snake 19 years old in 1996)

Monkeys of marriageable age are those born in 1968 (earth Monkey, 28 years of age in 1996) or in 1980 (metal Monkey, 16 years old in 1996)

In any cycle, the Snake will be older than the Monkey. It is highly probable the Snake will be the male and the Monkey will be the female.

Marriage between a fire Snake and a metal Monkey strengthens the fire of the Snake, and the metal of the Monkey. Any conflict between the two will be magnified, but the Snake stays in control. Likewise, a marriage between a wood Snake and an earth Monkey also enhances both parties. These two pairings of the Snake and the Monkey will either be very successful, or very bad ! The indications are that with the wise perseverance of the Snake, who stays in control, difficulties should be sorted out.

HORSE/SHEEP
a mutually enriching liaison

This is potentially an extremely satisfying and happy match. The mild mannered and soft spoken Sheep is deeply attracted to the more impetuous Horse personality, seeing in him/her all that is admirable and attractive. The Horse brings confident decisiveness to the couple's deliberations, while the Sheep has more than enough tolerance and diplomacy for the two of them. In building their life together, the Sheep will be content to let the Horse manage their joint affairs, and will place trust in his/her mate. Where the Sheep has special talents, the Horse will not hold her/him back. The generous nature of the Horse personality will be supportive and encouraging. This is match which will be a deeply enriching experience for both parties, and chances are, it will last for a very long time.

The influence of the Elements
The Horse's natural element is fire while the Sheep's natural element is earth. In the cycle, fire produces earth. The Horse, in this marriage will support and sustain the Sheep. He/she will take command and steer the relationship accordingly, and the Sheep will accept, and benefit from, the Horse's superior management of their affairs. Being a noble and amiable person by nature, the Horse's way of taking charge will never grate on the Sheep's nerves.

Horse of marriageable age are those born in 1966 (fire Horse 30 years old in 1996) or 1978(earth Horse, 18 years old in 1996)

Sheep of marriageable age are those born in 1967 (fire Sheep 29 years of age in 1996) or in 1979 (earth Sheep 17 years old in 1996)

Marriage between a fire Horse and a fire Sheep introduces the additional elements of fire for the Horse (which enhances its fire), and fire for the Sheep which exhausts the energy of the Sheep. In this case the Horse's fire will give him even greater strength and patience, which will be excellent for the union.

A marriage between an earth Horse and an earth Sheep weakens the Horse and strengthens the Sheep, which might not be so good for the relationship because the Horse has to be in charge. The influence of the additional elements in this second case, could cause friction between the two.

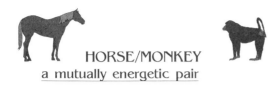

HORSE/MONKEY
a mutually energetic pair

Both are energetic, restless and amiable personalities. Their naturally friendly natures, however make for a great relationship. These are two people who will take the trouble to be *nice* to each other, rarely taking offense, and seldom getting into disagreements over petty small issues. As a result the union is productive and successful, and they accomplish significant things together. They are also able to bring out the best in each other. On top of which they are independently clever people, so there will not be any annoying *clinging* to each other on the part of either party. Yet there is much one can teach the other, and the alliance will benefit from shared intimacies and ambitions. They work well as a team because their talents are complementary, the Horse being a solid worker (when he buckles down to work), the Monkey being shrewd and resourceful.

The influence of the Elements
The Horse's natural element is fire while the Monkey's natural element is metal. In the cycle, fire destroys metal. The Horse, in this marriage will tend to dominate the Monkey. He/she will take command and steer the relationship accordingly, and the Monkey will accept, and benefit from, the Horses hardworking husbanding of their affairs. But the Monkey will also be able to teach the Horse a few tricks, and because the Horse is amiable and agreeable by nature, he will welcome rather than resent the Monkey's inputs.

Horse of marriageable age are those born in 1966 (fire Horse 30 years old in 1996) or 1978(earth Horse, 18 years old in 1996)

Monkey of marriageable age are those born in 1968 (earth Monkey 28 years of age in 1996) or in 1980 (metal Monkey, 16 years old in 1996)

Marriage between a fire Horse and an earth Monkey introduces the additional elements of fire for the Horse (which enhances its fire), and earth for the Monkey which also enhances its energy. The union becomes auspicious from this enhancement because both parties benefit equally, and are able to synergism the additional luck brought by the elements.

A marriage between an earth Horse and a metal Monkey weakens the Horse and strengthens the Monkey, which might not be so good for the relationship because the Horse has to be in charge. The influence of the additional elements in this second case, could cause misunderstandings and drive a wedge between the two.

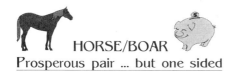

HORSE/BOAR
<u>Prosperous pair ... but one sided</u>

It will be their independent spirits, their need to be free and unshackled that will bring these two fun loving people together. The Boar will usually have the resources to enjoy a relatively undisciplined, and fairly comfortable lifestyle, and the Horse will be more than happy to enjoy the Boar's generosity. At least during the early days ... They should both use the happiness of the early years to develop genuine respect and tolerance for each other, in the process building a solid and deep relationship. They must guard against allowing the natural resentment of one being better off than the other, spill into serious conflict. This is a match that could bring happiness to both. But the Boar has a tendency to turn aggressive when things don't work out the way he/she expected; and the Horse will never allow his/her spirit to be broken. Theirs will be a fire/water relationship, it could either become a genuinely powerful alliance, as when fire turns water into powerful steam, or they could end up hurting each other horribly.

The influence of the Elements
The Horse's natural element is fire while the Boar's natural element is water. In the cycle, <u>water destroys fire.</u> The Boar in this marriage will tend to dominate the Horse. He/she will take command and steer the relationship, but the Horse is by nature a free spirit, and it will not be easy to tame this animal ! If he/she will accepts the Boar's lead, things will stand a better chance of working out. Otherwise there could be conflict. The fact that the Boar is a yin animal and the Horse is a yang animal could add to the difficulty.

<u>Horse</u> of marriageable age are those born in 1966 (fire Horse 30 years old in 1996) or 1978(earth Horse, 18 years old in 1996)

Boar of marriageable age are those born in 1959 (earth Boar 37 years of age in 1996) or in 1971 (metal Boar 25years old in 1996)

Marriage between a <u>fire Horse</u> and a <u>metal Boar</u> introduces the additional elements of fire for the Horse (which enhances its fire), and metal for the Boar which also enhances its energy. The union becomes auspicious from this enhancement because both parties benefit equally, and should be able to take advantage of the wonderful balance provided by the elements.

A marriage between an <u>earth Boar</u> and a <u>fire Horse</u> weakens the Boar and strengthens the Horse. This could cause problems for the union.

 SHEEP/SHEEP

Immediate and total synergy ... but ...

They agree wholeheartedly with each other all the time ! They defer to each other. They like and dislike the same people. They believe in the same values ... there is complete and total similiarity of thought processes. Which makes for a great relationship ... Right ? ... Wrong ! This is a union characterized by so little real discussion and communication, that as long as things go smoothly, everything will be fine. But introduce some difficulty, or when faced with problems, all that deferment to each other leads nowhere ! There is no leadership and little real decision making in this relationship. And the sad thing will be that neither will know what's gone wrong. Sure they will be good friends, and they will be true and faithful to each other ... as long as no third party comes in to disturb. But reality could shake this couple out of their elegant stupor. Having said all of that if either of this pair of Sheep is helped along by a strong element in his/her hour of birth, chances of this union working long term gets enormously better. Because then there will be direction and they will both know where they are headed for !

The influence of the Elements

The Sheep's natural element is earth. The excess of earth could induce excesses that seriously weaken the union, and work against them, but the similiarity of element could also enhance the communication and understanding between them. The Sheep is a yin animal, they yield and give in easily, especially to those they love. This pair must be careful not to give in so much that neither is prepared to disagree, take the initiative or lead ! There is obviously much to much yin energy in this union !

Sheep of marriageable age are those born in 1967 (fire Sheep, 29 years old in 1996) or 1979 (earth Sheep 17 years old in 1996)

A marriage between two earth Sheep strengthen the yin nature of both thereby making things worse rather than better. The marriage of two fire Sheep could be better since they both get strengthened but the strength comes from fire which could activate their respective fiery natures,

This increases their propensity to look out for each other, and loyalty becomes a keynote of the relationship. The elements also add to the couple's luck, thereby broadening the chances of success for the marriage..

MONKEY/SHEEP
Better if the Monkey is the male

This is will be more of a partnership than a marriage, with the ingenious Monkey calling the shots ! The Sheep, while clever and skillful in many ways, is really naive when compared to the worldly wise and crafty Monkey, and he/she will tend to be dependent on the Monkey to steer them through the potholes and the byways of their life. Yet it is also a mutually beneficial relationship, and while the Monkey could tend to be a bit of a nag, and often get impatient with the Sheep's relatively more ponderous style, there will nevertheless be genuine caring on both sides. This is because both parties will pull their weight to make the union work ... the Monkey will likely make sure of that. The Monkey will also be very good at motivating, inspiring and bringing out the best in the Sheep. All in all, it will be much better if the Monkey were the male since it will be he who will make or break the partnership. Plus it is the Monkey who is the Yang animal and the Sheep that is yin. The leadership role thrust on him in this relationship is thus inevitable.

The influence of the Elements
The Sheep's natural element is earth. That of the Monkey is metal. In the cycle, earth produces metal. This indicates that while the Monkey is the hands on leader in this relationship, it will be the Sheep that will provide the real sustenance and support. Since the Sheep nature is giving and very amiable, the relationship has a good chance of working.

Sheep of marriageable age are those born in 1967 (fire Sheep, 29 years old in 1996) or 1979 (earth Sheep 17 years old in 1996)

Monkey of marriageable age are those born in 1968 (earth Monkey 28 years old in 1996) or 1980 (metal Monkey 16 years old in 1996)

A marriage between the earth Sheep and the metal Monkey strengthens the respective yin and yang natures of both which indicates that it would be better for the Monkey to be the husband, even though he will be one year younger. At any rate, the elements are deemed to be auspicious as there is good balance.. The marriage of a fire Sheep and an earth Monkey is even better since they both get strengthened. Fire produces earth while earth produces metal. The cycle works in favour of the couple, and the indications are auspicious.

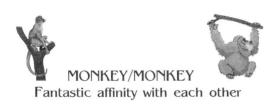

MONKEY/MONKEY
Fantastic affinity with each other

Oh what a fun and happy pair this will be ! Their sense of humour will pervade all their plotting and planning as they hatch up one scheme after another. Life to them, is one huge game, as they wheedle their mutual friends and fight their common adversaries. They are loyal and faithful to each other's interests, and they love doing things together. They also both have a passion for travel and adventure and their shared pursuits ... roaming the world for instance ... will bring them closer together. This is an energetic and spirited pair, always talking, always debating, and seldom lapsing into silences. Their household will be chatty and alive with people because both adore entertaining, and are gregarious. The main danger in this relationship is if, and when they start getting competitive with each other. This will be when the fun and games could stop being jolly, and start getting serious ... even dangerous. They could also get themselves over extended, but should this happen, they can depend on their Monkey nature to get them out of the woods ... altogether this coupling is a safe bet ...

The influence of the Elements
The Monkey's natural element is metal. The excess of metal here could work against them in the long term, making their restless and competitive natures even more so. Exactly how much this will affect them in a negative way will depend on whether there are other elements in their hour of birth, which could serve to reduce their energy, by infusing them with a huge dose of common sense. However, because the Monkey is also frequently practical, the danger of being over active can be safely discounted.

Monkey of marriageable age are those born in 1968 (earth Monkey 28 years old in 1996) or 1980 (metal Monkey 16 years old in 1996)

Marriages between two earth Monkeys or two metal Monkeys, will energize them even further. The surfeit of the earth element makes things unbalanced, and the couples here would be wise to temper the earth element with some water ... which would in effect help to cool down their energies to some extent. If water features in their respective hour of birth, it will add to the relationship. This is because water exhausts metal, but does not destroy it. The element of fire could also be suitable, but since fire destroys metal, too much fire could have the opposite effect.

MONKEY/BOAR

<u>Compatibility there sure is</u>

These two outgoing extroverts make a great couple. They are positive and optimistic about life in general, seeing in one another a perfect blend of two complementary natures. Each has much to bring to the synergy of the relationship and this not lost on either party. The Monkey's astute and quick thinking mind livens up dialogue between the two. The Boar will appreciate this, to the extent of deferring to the Monkey in important decision making situation. As a result, the Monkey will not meet up with too much resistance when he/she attempts to curb the Boar's extravagant spending habits, and could also succeed in getting the Boar to work, thereby making him/her less laid back and indolent.

This is a match where there will be a great deal of communication, since both parties love to talk. But it is also an effective partnership of two achievement oriented individuals. In all likelihood the yin Boar will defer to the manipulative yang Monkey to the greater good of both parties.

The influence of the Elements
The Monkey's natural element is metal. That of the Boar is water. In the cycle of element relationships, metal produces water, which in this case indicates that the Monkey will provide support and encouragement to the Boar. And because he/she is manipulative rather than autocratic, the relationship holds out the promise of great happiness. This is because the Boar generally responds better to persuasion than dominance.

Monkey of marriageable age are those born in 1968 (earth Monkey 28 years old in 1996) or 1980 (metal Monkey 16 years old in 1996)

Boar of marriageable age are those born in 1959 (earth Boar 37 years old in 1996) or 1971 (metal Boar, 25 years old in 1996).

Marriage between <u>an earth Monkey</u> and a <u>metal Boar</u>, will energize them both. This is because the Monkey's natural element is strengthened by earth, which produces metal; and the Boar's natural element is strengthened by metal, which produces water. The cycle flows smoothly, and the couple continually support each other in their ventures and endeavors. The teamwork between them is easily perceived, as the elements work auspiciously in their favour.

 DOG/BOAR

An enduring and intimate couple

While these two individuals are not terribly alike, they do share one thing in common, and that is their amiable and accommodating natures. If they come together in a love match, their relationship will be characterized by a great deal of intimacy, and possibly a deep and abiding affection. Loyalty and support of each other come naturally to them both, and chances of the two of them staying faithful to each other are indeed high. The union will also be characterized by a great deal of trust and sincerity, since the Boar and the Dog are by nature, honest individuals who are neither crafty nor manipulative.

Both will also have healthy sensual appetites for each other making for a happy and fulfilled sex life ... if there are any dark clouds that could cause trouble between the two, it could come from the Boars' tendency to take advantage of the Dog's seeming good nature, although being no pushover, the Dog deals with this in his stride. The yang Dog and the yin Boar have little difficulty in building a comfortable life together.

The influence of the Elements

The Dog's natural element is earth. That of the Boar is water. In the cycle of element relationships, earth destroys water, which in this case indicates that the Dog will be the one controlling the Union, which will balance out the Boar's tendency to bully the Dog, and hence the element influence is excellent in terms of balancing out their natures.

Dog of marriageable age are those born in 1970 (metal Dog, 26 years old in 1996) or 1982 (water Dog 14 years old in 1996)

Boar of marriageable age are those born in 1959 (earth Boar 37 years old in 1996) or 1971 (metal Boar, 25 years old in 1996).

Marriage between a metal Dog and a metal Boar, will exhaust the Dog and energize the Boar. This will be good for the match since the Boar's natural element has been strengthened by metal, making him/her behave even more true to type, i.e. being compliant and yielding. . When analyzing the effect of the elements, it is always necessary to combine the analysis with an understanding of the true natures of the respective animal signs, since elements react differently on different substances and situations. In this case the yang nature of the Dog makes him the natural leader, while the yin nature of the Boar makes her a naturally yielding person.

ROOSTER/BOAR
Flashes of brilliance

The domineering and aggressive Rooster finds love and comfort in the arms of the easy going and affable Boar, whose disorganized and undisciplined approach to life brings out the Rooster's protective instincts. Funnily enough the Boar also feels protective of the Rooster, and is able to tolerate the Rooster's loud singing and dancing about ! The Boar knows that the Rooster's industrious nature will tend to make him/her a perfectionist, so that any nagging tendencies on the part of the Rooster is well absorbed and understood. The Boar listens patiently, agrees amicably and proceeds to do things his/her way. Discussion is mostly one sided, but it never leads to controversy or fights. The Boar really knows how to handle the Rooster, and vice versa, as a result of which there will be flashes of brilliance in this match. Spurred on by the Boar's quiet encouragement, and helped along by his/her mate's admirable networking skills, the Rooster will have much to crow about in terms of career and business accomplishments. This is a good match indeed. Both parties can look forward to a happy time together.

The influence of the Elements
The Rooster's natural element is metal. That of the Boar is water. In the cycle of element relationships, metal produces water, which in this case indicates that the Rooster will provide support and sustenance to the Boar. It is likely that he/she will be the breadwinner of the family. And because he/she is protective as well as responsible, the relationship holds out the promise of great happiness. This is because the Boar generally responds in an appreciative manner thereby providing motivation to the Rooster..

Rooster of marriageable age are those born in 1969 (earth Rooster 27 years old in 1996) or 1981 (metal Rooster, 15 years old in 1996)

Boar of marriageable age are those born in 1959 (earth Boar 37 years old in 1996) or 1971 (metal Boar, 25 years old in 1996).

Marriage between an earth Rooster and a metal Boar, will energize them both. This is because the Rooster's natural element is strengthened by earth, which produces metal; and the Boar's natural element is strengthened by metal, which produces water. The cycle flows smoothly, and the couple continually support each other in their ventures and endeavors.

THE CHINESE ZODIAC WHEEL

The Chinese Zodiac Wheel, featured on the cover of this book indicates many things ! The twelve animal signs are placed round the wheel in their order of appearance in the Chinese calendar of twelve year cycles, starting with the rat and then followed in a clockwise direction, by the ox, the tiger, the rabbit, the dragon, the snake, the horse, the sheep, the monkey, the rooster, the dog, and the boar. In case there is confusion in the minds of readers who refer to other texts on the subject, the sheep is sometimes referred to as the goat; the rooster as the chicken, and the boar as the pig. The cat does not feature in the Chinese Zodiac, and the Tiger is deemed to represent the cat family, in the same way the Rooster represent all the winged creatures, which is why some outstanding Roosters are said to symbolize the Phoenix ! And the Snake represent the reptiles, while the Monkey represents the apes, the gorillas and the baboons ...

The Wheel shows the triangles of affinity made up the four groupings of Rat, Dragon and Monkey: the Ox, Snake and Rooster; the Tiger, Horse, and Dog; and the Rabbit, Sheep and Boar. These animal trinities get along.

The wheel also shows the arrows of antagonism, which indicate animals directly opposite each other not getting along at all !

Finally the wheel also shows the yin/or yang nature of the animals, as well as the natural element of each animal. These refer to the element of the earthly branch, which is another way of describing the animals themselves !

112 CLASHING COMPATABILITIES
THE ARROWS OF ANTAGONISM

In the Chinese Zodiac Wheel, *poison arrows of antagonism* are said to be created between animal signs that are placed directly opposite each other. These indicate generalised readings of incompatibility between the signs affected. Based on this belief, there are six major incompatabilities amongst the twelve animal signs. Hence:, if you examine the Zodiac Wheel reproduced on the preceding page (and also on the cover) you will see that:

the Rat clashes with the Horse ....the Ox clashes with the Sheep
the Tiger clashes with the Monkey .....the Rabbit clashes with the Rooster
the Dragon clashes with the Dog and the Snake clashes with the Boar.

The arrows of antagonism
of the Chinese Zodiac Wheel

These pairings have thus been listed as basically incompatible, or clashing. Some Astrologers interpret these opposing signs as being the natural enemies of the Chinese Zodiac, and indeed, viewed in general terms, partnerships and marriages between them are rarely happy, and often break up amid recriminations. Even when there is no breakup, there will be persistent tensions in the relationship.

In addition to incompatibilities caused by opposing arrows of antagonism, there are also other pairings where severe conflicts are caused by the intrinsic nature of the signs.

All individuals, depending on the signs they are born under, will tend to reveal specific types of behavior, especially with respect to the way they respond and react to others. This inner nature is often the cause of conflict between incompatible partners. Nevertheless, the reader should understand that characteristics of individuals often get magnified, or diminished by element influences and ascendant hours of birth. In addition, please note that incompatibilities between clashing animal signs show up and become evident only within close relationships as in a marriage or a close business partnership. Incompatibilites often do not prevent them from becoming good friends. This is because good friends do not live or work together.

 RAT/RABBIT

Potentially disastrous ... cut

There will be precious little affection between these two, and quite definitely a lack of trust. The insecure but demonstrative Rat will react negatively to the Rabbit's aloof reserve, and will misinterpret everything the Rabbit does, and does not do. Thus, there will be an absence of communication. The Rabbit will regard the Rat's many grand schemes with disdain, and is unable to provide either support or encouragement. Rebuffed, the Rat's already massive insecurities will get magnified, to an extent where there will grow a coldness between them, which even the grandest windfall cannot thaw. In the early stages of the relationship, expectations of both parties will be too high. There is no sincere effort to understand or compromise. Instead both are devious and calculating. Each is interested only in what can be got out of the relationship. It is thus better if the match is severed at the outset. Otherwise, they are merely setting themselves up for heartbreak and disappointment.

The influence of the Elements

The Rat 's natural element is water. The Rabbit's natural element is wood. In the cycle, water produces wood. The Rat will thus be expected to be the provider in this relationship, and will attempt to control or restrict the rabbit. This leads to resentment on the part of the sensitive Rabbit, who does not take kindly to the Rat encroaching on his/her independence.. The Rabbit will not defer to the Rat, and the Rat is not strong enough to impose his will ... leading to resentment on both sides.

Rat of marriageable age are those born in 1960 (metal Rat 36 years of age in 1996) or 1972 (water Rat 24 years old in 1996)

Rabbit of marriageable age are those born in 1963 (water Rabbit 33 years of age in 1996) or in 1975 (wood Rabbit 21 years of age in 1996)

Marriages between a metal Rat and a water Rabbit could work, since the elements strengthen both sides, giving them much needed energy to overcome their personality clashes. Metal produces the Rat's water; while water produces the Rabbit's wood, a smooth cycle of auspicious indications. A marriage between a water Rat and a wood Rabbit is similiarly favourable to both, their respective elements being once again enhanced. With the Rats being probably older, and more likely to be the husband, his yang nature will also work in his favour, and provide him with the will power to win the Rabbit's respect, thereby making the match work.

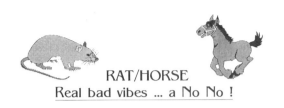

RAT/HORSE
Real bad vibes ... a No No !

This is one of the worse pairing of the Chinese Zodiac. It represents a strong clash of wills, and a total absence of communication and unless the ascendant hours contribute towards the compatibility of these two it is a match best broken off before it gets too far along. The Horse is a restless free spirit, completely devoid of snobbish tendencies or insecure behavior. The Horse also does not have the kind of intense ambition which the Rat has. He/she simply cannot understand why the Rat needs to be so calculating, or to be so concerned about other people's opinions. The Rat on the other hand, cannot abide by the Horse's impulsive nature, and strongly disapproves of what he/she sees as an irresponsible attitude. Both sides will get agitated and disappointed with one another, and because they are both yang, neither side will be inclined to give in. Their elements, fire and water also clash !

Influence of the elements
The Rat's natural element is water while the Horse's natural element is fire. In the cycle, water destroys fire. The Rat will dominate the Horse, who will not accept any attempts to curtail either his freedom or his restless spirit. The stage is set for a quite explosive face off !

Rat of marriageable age are those born in 1960 (metal Rat 36 years of age in 1996) or 1972 (water Rat 24 years old in 1996)

Horse of marriageable age are those born in 1966 (fire Horse 30 years of age in 1996) or in 1978 (earth Horse 18 years of age in 1996)

Marriages between a water Rat and a fire Horse might succeed since the elements strengthen both sides, giving them additional impetus to overcome their resentments. Water expands the Rat's own water; while fire does the same for the Horse's fire. Here the Horse is male and this could work help the match along.

A marriage between a metal Rat and a fire Horse is similiarly favourable to both, their respective elements being once again augmented. With the Rat being older, and more likely to be the husband, this configuration of elements could be auspicious.

Note: While the Rat/Horse pairing is deemed incompatible under the *arrows of antagonism* theory, friends born under these signs could well get along famously, that is unless they get too close, and into each other's hair. Readers should not be surprised at good solid friendships between the two. It is only when they live together that severe problems arise.

RAT/SNAKE
Only skin deep ... look elsewhere

Any relationship between these two individuals can only be skin deep. There is, at best, a superficial interaction between them, and at worst, no communication at all. When the honeymoon is over, the Rat's talkative nature and his need to be always doing something, exhausts the Snake's patience. Indeed, the Snake's serious and almost secretive nature contrasts sharply with the Rat's gregarious need for loud and boisterous behaviour. Things could even reach a stage where the Snake would start to resent the Rat's many clumsy attempts to pry into the inner recesses of her/his mind, as a result of which she/he could totally switch off. Even if the two are involved in a partnership, their totally different styles of working and thinking make the going tough and an uphill climb. Interests clash, as do goals and strategies. Neither party can or will give way, not due to stubbornness, but simply because there will be a very serious lack of understanding ... it will take real effort to make this match work. The Rat here is at a disadvantage.

The influence of the Elements
The Rat 's natural element is water. The Snake's natural element is fire. In the cycle, water destroys fire, resulting in the Rat being the more domineering of the two. The problem is, the more the Rat tries to dominate the Snake, the worse the problem becomes. The Snake does not respond to autocratic behavior that is too direct and obvious. The Snake has to be persuaded and cajoled. She/he is seldom pliable, and never compliant.

Rat of marriageable age are those born in 1960 (metal Rat 36 years of age in 1996) or 1972 (water Rat 24 years old in 1996)

Snake of marriageable age are those born in 1965 (wood Snake 31 years of age in 1996) or in 1977 (fire Snake 19 years of age in 1996)

Marriages between a metal Rat and a wood Snake might succeed since the elements strengthen both sides, giving them much needed energy to overcome their different dispositions. Metal produces the Rat's water; while wood produces the Snake's fire, a smooth cycle of auspicious indications. A marriage between a water Rat and a fire Snake is similarly favourable to both, their respective elements being once again augmented. With the Rat being older, and more likely to be the husband, his yang nature will help him by providing him with the will power to win the Snake's respect. Only by doing so can the match work.

RAT/SHEEP
Not an easy match ... let go

It will require a great deal of effort and patience for these two very different personalities to create an amicable and long lasting relationship. Both the Rat and the Sheep require constant reassurance, yet they are probably the very types who are unable to provide this for each other. There is a tendency to be selfish on both their parts ! The Rat is insecure and loud, and could even be abrasive. The Sheep is gentle and peace loving and could be scared off by the Rat's very forward and direct nature. ! On top of which, it is in the Rat's make up to hoard, and to save for a rainy day, reflecting his careful nature. The Sheep on the other hand is quite relaxed about the future and certainly has none of the Rat's stinginess. This serious difference of attitude could well be a bone of contention between the two and could cause major disagreements to occur. Both are sociable and mix easily, but the difference in attitudes and responses to friends and associates could also cause a serious rift. This is not a match that has good long term success potential.

Influence of the elements
The Rat's natural element is water while the Sheep's natural element is earth. In the cycle, earth destroys water. The Rat's insecurities could be fanned by the Sheep's indifference. The Rat will also not take kindly to the Sheep's persistent nagging and criticisms, or his/her attempts to take charge of the relationship. The news really is not very good at all.

Rat of marriageable age are those born in 1960 (metal Rat 36 years of age in 1996) or 1972 (water Rat 24 years old in 1996)

Sheep of marriageable age are those born in 1967 (fire Sheep 29 years of age in 1996) or in 1979 (earth Sheep 17 years of age in 1996)

Marriages between a water Rat and a fire Sheep could work since the elements strengthen both parties, giving them additional impetus to deal with conflicts and disagreements. Water expands the Rat's own water, and also soothes the Rat's nature while fire expands the Sheep's earth.. With the Sheep being older as the husband, this pair could work through their problems. A marriage between a water Rat and a earth Sheep is similiarly favourable to both.

RAT/ROOSTER
No compatibility ... best to avoid

This is such a serious mismatch ... that to avoid later pain and mental anguish, it is best to let go of the relationship, and look elsewhere ! In this marriage of the Rooster with the Rat, there is so much quarreling, so much incessant recriminations and shouting matches ... that there will be no peace in the house. The Rooster's superior attitude grates on the Rat's nerves and gnaws into his/her confidence, fueling feelings of inadequacy and insecurity. The Rat takes out his/her frustrations by constantly nagging and brooding, repeatedly letting the other party down through sheer stubbornness and a real intention to hurt. Neither side will give in, and the two get caught in a terrible downward spiral that could well destroy one or both together. There is no understanding here because neither party wishes to make the effort to do so. This is such a bad match that I repeat the advice to look elsewhere. There is no love and definitely no sensitivity in this relationship !.

Influence of the elements
The Rat's natural element is water while the Rooster's natural element is metal. In the cycle, metal produces water. In this relationship, it will be the Rooster who will support and sustain the relationship. This will further exacerbate the Rat's resentments, and cause the match to flounder. The Rooster also lacks the patience to tolerate the Rat's insensitivity and insecurities. The elements reflect the incompatibility between the two.

Rat of marriageable age are those born in 1960 (metal Rat 36 years of age in 1996) or 1972 (water Rat 24 years old in 1996)

Rooster of marriageable age are those born in 1969 (earth Rooster 27 years of age in 1996) or in 1981 (metal Rooster 15 years of age in 1996)

Marriages between a water Rat and an earth Rooster could work since the elements strengthen both parties, giving them additional impetus to deal with conflicts and disagreements. Water soothes the Rat's insecure nature while earth brings inner fortitude to the Rooster. Also, since the Rooster is older, he is very likely the husband in this match, and this assists the relationship ... since pressure on the Rat to perform, so to speak, will be eased. Since she does not need to be the breadwinner, her pragmatic character will induce her to occasionally give in to the domineering Rooster, thereby setting the stage for some peace between them. Nevertheless, because of their basic incompatibility, the match will be difficult.

RAT/DOG
A tiresome match ... give up

A quite impractical and potentially sad match. These two bring out the worse in each other. The Dog, so normally faithful and loyal will be put off by the Rat's insensitivity and selfishness, viewing him/her as self centered and not worth loving. The Rat discovers that the Dog's initial warm hearted nature does not last, and starts to mistrust and questions the Dog's motives. The mix up in communication cause a great deal of barking and shouting, and things will, instead of getting better over the years, get a whole lot worse. This is because, the Rat's insecure nature will get in the way of there being any genuine communication; and the Dog will simply give up trying to make things work ... and instead, look elsewhere for love, encouragement and support. This match could end up sad and loveless, as each retreats into his/her own shell. The chill between the two will be unlikely to thaw.

Influence of the elements
The Rat's natural element is water while the Dog's natural element is earth. In the cycle, earth destroys water. In this relationship, it will be the Rat who will be the dominant party, and all his attempts to take charge will meet with resistance from the Dog. Because there is little communication between the two, and because the Dog will basically have dwindling respect for the Rat, he/she will resist all efforts to be controlled by the Rat.

Rat of marriageable age are those born in 1960 (metal Rat 36 years of age in 1996) or 1972 (water Rat 24 years old in 1996)

Dog of marriageable age are those born in 1958 (earth Dog 38 years of age in 1996) or in 1970 (metal Dog 26 years of age in 1996)

Marriages between a water Rat and an metal Dog indicate a pairing of a stronger Rat and an exhausted Dog. This is because water is the Rat's natural element, and earth produces metal, so that metal in effect exhausts anyone of the earth element. In this case the Rat's more aggressive approach and stronger mental attitude could wear the Dog down. Whether or not it will be good for the marriage will depend on the Dog's acceptance (or not) of the Rat's attempts to dominate. It is also possible that the much energized Rat's eyes could stray ... leaving the hapless Dog to his/her own devices. Because of the basic incompatibility in the first place, the elements, instead of helping the relationship could well make things a lot worse, and even hasten the demise of the relationship altogether.

Note: Although the Zodiac indicates strife between these two animal signs, they can still be friends. But it is recommended that they should not get too close, and sharing rooms or accommodation is not a good idea.

 OX/TIGER
A disastrous relationship ...sad !

These are two extremely strong individuals, whose personalities are as different as day and night ! The Ox is steady and disciplined ... not one to go for dramatic theatrics. The Tiger is undisciplined and something of a rebel at heart, a person who will growl his way through life ... Between the two, it will be tough to find common ground. Both their goals, as well as their way of doing things will differ substantially. If one could give in, or defer to the other, this match might well work ... for both have formidable qualities and are people of substance. Yet precisely because of their intrinsic powerful natures, and also their tremendous egos, pride will always stand in the way. The Ox will be slow to anger but when aroused will charge like a bull in a china shop. The Tiger is ferocious when crossed. Quick to anger, he/she will be impatient with, and retaliate against, the Ox's icy coldness. Unless the ascendant hours of birth introduce soothing elements to the relationship, the match will fall apart ... which is sad really, because if they could only cooperate, the courage of the Tiger and the determination of the Ox could carry this couple aloft into heady spheres of accomplishments.

The influence of the Elements
The Tiger's natural element is wood, while the Ox's natural element is earth. In the cycle, wood destroys earth. The yang Tiger will dominate the yin Ox, setting the stage for a confrontational stance where neither will win. This is because the erstwhile Ox is neither pliable nor compliant by nature.

Ox of marriageable age are those born in 1961 (metal Ox 35 years of age in 1996) or in 1973 (water Ox 23 years old in 1996)

Tigers of marriageable age are those born in 1962 (water Tiger, 34 years old in 1996) or 1974 (wood Tiger, 22 years old in 1996)

A marriage between a metal Ox and a water Tiger weakens the Ox and strengthens the Tiger. This provides additional energy to an already energetic Tiger. If the relationship works, the weakened Ox will be under the thumb of the Tiger, but there will be inner conflicts and resentments. This match is not recommended.

In a marriage between the water Ox and the wood Tiger both overcome the influence of the elements. The match does not get better or worse. It is advisable for both parties to find someone else more compatible.

 OX/DRAGON

<u>Spells eventual heartbreak</u>

If only they could be supportive of each other, the steady Ox helping the idealistic Dragon ... as it at first appears during the initial months of courtship, this pair could forge a satisfying and fulfilling relationship. But their natures are basically incompatible because the reality is that the down to earth Ox will have little time or patience for what he/she will regard as the Dragon's wild flights of fancy. Idealism has little place in the deliberations of the pragmatic Ox. Impatience and irritation becomes the order of the day, and the relationship could spiral into heartbreak ... this is because frustration and despondency will set the stage for a major turning away from one another. And where under normal circumstances, the faithful Ox could have been a magnificent and responsible supporter, their paths diverge instead. Devoid of encouragement and applause, the Dragon's enthusiasm will be seriously undermined. If the ascendants and the elements help the pair by giving greater strength to the Dragon, things will be a whole lot better.

The influence of the Elements
Both the Dragon and the Ox's natural elements are earth. But where the Dragon is yang, the Ox is a yin animal. The yang Dragon will want to dominate the yin Ox, and if he/she has the strength to do so, this match might work. But while the Ox might be easier to manipulate, he/she is seldom easy to control with brute strength.

Ox of marriageable age are those born in 1961 (metal Ox 35 years of age in 1996) or in 1973 (water Ox 23 years old in 1996)

Dragon of marriageable age are those born in 1964 (wood Dragon, 32 years old in 1996) or 1976 (fire Dragon 20 years old in 1996)

A marriage between a <u>metal Ox</u> and a <u>wood Dragon</u> depletes the Ox's energy, and strengthens the Dragon considerably, making the match more likely to work, and indeed could even transform the pair into a dynamic team together. Energized, the Dragon is more confident and self sufficient, which will bring the Ox round to his/her way of thinking and doing things.

In a marriage between the <u>water Ox</u> and the <u>fire Dragon</u> both overcome the influence of the elements although in different ways, and the Dragon is also strengthened as well. This confluence of elements also benefits the match, making the Dragon strong, and the Ox more tolerant. The marriage could work if Both sides try real hard !

OX/HORSE
Exhausting, trying union

The two of them together think along parallel lines, their minds seldom meeting, and their intellects usually not communicating. Any attempts on the part of either person to find common ground is an uphill battle, simply because they truly are so different. The Horse is quick witted and impulsive ... the ultimate free spirit. He/she is restless, always on the move, always having to keep busy. The Ox, on the other hand can be slow and plodding, always deliberating ever so carefully before making a move. He/she respects tradition, prefers to follow the well worn path, and could even be described as unadventurous by the Horse, to whom anyone who is not immediately enthusiastic about anything, is seen as unadventurous. The Horse is unable to appreciate the Ox's leadership qualities nor perceive his/her great substance of intellect. Sometimes the Horse could even dismiss the Ox as dumb ... which would be a huge mistake since this will lead to the Horse seriously underestimating the Ox. In the end, the sorry lack of understanding gets worse and both sides become depressed. Not a good match.

The influence of the Elements
The Horse's natural element is fire, while that of the Ox is earth. In the cycle of relationships, fire produces earth. This means that it is the Horse who will sustain this relationship, and set the tone for it working or not working. Put another way, it will be the Horse who will have to work harder, either in terms of curbing his/her temperament, or in being more tolerant. The Horse is a yang animal, capable of leadership; the Ox is a yin animal and his/her leadership qualities are also very much in evidence. The yang Horse must coax the yin Ox to yield !

Ox of marriageable age are those born in 1961 (metal Ox 35 years of age in 1996) or in 1973 (water Ox 23 years old in 1996)

Horse of marriageable age are those born in 1966 (fire Horse 30 years old in 1996) or 1978 (earth Horse 18 years old in 1996)

A marriage between a water Ox and an earth Horse does not hurt the Ox's energy level, but it weakens and exhausts the Horse considerably, making the match less likely to work.

In a marriage between the metal Ox and the fire Horse the Ox is weakened while the Horse gets strengthened. This helps the relationship since the Horse now has the energy to be more patient and understanding.

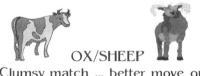 OX/SHEEP

Clumsy match ... better move on

Petulance and exasperation will characterize this relationship. The nature of the Ox and the Sheep are entirely dissimiliar. The Ox is a no nonsense sort of person who has little time to waste on emotion, while the Sheep, who is not necessarily headstrong or impulsive, tends nevertheless to be emotional. The two have different priorities and their views about life and love are divergent. One sees the other as doing things the wrong way, and going off in wrong directions. Thus while both are ambitious, and can be highly motivated, their character does not allow them to see eye to eye or appreciate each other. This is a pity of course, since their skills could well make them a great pair. Unfortunately they are not sufficiently compatible to take advantage of each other's attributes and strengths. Usually the Ox person likes to think things through sensibly and surely, but preferring his/her own counsel. The Sheep on the other hand likes consulting others, and listening to other people's viewpoints. And the fact that both can be dogmatic and stubborn does not help. Theirs will be more of an adversarial than a cooperative situation. This truly is a clumsy match ... with little potential. Much better for both to move on ...

The influence of the Elements
The Sheep's natural element is earth while that of the Ox is also earth. There really seems like an excess of earth energy here except that the energies are being channeled into different directions. There is too much stubbornness in this pair, and their stamina are not compatible.

Ox of marriageable age are those born in 1961 (metal Ox 35 years of age in 1996) or in 1973 (water Ox 23 years old in 1996)

Sheep of marriageable age are those born in 1967 (fire Sheep 29 years old in 1996) or 1979 (earth Sheep 17 years old in 1996)

A marriage between a water Ox and an earth Sheep favours the Sheep since the element of the year strengthens his/her spirit, although the Ox is not in any way handicapped by the elements. But the nagging dogmatism between the two remains, and the match stays clumsy and uninspiring.
In a marriage between the metal Ox and the fire Sheep the Ox is weakened while the Sheep gets strengthened. This could help the relationship since the Sheep now has the energy to bear with the Ox's ponderous nature.

Note: There are severe arrows of antagonism aimed at each other in an Ox/Sheep match. This does not necessarily mean every Ox cannot get along with every single Sheep. Amongst friends and acquaintances, and even amongst colleagues, the two could achieve some kind of familiarity. It is when they get too intimate and too close that troubles arise.

 TIGER/TIGER
No, no, no ! Ugh ! Exhausting !

Will the law of the jungle prevail each time these two Tigers fight ? Will they get at one another's throats, fiercely intent on demolishing each other everytime they disagree ? Not at all ! Indeed, Tigers are not by nature quarrelsome or vindictive creatures. Fierce yes, and quite outstandingly courageous, but Tigers are like pussycats ... when they are stroked, they purr in contentment. The thing that goes wrong when two Tigers come together however, is that they will exhaust and debilitate one another, all the time competing and never knowing when to relax or take things easy. Tigers are extremely colourful and passionate people, whose natures make them require frequent acknowledgment and constant recognition. They need to be applauded, encouraged and motivated. Yet they also tend to be insensitive, and will not understand that their mates also require support. This insensitivity lies at the core of their problems and it will be serious enough to make them wish they had never got stuck togethe. Sadly, all their intrinsic generosity and sense of humour is lost on each other.

The influence of the Elements
The Tiger's natural element is wood. Marriage between two Tigers will be affected by the respective elements of their ascendant hours of birth.

Tigers of marriageable age are those born in 1962 (water Tiger, 34 years old in 1996) or 1974 (wood Tiger, 22 years old in 1996)

A marriage between two water Tigers strengthens them both equally. This provides additional energy to already energetic Tigers, and could increase the competitive nature in them, not necessarily a good thing for the couple. Excess of energy leads to too much activity. Besides, the Tiger is also a yang animal, and the relationship is not sufficiently balanced to be really auspicious. Yet the water element does have a soothing effect on their natures, and if properly directed and motivated, their combined energy could be channeled onto a single shared objective which could be productive. The relationship might then work ... but one of them must be willing to take a back seat. This will depend on their hours of birth. Otherwise both will get exhausted.

A marriage between two wood Tigers also strengthens their inherent natures, except that in this case the possibility of them cooperating together is quite remote. Each goes his/her own way ... and the relationship will flounder.

TIGER/MONKEY
A love hate relationship

These two impetuous yang individuals are strongly and irresistibly drawn towards each other at the start. Theirs is a relationship that is full of laughter and high adventure, with loads of intensity and energy. There is also a great deal of passion, characterized by dramatic breakups and equally emotional reconciliation. But this is an intense *love hate* relationship. They continually match wits with, and challenge each other, viewing life as a game, with neither one prepared to give in to the other. They are also both poor losers, and there is nothing graceful or diplomatic in their interface with each other. Both the Tiger and the Monkey are highly individualistic. They are determined and impulsive people. If their relationship works it will be because they understand their own strong and extrovert natures, but because they are also naturally incompatible, more likely the relationship will experience a dramatic breakup. Their magnificent fights will exhaust them, to the point of breakdown. A Tiger/Monkey match could end up being one long yelling match ! If the relationship does go sour, the breakup will be explosive and hostile !

The influence of the Elements
The Tiger's natural element is wood. The Monkey's natural element is metal. In the cycle, <u>metal destroys wood</u>, as a result of which it will be the Monkey who dominates the relationship, and takes the lead. Which is just as well since the Tiger's ferocity is no match for the Monkey's ingenuity. Yet this will also cause them to fight back below the belt. Neither sign will easily give in or play fair !

<u>Tigers</u> of marriageable age are those born in 1962 (water Tiger 34 years of age in 1996) or in 1974 (wood Tiger 22 years of age in 1996)

<u>Monkeys</u> of marriageable age are those born in 1968 (earth Monkey 28 years of age in 1996) or 1980 (metal Monkey 16 years of age in 1996)

Marriage between the <u>wood Tiger</u> and the <u>earth Monkey</u> is an excellent pairing. The elements are working in favour of this match. This is because the Tiger benefits hugely from the strengthening provided by the wood element; while the Monkey is likewise energized by the earth element, which produces metal ! The favourable element influence gives this marriage a chance of success, bringing resilience and strength to both parties. It is the Monkey who will have to set the tone for this marriage.

<u>Note:</u> the Tiger/Monkey match suggests a clash of relationships which can be quite severe, since the two are diametrically facing each other in the Zodiac wheel. If they do appear to get along, it will only be superficial, and cannot hold up in times of real crisis and stress.

TIGER/RABBIT
Clash of style and values

There is much repressed antagonism between these two very different personalities. The Tiger's brash ferocity is not looked at kindly by the seemingly docile Rabbit ! It is unlikely that they will be attracted to each other in the first place, but even if they are, the match cannot endure the great divide that exists between them. Their values and styles are too different. While the Tiger tends to be direct and confrontational, the suave and prudent Rabbit prefers diplomacy; and where the Tiger's nature is a domineering one, the Rabbit finds such behaviour crass and vulgar. The Rabbit can usually only respect people of similiar intellectual interests, and his/her tastes are normally too refined for the Tiger. Thus, he/she will view the Tiger as something of a bully, not worthy of too much attention, and definitely best avoided. In the event that two people under these signs do come together, the Tiger will tend to under estimate the Rabbit, but it will be the tactful and secretive Rabbit who will out maneuver the Tiger.

The influence of the Elements
The Tiger's natural element is wood. The Rabbit's natural element is also wood. This excess of wood in their respective year elements, makes their hour ascendants significant, since the introduction of other elements will offer clues as to the tone and direction of their relationship.

Tigers of marriageable age are those born in 1962 (water Tiger 34 years of age in 1996) or in 1974 (wood Tiger 22 years of age in 1996)

Rabbits of marriageable age are those born in 1963 (water Rabbit 33 years of age in 1996) or 1975 (wood Rabbit, 21 years of age in 1996)

Marriage between the water Tiger and the water Rabbit represents a stalemate between the pair. The elements are working equally in favour of both individuals. This is because water produces wood in the cycle. But whether or not this will be good for the match is something else again since the two are not really compatible, and is unlikely to be engaged in any joint project where the favourable elements can enhance their chances of success. Instead the elements merely embellish them separately in effect strengthening their innate nature, thereby enlarging the gulf between them. The same is true of a wood Tiger/wood Rabbit pairing.

Note: Indications of incompatibility between these two animal signs does not mean they cannot be friends. But they should not live together and sharing rooms/flats is not recommended.

 TIGER/SNAKE
No good for each other ... Split !

If a Tiger man were to pair up with Snake lady, he could well go out of his mind with frustration and anger ! Persons born of these two signs should best avoid each other, and not waste time on chasing a hopeless cause. Between the two there can be little attraction. But more important than that, they will be no good for one another. One will bring out the worst in the other. The Tiger's view of the world, and of how he/she should behave is totally out of sync with that of the Snake. Thus while the Tiger is open and forthright, wearing his/her heart on the sleeve, the Snake is secretive, keeping things close to the chest. One is dramatic and gushing, while the other is cool and aloof. Much conflict is thus indicated when these two get together, caused as much by misunderstandings of intentions and motives, as by massive failure of communication. In the end they can only harm each other and it is better to run ...

The influence of the Elements
The Tiger's natural element is wood. The Snake's natural element is fire. In the cycle wood feeds the fire, and indeed fire could well destroy wood ! It is the Tiger who will ultimately suffer in this relationship, for truly, his/her clumsy courage is no match for the seductive and mesmerizing Snake, man or woman ! In a marriage between the two, it will have to be the Tiger who will need to make the effort ... the Snake merely stays reserved and far removed from it all ....

Tigers of marriageable age are those born in 1962 (water Tiger 34 years of age in 1996) or in 1974 (wood Tiger 22 years of age in 1996)

Snakes of marriageable age are those born in 1965 (wood Snake 31 years of age in 1996) or 1977 (fire Snake, 19 years of age in 1996)

Marriage between the water Tiger and the wood Snake represents a standoff between the pair. The elements work equally in favour of both individuals. This is because water produces wood for the Tiger; while wood produces fire for the Snake. And where normally this would be great if they were compatible, this simultaneous strengthening merely enlarges the gulf between them. In the case of a marriage between a wood Tiger and a fire Snake the elements cause the Tiger to truly have a terrible time. His excess wood merely makes the Snake's fire burn brighter and bigger. He will be no match at all for the Snake. The wood Tiger should run far away from the fire Snake !

TIGER/SHEEP
Bad ! downhill all the way

How does a one sided relationship where one party gets continually intimidated and bullied by the other ever really work ? While the Sheep is no doormat, and indeed is often possessed of a superior and clever mind, he/she will not be able to stand up to the fierce and highly egoistic Tiger. In a pairing between the two, the docile and agreeable Sheep could find the Tiger extremely difficult to live with. Despite the Sheep's skills at reducing tension and confrontations, the high powered Tiger will nevertheless wear him/her down, and patience and tolerance quickly flies out of the door. This is a match that is traditionally frowned upon by most Chinese grandmothers, who according to superstition, seldom smile on a match between a Tiger and a small animal, believing in this case, that the fierce Tiger *will eat up the Sheep*. Certainly, no self respecting mother would allow her son to be married to a Tiger woman ! This fallacious belief probably has its roots in the Tiger's basic inability to live in harmony with animal signs like the Sheep, the Rabbit and the Rooster, all delicious dishes for the hungry Tiger ! ...

The influence of the Elements
The Tiger's natural element is wood. The Sheep's natural element is earth. In the cycle wood destroys earth, and this merely compounds the Tiger's ferocious character. The elements in this case are indicating a serious warning to those of you Sheep who maybe presently romantically involved with a Tiger. If you can, better cool it ... otherwise the Tiger's fierce stamina could eventually demolish your peace of mind, and your happiness. Plus remember that the Tiger is a yang animal and you are yin ... all the signs show the Tiger strongly in control. The relationship is thus unbalanced.

Tigers of marriageable age are those born in 1962 (water Tiger 34 years of age in 1996) or in 1974 (wood Tiger 22 years of age in 1996)
Sheep of marriageable age are those born in 1967 (fire Sheep 29 years of age in 1996) or 1979 (earth Sheep 17 years of age in 1996)

Marriage between the wood Tiger and the earth Sheep represents an impasse. The elements equally strengthen the inherent natures of both. This is because wood adds to the Tiger; while earth adds to the Sheep. But this simultaneous strengthening merely makes the Tiger more fierce and the Sheep more docile. In the case of a marriage between a wood Tiger and a fire Sheep, the effect will be similiar.

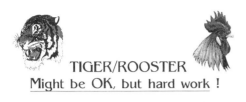

TIGER/ROOSTER
Might be OK, but hard work !

A match between the Tiger and the Rooster is the classical example of clashing personalities. The Rooster, though symbolically smaller in size than the Tiger, and certainly not possessed of the Tiger's physical strength, is nevertheless just as fierce, and equally domineering in character. The Rooster is as much an egoist, and definitely as strong willed as the Tiger. This is a case where two strong wills challenge each other ... and no matter which side wins or loses, both will bear a grudge and not forget any humiliation caused by a loss of face. Between this two there is no cooperation, They cannot work together. The Rooster is too much of a perfectionist and too much of nag, and the Tiger's independent spirit will rebel against the Rooster's obvious efforts to take charge. If the elements of the year and hour of birth favour the match, it could work out, but not without a great deal of effort on both sides. Far better to break off ...

The influence of the Elements
The Tiger's natural element is wood. The Rooster's natural element is metal. In the cycle metal destroys wood. The Rooster will clearly have the upper hand in this relationship, and the Tiger will not easily accept this. The Tiger is the yang, and the Rooster is yin. These indications, together with their inherent natures work against the pair getting close to each other. Nevertheless, if they do, the bossy Rooster will have the edge over the Tiger, unless other elements modify this.

Tigers of marriageable age are those born in 1962 (water Tiger 34 years of age in 1996) or in 1974 (wood Tiger 22 years of age in 1996)

Roosters of marriageable age are those born in 1969 (earth Rooster 27 years of age in 1996) or 1981 (metal Rooster 15 years of age in 1996)

Surprisingly, the indications of the elements for a marriage between the wood Tiger and the earth Rooster where the Rooster is probably the husband, are that the marriage could work ! This is because wood adds to the Tiger; while earth supplements the Rooster's metal. The elements are balanced in favour of the couple, and indeed, with the Rooster in control of the situation, the pair might yet find common ground. Perhaps their success together might motivate both to make the effort ... the Rooster to being more compromising, and the Tiger to being less of a rebel. Having said this, the Tiger could growl her way out of the marriage !

RABBIT/DRAGON
A one sided relationship

When a Rabbit meets with a Dragon, much of his/her legendary reasoning capabilities could fly out the window. Not normally overly emotional, the Rabbit's infatuation for the Dragon arises from perceived synergy in a fantasy match between, them. As it turns out, much of this will be sad misconceptions. For of course the reality is that the Dragon's outward flamboyance and glamour hides a distinctly impulsive soul, and the two can hardly be said to be compatible ! The Dragon is in reality a very impetuous sort, prone to making headlong decisions and dashing into wild schemes and deals ... most of which will confuse, and even mortify the staid Rabbit's well ordered view of how things should be done. The rabbit seriously misreads the Dragon's intentions ! Also, the Dragon can be supercilious and over bearing, and full of his/her own visions and dreams, wanting recognition and applause. This is all quite tiresome for the Rabbit who harbours none of these lofty ambitions, actually preferring to stay low profile and work from behind the scenes. The relationship thus becomes one sided and frustrating for the Rabbit.

The influence of the Elements
The Dragon's natural element is earth. The Rabbit's natural element is also wood. In the cycle wood destroys earth. This indicates that it is the Rabbit who will control and dominate the Dragon. If he/she succeeds in breaking the spirit of the Dragon, there could be a modicum of acceptability in the relationship, but the victory will be a hollow one since then, much of the Dragon's vitality will have been repressed. But chances are, the yin Rabbit does not have it in him/her to contain the all mighty yang Dragon, simply because it is not in his/her nature to do so. Herein will lie the root of all their problems !

Dragons of marriageable age are those born in 1964 (wood Dragon 32 years of age in 1996) or in 1976 (fire Dragon, 20 years of age in 1996)

Rabbits of marriageable age are those born in 1963 (water Rabbit 33 years of age in 1996) or 1975 (wood Rabbit, 21 years of age in 1996)

Marriage between the fire Dragon and the wood Rabbit creates extra energy in equal measures for both the Dragon and the Rabbit. For the Dragon, the fire supplements its natural earth element, while the wood is of course the Rabbit's own element. The favourable effect of the elements does not necessarily favour the match.

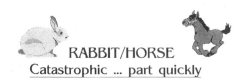

RABBIT/HORSE
Catastrophic ... part quickly

The total absence of compatibility between these two individuals is so obvious as to be glaring. They can neither live nor work amicably together, and any attempts to do so will be catastrophic.. Tempers will flare, frustrations will set in, and misunderstandings will be legion. The match brings out all of the Horse's fiery personality, as he/she tries to grapple with the disappointment of having to cope with the seemingly dull, passive and unexciting Rabbit. Meanwhile the Rabbit finds the Horse's impetuousness exhausting, and cannot understand all this talk about adventure and wanting to see the world, and wanting a change ... et al !! The Rabbit's outlook is more sedentary. Being home loving, he/she finds the Horse's restlessness disquieting and distracting, and will be unable to adapt to the kind of lifestyle favoured by the Horse. An altogether mismatch that shouldn't have taken place at all.

The influence of the Elements
The Horse's natural element is fire. The Rabbit's natural element is wood. In the cycle wood produces fire. This indicates that it is the Rabbit that must provide support and sustenance for the Horse; but the Horse also exhausts the Rabbit.

Horses of marriageable age are those born in 1966 (fire Horse 30 years of age in 1996) or in 1978 (earth Horse 18 years of age in 1996)

Rabbits of marriageable age are those born in 1963 (water Rabbit 33 years of age in 1996) or 1975 (wood Rabbit, 21 years of age in 1996)

Marriage between the earth Horse and the older wood Rabbit favours the Rabbit whose energies are supplemented by the favourable element relationship. The Horse however gets exhausted by the earth element because fire produces earth. This might not be such a bad thing for the relationship since it somewhat reduces the Horse's fiery outbursts. Nevertheless, the match is an incompatible one. The two should much rather stay friends by not becoming husband and wife ... than make for much unhappiness by getting hitched to each other.

A marriage between a fire Horse and a water Rabbit is a match between two individuals whose characteristics have been strengthened by the elements. It has an even lesser chance of working out since the incompaitibility between the two will be magnified. Not recommended.

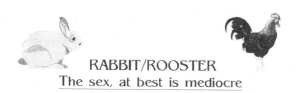

RABBIT/ROOSTER
The sex, at best is mediocre

This pair could not be further apart in terms of what each consider to be proper behaviour. The Rooster finds the Rabbit's righteous morality insufferable, and the Rabbit regards the Rooster's arrogance and pretensions annoying. One is low profile and understated, while the other is smug and conceited, carrying his/her *know it all* attitude in a manner that thoroughly grates on the Rabbit's nerves. Plus in the Zodiac, these two are supposedly natural enemies. They suffer the negative effects of each other's poison arrows, thereby bringing out the worst in one another. The Rabbit's traditional reserve turns into disdainful indifference while the Rooster's boastful nature is carried to such extremes, as to become genuinely distasteful ! They are truly bad for one another. As long as they don't have to live with each other, or see and interact with each other on a daily basis they could perhaps be good friends ... but once married, the Rabbit will regard the Rooster as nothing but a pompous show off while the Rooster will sniff haughtily at and reject the Rabbit's virtuous *holier than thou* attitude. Besides, sex between the Rooster and the Rabbit, is at best mediocre !

The influence of the Elements
The Rooster's natural element is metal. The Rabbit's natural element is wood. In the cycle metal destroys wood. This indicates that it is the Rooster who will control and dominate the Rabbit, or at least attempt to do so. But whether the Rabbit is prepared to accept the Rooster's leadership is something else again ! Based on the Zodiac readings this is quite unlikely, and being a yin animal, the Rooster will be unable to really achieve much in terms of domination over the similiarly yin Rabbit.

Roosters of marriageable age are those born in 1969 (earth Rooster 27 years of age in 1996) or in 1981 (metal Rooster, 15 years of age in 1996)

Rabbits of marriageable age are those born in 1963 (water Rabbit 33 years of age in 1996) or 1975 (wood Rabbit, 21 years of age in 1996)

Marriage between the earth Rooster and the older wood Rabbit favours the Rabbit and the Rooster equally, and their energies are supplemented by the favourable element relationship. Being the older of the two, it is likely that the Rooster is the husband. With earth producing metal, his nature is considerably strengthened but this does not do him much good since the Rabbit is also being strengthened with her own wood element.

Note: I have known Roosters who get along famously with Rabbits, despite the so called *arrows of antagonism*. But these relationships often crack when they get too close. Friendships are fine but keep your distance.

DRAGON/DRAGON
Whoa ! Squabbles galore !

The Dragon personality is strong willed, determined and thoroughly impulsive. They dash into places and situations with a great deal of courage and bravado, but often without sufficient thought. And it is the same in their love life ! When two Dragons meet, the initial enthusiasm of finding a kindred soul could cause there to be instant attraction; these are two powerful individuals whose zest for life in all its ramifications boil down to being fast, action oriented and vivacious .... two Dragons could well fall instantly and madly for each other ... but alas, the pair will find it difficult to live together. Both will want to have the upper hand, and both being strong willed, are loathe to give in. Differences of opinion when they arise will become serious issues involving emotions as well as the powerful egos of both, setting the stage for loads of spirited disagreements ! Dragons are not known for great diplomacy either, so there could be squalls and fights galore. But Dragons are also famous for not admitting defeat, and where the Elements work in their favour, this pair could well come together in a sincere effort to build something worthwhile and valuable together. This happens when their respective hours of birth contribute to a peaceful acceptance of one party as the leader. When their energies get directed in a positive and cooperative manner, the match could work ... but there will still be quarrels !

The influence of the Elements
The Dragon's natural element is earth.! They are also both yang animals, born to lead and dominate. The elements will come into play when a pair of Dragons, born of different ascendant hours come together.

Dragons of marriageable age are those born in 1964 (wood Dragon 32 years of age in 1996) or in 1976 (fire Dragon, 20 years of age in 1996)

Marriage between two fire Dragons creates extra energy in equal measures for both. Fire supplements their natural earth element. This favourable effect of the elements does not necessarily favour the match, on the other hand it could well make them more fiery and hot tempered with each other.

Marriage between two wood Dragons, results in their natural elements being reduced since wood destroys earth. This could have the effect of modifying their powerful energies, making it easier for both to get along. But a lessening of elements can also cause imbalance. It will be useful to examine the elements of the hour ascendants.

DRAGON/DOG
Exhaling and barking all night long !

These two are naturally incompatible ! It is improbable they will even find each other attractive. The spirited and impulsive Dragon has no time for the cynically inclined Dog personality. They will not be able to hold a conversation without either one coming near to losing his/her cool, and it is better that such a match does not become permanent. In the Zodiac their signs are placed directly in the path of each other's *arrow of antagonism*; they are regarded as intrinsic enemies. The Dog will sniff with disdain at the Dragon's ideas and opinions, while the Dragon finds the Dog hostile, unsupportive and a wet blanket ! The match is a serious example of clashing personalities. Not only is there little communication between them, there will be much exhaling in exasperation on the part of the Dragon, and a great deal of shrill barking from the Dog ! The continious friction between them is best dealt with by the two avoiding each other altogether; otherwise both will get hurt.

The influence of the Elements
Both the Dog and the Dragon are earth signs, and both are yang. This preponderance of earth and yang energy will accentuate the hostility between them, and bring out all their naturally aggressive instincts. Unless the hour ascendants cool down tempers, it is best they part !

Dragons of marriageable age are those born in 1964 (wood Dragon 32 years of age in 1996) or in 1976 (fire Dragon, 20 years of age in 1996)

Dogs of marriageable age are those born in 1970 (metal Dog, 26 years of age in 1996) or 1982 (water Dog, 14 years of age in 1996)

Marriage between the fire Dragon and the metal Dog creates extra energy the Dragon and exhausts the Dog. If the Dragon completely dominates the relationship, the friction will not be so pronounced. But it is still an unhappy situation. If the Dog is the male (as is likely as he is older), we will have a case of a thoroughly hen pecked husband, and a wife who will have her own agenda !

A marriage between a wood Dragon and a metal Dog is inauspicious for both ! The Dragon is weakened, and the Dog is exhausted ... a sorry state of affairs indeed. This marriage will likely end in separation or divorce, which will be just as well for the two of them, otherwise both will suffer.

Note: Dragon/Dog friendships may work sometimes, but these two really are the natural enemies of the Zodiac and cannot get too close to each other.

 SNAKE/SNAKE
Passion, promiscuity and jealousy

How can two Snakes stay faithful to each other ? How can a relationship between these two seductive, and often highly sexed individuals not have to cope with suspicions and jealousies ? Snakes are such natural charmers, and they would normally find one another madly attractive ... plus they can also work well together because both are cool and clever strategists ... they cannot fail to see and appreciate the attributes in each other. And yet, the very nature that brings them together could also cause them heartbreak ... either within a love triangle where an outside third party create havoc in their love nest, or because one gets inordinately jealous of the other's success with the opposite sex ! And even if they accept and condone marital infidelities, any commitment between them then becomes quite superficial. One thing that works in their favour is their naturally patient and calm demeanours. Snakes seldom shout or indulge in loud recriminations ... when things get too difficult, they will just quietly slither away ...

The influence of the Elements
The Snake's natural element is fire. In the cycle of elements fire is said to represent aggressive instincts. How these instincts surface differ according to the animal sign ! In the case of the yin Snake, the fire is manifested in their inherent passionate and sometimes promiscuous natures. And because the Snake is yin, any aggressiveness seen is subtle, and therefore quite inordinately effective.

Snakes of marriageable age are those born in 1965 (wood Snake 31 years of age in 1996) or 1977 (fire Snake, 19 years of age in 1996)

Marriage between two wood Snakes represents a standoff between the pair. The elements work equally in favour of both individuals. Wood produces fire for the Snake, making their Snake nature all the more in evidence. If jealousy does rear its ugly head in this relationship, it could get quite ugly. Both will scheme against the other.

In a marriage between two fire Snakes the effect of the elements is similiar because the Snake's fire is also enhanced. In such a match there will be excitement, sexual promiscuity and a great deal of jealousy. To an extent where it could cause real problems for the couple.

Note: While the Zodiac indicates inability to live in harmony between these two animal signs, this does not suggest they cannot be friends. But they should not try to get too close..

SNAKE/DOG
So lopsided its not worth it

On the surface the characters of these two individuals seem highly compatible, with one party being ambitious and apparently unselfish, (the Snake) and the other being supportive and faithful . But this merely addresses their best aspects. In reality the Snake's intense and secretive nature hides lofty ambitions which the Dog can neither appreciate nor be sympathetic with, nor indeed even understand very well ! The Dog is often straightforward, direct and naively forthright, quite the opposite of the subtle, conniving and clever Snake. Besides, the Dog is seldom very ambitious. Loyal yes, and idealistic as well. But the Snake is practical and usually all knowing. He/she can see what the Dog cannot see. To the Snake, the Dog seems too simplistic ! There is thus no meeting of the minds, and no great appreciation of each other's intellect. In many instances the Dog will plainly not be clever enough to excite and thrill the Snake for long ... indeed the Snake could well deceive the Dog without him/her ever finding out ! This will not be a relationship of mutual respect ... but both are tolerant ...

The influence of the Elements
The Snake's natural element is fire. The Dog's natural element is earth. In the cycle of elements fire produces earth. It is the Snake that calls the shots in this alliance, and it will depend on the Snake whether or not to make the relationship work ! Both are yin signs, and with one party taking the lead will quite naturally yield. The match could work.

Snakes of marriageable age are those born in 1965 (wood Snake 31 years of age in 1996) or 1977 (fire Snake, 19 years of age in 1996)
Dogs of marriageable age are those born in 1970 (metal Dog, 26 years old in 1996) or in 1982 (water Dog, 14 years of age in 1996)

Marriage between the wood Snake and the metal Dog, with the Snake as husband, strengthens the Snake and exhausts the Dog. The relationship will be totally dependent on the Snake who will have the upper hand. The Snake could have a roving eye but the marriage will stay intact. The same thing could happen in a marriage between a fire Snake and a metal Dog, except in this case it is the wife who will stray ...

In a marriage between the fire Snake and the water Dog, the Dog will not be such a doormat. The relationship will be a little more spirited, but the Snake is once again clearly in charge.

SNAKE/BOAR
Terrible, run Boar run ..

This is one of the worst matches of the Zodiac. There is absolutely no compatibility between these two. The Snake and the Boar will never see eye to eye and will disagree on everything. Anything done by one for the other will not be appreciated, and will be purely a waste of time, effort, and money ! Thus all the good intentions in the world cannot save this match from degenerating into unhappiness. Misunderstanding of motives and intentions rule the day, and in the end both sides will give up trying altogether. Besides, the two are different in so many ways as well ...so that communication between them is often completely absent. Thus while ordinarily, the Boar is obliging, considerate and kind, all of this will come across as naive, weak and dumb in the eyes of the haughty Snake ! The same is true of the Snake's good intentions. His/her propensity towards deep thought and planning will be interpreted as pretension and indecisiveness. Both cannot win in this match !

The influence of the Elements
The Snake's natural element is fire. The Boar's natural element is water. In the cycle of elements water destroys fire. It is the Boar who will want to control and dominate the relationship. Both signs are yin, and yielding comes easily and naturally tothem. Thus if the Boar has favourable additional elements that strengthen him/her, to the extent that Snake accepts it, the match could last.

Snakes of marriageable age are those born in 1965 (wood Snake 31 years of age in 1996) or 1977 (fire Snake, 19 years of age in 1996)
Boars of marriageable age are those born in 1971 (metal Boar, 25 years old in 1996) or in 1959 (earth Boar, 37 years of age in 1996)

Marriage between the wood Snake and the metal Boar, (with the Snake as husband) strengthens the Snake and the Boar equally. Neither has the advantage in terms of control and dominance of the relationship. It is the same in a marriage between the fire Snake and the metal Boar. Both signs have productive and helpful elements that add sparkle and energy to their intrinsic natures. This is not necessarily such a good thing, because although the elements bring luck to the pair, it may not necessarily bring lasting happiness. Indeed, if the Snake reverts to his/her true self, there could be a great deal of unhappiness in store for the Boar, who is therefore strongly advised to run the demanding Snake.

Note: The Snake/Boar friendship could start off well, but the two are so different, it is unlikely any friendship can stand the test of time. Scratch beneath the surface and there will be hidden resentments.

HORSE/HORSE
Early attraction withers ... ouch

Two Horses of the opposite sex will be instantly attracted to each other. Their spirited approach to life finds immediate gratification in each other's company, especially during their early years when the shared sense of adventure, and mutual love of travel could bring together. The courtship will thus be an enjoyable time. But this early attraction could shrivel as both individuals start to mature. When forced to confront the realities of working life and the shouldering of responsibilities what seemed at first exciting and thrilling will begin to lose some of its gloss. This will be when trouble between the two will start being felt.. The Horse nature possesses an impulsive and rebellious streak, and unless this is handled with care, or is somewhat tamed by a stronger willed or more determined, or more sensible person, the Horse could waffle through life quite unconcerned about his/her duty to family and friends. There will be lack of discipline and direction. And neither party will be able to motivate the other simply because both are made of the same stuff ! Two Horses with this same attitude could spell trouble with neither prepared to take responsibility for the relationship. The attraction of early days withers ...

The influence of the Elements
The Horse's natural element is fire. In the cycle of elements, fire symbolizes energy and power. In the Horse character, fire fuels the rebel spirit. When the fire element is affected by the cycle of other interactive elements in the birth chart, the Horse character is modified, and this will affect the relationship between two people born of the Horse year.

Horse of marriageable age are those born in 1966 (fire Horse 30 years old in 1996) or 1978 (earth Horse 18 years old in 1996)

A marriage between two earth Horses is probably better than marriage between two fire Horses. This is because the earth element will exhaust the fire of the Horse, thereby reducing the impulsive and irresponsible steak that is so much a part of the Horse nature. Where the additional element is also fire, the same tendency towards impulsiveness merely gets strengthened ... and this could well work against the pair.

If either one of the Horse individual has water in his/her hour ascendant, the water will cool the Horse's natural ardour somewhat, leading to a cooler head prevailing. The water element could thus work in their favour.

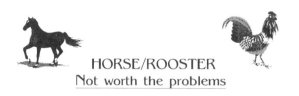

HORSE/ROOSTER
Not worth the problems

There are so many matters that cause misunderstanding and unhappiness between these two individuals, it is probably not worth it to both parties, trying to make things work. A great deal of effort, tolerance and understanding is called for simply because the two natures are quite incompatible. The Horse is affable, easy going and generally likable and diplomatic. The Rooster is a perfectionist with a strong sense of responsibility. He/she also tends to be opinionated and self centered, unable to shift from his/her rigid opinions and dogmatic attitudes. Both parties suffer from miscommunication and a total lack of appreciation of each other's aspirations and motives. Tempers flare up between them The Horse will lose patience as he/she struggles to cope with the Rooster's eloquent rhetoric. The Rooster personality will be too strong and too domineering to find acceptance with the otherwise quite adaptable Horse. The effort required to make this match work is not worth it ... since there will be little happiness in the match even when both parties compromise.

The influence of the Elements
The Horse's natural element is fire. The Rooster's element is metal. In the cycle of elements, fire destroys metal. The Horse will want to dominate and indeed will attempt to, being a yang animal. But the Rooster is impossible to subdue, and will resist all attempts to control him/her. It is truly an impossible situation fraught with difficulties.

Horse of marriageable age are those born in 1966 (fire Horse 30 years old in 1996) or 1978 (earth Horse 18 years old in 1996)

Rooster of marriageable age are those born in 1969 (earth Rooster 27 years old in 1996), or in 1981 (metal Rooster, 15 years old in 1996)

A marriage between the fire Horse and the earth Rooster energizes both parties equally. The additional fire element adds to the Horse's intrinsic and basic instincts, while the additional earth element replenishes the Rooster's metal, thereby constantly feeding it strength. This combination of elements does not ease matters between the two, and could even add to their clashing compatibility.

A marriage between an earth Horse and an earth Rooster, exhausts the Horse, causing the formidable Rooster to have the stronger hand.

Note: Even though the Zodiac indicate conflict between these two animal signs, it is not impossible for them to be chums. But they should not live together or share rooms/flats together.

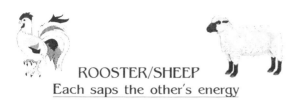

ROOSTER/SHEEP
Each saps the other's energy

Could there be anything worse than a relationship where attempts at humour are regarded with suspicion, and where relentless nagging instead, becomes a daily ritual ? This state of affairs describe a typical Rooster/Sheep couple. The Rooster in this situation tends to be rigid, autocratic and quite lacking in a sense of humour. He/she will try to take advantage of the Sheep's apparently amiable and seemingly tolerant nature. But the Sheep reacts to all of the Rooster's endless complaints with passive non resistance. Worn down and frustrated, the Sheep will use the one method that comes easily and naturally to his/her nature, and that will be to ignore the Rooster, and appear completely oblivious and indifferent. Which will only make the Rooster even more determined to get his/her opinions across. Looked at in any way, this is a relationship that exhausts both sides. There's will be silly game of one upmanship, to see who will be able to tolerate the chilly silences that arise between them. Instead of motivating and encouraging each other, the Rooster and the Sheep succeed instead, in sabotaging one another's efforts. The incompatibility of these two individuals is painful to watch as one tries to destroy the other. Sad of course, because in truth their attributes are perfectly complementary.

The influence of the Elements
The Sheep's natural element is earth. The Rooster's element is metal. In the cycle of elements, earth produces metal. The Sheep is the one who will sustain this relationship. But the Rooster is too proud to accept a situation where he/she is totally reliant on the Sheep. A great deal of tact and diplomacy on the part of the Sheep is called for. Otherwise the Rooster will bristle with resentment.

Sheep of marriageable age are those born in 1967 (fire Sheep 29 years old in 1996) or 1979 (earth Sheep 17 years old in 1996)

Rooster of marriageable age are those born in 1969 (earth Rooster 27 years old in 1996), or in 1981 (metal Rooster, 15 years old in 1996)

A marriage between the fire Sheep and the earth Rooster energizes both parties equally. The additional fire element adds to the Sheep's diplomatic and amiable nature, even while strengthening his/her resolve. This will be good for the match since firm treatment will win the Rooster's respect.

Note: Notwithstanding that the Zodiac indicates incompatibility between these two animal signs, they can be good friends, but living together or sharing accommodation is not, generally, a good idea.

SHEEP/DOG
Utterly unsuited for each other

This is a match where one party becomes completely dependent on the other. The Sheep's apparent vulnerability at first brings out all of the protective Dog's instincts. He is filled with the urge to take care of his seemingly helpless wife, while she will be want to mother the *little boy* in her mate. Eventually however the Sheep's helplessness begins to irritate the Dog, and the more the Sheep exploits the Dog's compassionate and kind nature, the more the Dog will come to resent the *clinging vine* his/her mate has become. When this happens, the Dog could turn away in annoyance, and the two will grow apart. All their differences begin to surface, and they soon discover that they really have nothing in common. However, despite the unhappiness that then overtakes this couple, the Dog is instinctively a family person, and it is unlikely that he/she will abandon the Sheep for greener and fresher pastures. The Dog has a strongly developed sense of moral duty,. He is not one for deserting the ship ... but there is little real and fulfilling happiness.

The influence of the Elements
The Sheep's natural element is earth. The Dog's element is also earth. This preponderance of earth imbues the relationship with a great deal of pragmatism. Both parties will try to make their match work, but whether or not they succeed will depend on the effect of additional elements in the birth ascendants.

Sheep of marriageable age are those born in 1967 (fire Sheep 29 years old in 1996) or 1979 (earth Sheep 17 years old in 1996)

Dog of marriageable age are those born in 1970 (metal Dog, 26 years old in 1996), or in 1982 (water Dog 14 years old in 1996)

A marriage between the fire Sheep and the metal Dog energizes the Sheep while exhausting the Dog, oh dear ! This could make the Sheep behave even more true to form, thereby exhausting the Dog further. The Sheep will need the Dog's strength, but the Dog could well disappoint ! This is because the fire element produces earth for the Sheep, thereby strengthening his/her basic nature. The Dog's earth element is busy producing the additional metal, and this is exhausting thereby sapping the Dog's strength. Not very encouraging at all.

Note: While the Zodiac indicates incompatibility between these two, it is not impossible for them to be friends. But living together is not recommended.

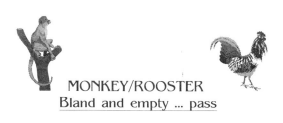

MONKEY/ROOSTER
Bland and empty ... pass

Neither side is able to see much worth in the other, and it is surprising they can even be attracted to each other sufficiently to get together in the first place. The Monkey is puzzled by the Rooster's stubborn insistence on logic and perfection and frowns at the seeming lack of creativity and imagination. Equipped with an ingenious mind and a quicksilver wit, the Monkey finds the Rooster's caustic cynicism tiring and discouraging. The erstwhile Rooster on the other hand considers the Monkey's attitude irresponsible and thinks little of his/her ideas. The two are wide apart in terms of attitude, temperament and style. They may be ambitious, but their ambitions differ substantially in nature. The Rooster wants all the material things of life ... and equates success with wealth and power, never mind how this is achieved. The Monkey's aspirations have more to do with intangibles, and he/she pursues dream projects and visions that inspire his/her creativity and imagination. The motivational factors for both are therefore different. As a result, neither can take joy in the other, and the relationship is at best, empty and boring for both of them, and at worst wildly unfulfilling.

The influence of the Elements
The yang Monkey's natural element is metal. The yin Rooster's element is also metal.. There is thus a preponderance of the metal element in this couple, and how well they can live amicably together depends on how the additional elements of their ascendants affect them.

Rooster of marriageable age are those born in 1969 (earth Rooster, 27 years old in 1996) or 1981 (metal Rooster, 15 years old in 1996)
Monkey of marriageable age are those born in 1968 (earth Monkey, 28 years old in 1996), or in 1980 (metal Monkey 16 years old in 1996)

A marriage between the earth Monkey and the earth Rooster energizes both parties equally. The additional earth element adds to both the Monkey's and the Rooster's basic instincts, and there is too much metal element as well, since the additional earth element is producing yet more metal. The Monkey becomes cheekier and craftier while the Rooster becomes more cynical and critical. Neither side can dominate, and neither side will give in. The match could flounder badly. A marriage between a metal Rooster and a metal Monkey likewise has too much metal !!

MONKEY/DOG
A match made in hell

There is little to recommend this match ! In addition to the two having completely different values, this is a couple whose initial attraction and love could turn into raging discontent. There will be much disappointment as they get to know each other ... the Dog cannot tolerate the Monkey's habitual economy with the truth, and sees it as a basic dishonesty that is totally unacceptable and out of line. Love will surely turn to resentment, and respect will be completely lacking. The Monkey will lose patience with the Dog's righteous attitudes, and he/she too will start to resent the innuendoes and criticisms leveled by the Dog. The two will bring out all that is ugly in each other. The danger here is that the strong willed and impetuous Monkey could take advantage of the Dog's generally forgiving nature. Expecting a certain amount of support and loyalty from his/her mate the Dog will only find disappointment, as all these noble virtues are quite alien to the Monkey nature.... all in all this will be a hypocritical match that is sadly coloured by a great deal of disillusionment.

The influence of the Elements
The yang Monkey's natural element is metal. The Dog, also yang, has earth as the natural element. In the cycle of relationships, earth produces metal. It is the Dog who will sustain and work at the relationship. The Monkey will not have the intrinsic nature to make this particular match work.

Dog of marriageable age are those born in 1970 (metal Dog 26 years old in 1996) or 1982 (water Dog 14 years old in 1996)

Monkey of marriageable age are those born in 1968 (earth Monkey, 28 years old in 1996), or in 1980 (metal Monkey 16 years old in 1996)

A marriage between the earth Monkey and the   metal Dog energizes the Monkey and weakens the Dog. This is based on the cycle of relationships which cause earth to produce metal. Thus the Monkey's metal element is strengthened by the additional earth; and the Dog's earth element is exhausted by the additional metal. (go slowly if you find this confusing). This arrangement of elements does not look good for the relationship since its success depends on the Dog. With the Dog weakened, any marriage between the two will surely flounder. Plus the strengthened Monkey could well take advantage of the Dog ...

ROOSTER/ROOSTER
Disastrous in a first marriage

When two Roosters get together, the obvious synergy suggests that this could well be a great match. It would seem that their perfect understanding of the things that motivate them, and that give them satisfaction would make them work congenially together, and indeed find strength and joy in each other. But the reality of the situation is that the Rooster is also self centered and opinionated. They can be dogmatic and intolerant of other viewpoints. Thus when two Roosters get together the attributes that could make them a great and synergistic pair, also work against them !

Hence in a first marriage of two Roosters, where neither side has yet learnt the great virtues of tolerance and diplomacy the match could be disastrous. This is because the Rooster will turn away from those that are critical and unsupportive of them. Plus two Roosters can get too much of each other's nagging and constant bickering. And most of all their king size egos create monumental resentment of each other. All these points notwithstanding, if they could somehow learn to bring out the best in each other, the match could be quite a success. It has a better chance as a second attempt at marriage.

The influence of the Elements
The yin Rooster's natural element is metal. Two Roosters together bring too much metal to the equation, and this could harden their nature in a way that is detrimental both to their match, and to themselves individually.

Rooster of marriageable age are those born in 1969 (earth Rooster, 27 years old in 1996), or in 1981 (metal Rooster, 15 years old in 1996)

A marriage between two earth Roosters energizes both equally. This is because earth produces metal in the cycle of relationships. But here of course there will definitely be much too much metal, thereby causing an imbalance which is not good for the relationship.

Where the hour ascendants can offer other elements that balance out the excess of metal, the pair will have an easier and much more peaceful time. Otherwise, the excess of metal spells ill fortune for the pair. At any rate the compatibility aspects of a Rooster/Rooster pairing leaves much to be desired, and it is best not to pursue this match ...

ROOSTER/DOG
A pairing best broken

When these two individuals first get together, they talk but do not communicate. This is because both give voice to lofty ideals, but do not listen to each other. The moral high ground is the Dog's favourite topic of conversation. He/she takes pride in the nobler instincts of Man. Virtues like honour, integrity, loyalty and honesty are important to the Dog, and the attraction of the Rooster is that the Dog believes he/ personifies these traits. But these high expectations merely set the Dog up for disillusionment and disappointment, not because the Rooster is dishonest or dishonourable, but only because the Dog's expectations and standards are unrealistic. The Rooster too sees much that is admirable in the Dog during the early stages of courtship, but any encouragement or moral support he/she expects from the Dog will be sadly lacking. As it turns out the Dog is a greater pessimist than is at first evident, and the Rooster will seem to have less integrity when he/she is observed up close, especially compromising principles and convictions in the interest of advancement. This pragmatic side of the Rooster annoys the Dog ... the match has difficulty working because neither side is prepared to make allowances. Both being dogmatic and stubborn, they view their disillusionment as being caused by the shortcomings of the other. This lack of understanding make better for them to part.

The influence of the Elements
The yin Rooster's natural element is metal. The yang Dog's element is earth. In the cycle of relationships, earth produces metal. It is the Dog who has to sustain and work at this relationship.

Dog of marriageable age are those born in 1970 (metal Dog 26 years old in 1996) or 1982 (water Dog 14 years old in 1996)

Rooster of marriageable age are those born in 1969 (earth Rooster, 27 years old in 1996), or in 1981 (metal Rooster, 15 years old in 1996)

A marriage between the earth Rooster and the metal Dog energizes the Rooster and weakens the Dog. This is based on the cycle of relationships which cause earth to produce metal. Thus the Rooster's metal element is strengthened by the additional earth; and the Dog's earth element is exhausted by the additional metal. (go slowly if you find this confusing). This arrangement of elements does not look good for the relationship since its success depends on the weakened Dog.

DOG   DOG

A dark union ... Cut !

There will be a constant struggle for dominance in a marriage between two Dogs. Contrary to conventional wisdom, these two will bring out all that is inherently negative and ugly in their natures, and life will be one temper tantrum after another. They will fight and squabble endlessly and unless ascendant elements introduce mitigating influences, this is a dark union that is better cut than carried on ! Although the Dog personality is usually amiable, loyal and not easily angered, much of these pleasant traits will, unfortunately be reserved for others. Instead, what surfaces will be their argumentative natures, with each one taking offense at the other's righteous attitudes and moral high ground.

They are also not loyal to, or supportive of each other. It seems like this is a situation where they are in a confrontational mode rather than a sympathetic mode. Hostility prevents rationale thinking, and common sense just will not prevail. If they can somehow cool their natures a little, and start to appreciate each other they might be able to make things work, but this will only happen if other elemental influences favour them. According to the Zodiac readings however their incompatibility unfortunately remains.

The influence of the Elements

The yang Dog's element is earth. The excess of earth in their yang nature makes them quarrelsome and hostile. It will be good if the birth hours of one of the pair, contains elements like metal, water or wood, which will lend greater balance to the relationship. Otherwise the match is not to be recommended since both will growl at each other from morning to night !

Dog of marriageable age are those born in 1970 (metal Dog 26 years old in 1996) or 1982 (water Dog 14 years old in 1996)

A marriage between two metal Dogs weakens them both. This is based on the cycle of relationships which cause earth to produce metal. Thus the Dog's earth element is exhausted by the additional metal. This arrangement of elements could assist the match to survive since the weakened natures of the dogs will allow for greater tolerance, which in turn will work in favour of the match.

Note: Although the Zodiac indicate incompatibility between these two animal signs, it is not impossible for them to be friends. But they should not live together or share rooms/flats together.

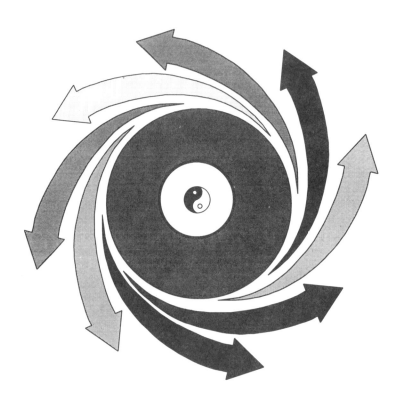

Interacting elements can fan the protective fires or create havoc in relationships. When trying to maximize the potential of a relationship, applying element analyses becomes a vital part of the process. From the preceding sections, it should have become clear that every year is symbolized by two elements which actually expresses the interaction between the *earthly branch* and the *heavenly stem* of that year. The earthly branch is the animal sign, while the heavenly stem is the element of a particular year. Together these two elements offer immediate clues pertaining to the character and personalities of people born in that year ... as well as other things !. Chinese fortune telling always starts with element analysis of the years being investigated. Understanding the positive and negative aspects of element interaction requires skillful interpretation. These are based on the Theory of Five Elements, and understanding this theory is vital, as it brings added dimensions to the animal compatibility readings.

 INTERACTING ELEMENTS

Knowledge of the five elements and their interactions with each other is a fundamental part of Chinese Zodiac analysis. This is because Chinese Astrological Sciences is based on the belief that everything in the entire Universe is made up of these five elements, which are Wood, Water, Fire, Metal and Earth, in no particular order or sequence ...

Instead there are PRODUCTIVE and DESTRUCTIVE CYCLES in the sequences, and upon these are based a wide range of possible interpretations ... of personality traits, outcomes, fortunes, and corrective measures. How skillful a Master Astrologer, or a Master Feng Shui man is, at interpreting the life manifestations of these elements (as they appear from year to year, from month to month, from day to day, and even from hour to hour) is one of the best measures of how good he/she is ! This is because the influence of the five elements is extremely important in every branch of the Chinese metaphysical and astrological sciences.

Before one can analyze one's personal elements however, it is necessary to know how to identify these elements. In Zodiac analyses of compatibility and fortunes, the elements of hours (1) days(2), months(3), and years(4) can be found in the Chinese 100 year calendar. Each of these so called four pillars of destiny contains two elements, one representing the *earthly branch*, and the other representing the *heavenly stem*. For every individual reading, the most important is the element relationship of the year of birth, followed, in descending order by the elements of the hour, the month and the day of birth. The elements of the year, month and hour of birth can be obtained by referring to the Tables in the first part of this book (Pages 8 to 13). The elements of the day of birth are based on a complicated formula, too unwieldy to present in this book. For compatibility readings the year and hour ascendant elements are usually sufficient to give very clear indications. This involves investigating how the ascendant elements of two people interact and relate to each other. If they are conducive and productive, they are *generally* said to be compatible, or exhausting, one for the other ... and when they are in a destructive or controlling sequence, the tone of the relationship is similiarly defined. Exact interpretations also require a deep understanding of the intrinsic natures of the respective animal signs. Element analysis cannot be done in a vacuum, but must instead be related to, and influenced by other relevant factors. Finally, one must also consider relativity. There are degrees of compatibility, just as there are scales of wealth and gradations of success ! Thus your interpretations of what the elements are saying should always relate to the applicable environment.

147

THE PRODUCTIVE CYCLE
<u>can fan the positive influences ...</u>

None of the elements is better, stronger or more important than another.
They exert equal importance to the human condition, but the effect of their
influence (good or bad) depends on their interaction with one another.
The productive cycle of the elements explains the positive or conducive
influences exerted by the elements on each other. This cycle also suggest
how one element can exhaust the other. Thus in this   cycle:

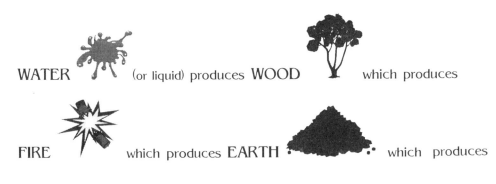

WATER   (or liquid) produces WOOD   which produces

FIRE   which produces EARTH   which   produces

METAL   which produces WATER .... and the cycle continues.

To understand this cycle, consider the simple logic behind the sequence.

<u>WATER</u> produces WOOD because water makes plants grow. Water can be
big or small water and can refer equally to the sea as to raindrops and dew.
In producing wood, it can also be said then that Wood exhausts water !

<u>WOOD</u> produces FIRE because rubbing two pieces of stick creates a fire.
Plus wood is the fuel that makes fire burn. Thus Fire exhausts Wood !

<u>FIRE</u> reduces everything to ashes thereby creating EARTH. Without the fire
burning, where can additional earth come from ? Thus Earth exhausts Fire !

<u>EARTH</u>, produces METAL, gold and silver and other precious stones deep
within its depths. It can be said that Metal exhausts Earth !

<u>METAL</u> produces WATER because it is the only element that can be
melted through heat to change into liquid ! Thus Water exhausts Metal !

THE DESTRUCTIVE CYCLE
creates havoc in relationships

It is vital to understand that the five elements are constantly reacting to each other. They are interdependent, and each element enjoys a productive and a destructive relationship simultaneously. This interactive dynamic is the crux of the element theory. In the destructive cycle, the factor of control is introduced. Thus the element which destroys another is said to be the element in control. The destructive cycle has the following sequence:

WATER (or liquid) destroys FIRE

FIRE destroys METAL

METAL destroys WOOD

WOOD destroys EARTH

EARTH destroys WATER ....
and the cycle continues.

To understand this cycle, consider the explanations behind the sequence.

WATER destroys, or is said to control Fire because water puts out a fire faster and more efficiently than any other element.
FIRE destroys or controls Metal because just about the only thing that can melt Metal thereby changing its form, is the intense heat of fire !
METAL destroys or controls Wood because in the form of tools (saws, blades, hammers etc.) metal can conquer any amount of wood, and even the largest tree can be felled with a metal ax..
WOOD destroys or controls Earth because the roots of plants are relentless in taking control of the soil beneath, which cannot resist.
EARTH destroys Water because it can control its direction and intensity of flow through drains, canals and protective walls and dikes.

 THE WATER ELEMENT

Water flows in rivers and seas, and seeps relentlessly into the earth, quietly chipping away ... infiltrating and restructuring things in its way. Water can also roar like a deluge, putting out fires and flooding the land, destroying everything in its path. Thus the element of water can suggest subtle and gentle persistence like the brook successfully wearing away the hardest rocks or rust destroying steel bars over time. Water is fluid and flexible, seeping through the tiniest pores and covering large surface areas.

People born of the water element i.e. those whose birth charts contain a dominance of water are usually excellent communicators. They are charming, likable and often extremely persuasive, relentlessly wearing down the most obstinate resistance. They are tenacious, but also have the capacity to compromise, to an extent which suggests weakness. Their attitude to life is flexible, and they prefer the soft approach. The water element always adds a calming influence, so that aggressive and hostile behaviour often get modified under its influence, just as passionate and emotional natures also get cooled with the addition of the water symbol.

The way of the water element is to infiltrate rather than dominate. They are also effective catalysts, and water influenced people have a knack for knowing the best people to approach to solve any given problem, the best time to get started on any project, and the most effective indirect way of getting things done. They are usually passive and conciliatory and often adopt the easiest and simplest course of action.

Water is usually an excellent additional element for those born under the influence of wood, since water enables the plant to grow and flourish. But too much water can cause the roots to rot, and plants to die. Balance is important. Water is usually not good for those born under the influence of the fire element, but when there is too much fire in the birth chart, water becomes an effective balancing agent.

For those born with a preponderance of water in the birthchart, metal is good for them and metal dominated people will suit them. Wearing gold accessories and carrying lots of coins is thus good for them. But earth people will take advantage of their good nature.

✳ If you need to enhance your fortunes or your relationships with water, wear the colours blue or black; drink plenty of water daily; and try to live near a river or a lake. But never overdo it by having too much water !

 THE WOOD ELEMENT

Wood is the only element which has the ability to expand and grow of its own accord. Yet to do so, and to flourish it needs all four of the other elements. Earth to give it home, water and minerals to feed it and the warmth and light of fire to make it bloom ! Thus people whose birthcharts are dominated by the wood element should ensure a healthy presence of other elements as well in order to reach their fullest potential.

The same reasoning should be applied in the search for a life partner. When his/her package of elements complement yours with the presence of elements which you have a deficiency of, he/she will often give you the balance needed to make for a fuller, more satisfying life.

Wood dominated people, especially those born in years which have wood as the *heavenly stem*, are usually self confident, and possess a natural attraction. This is because the wood element artlessly and successfully entices the other elements because of its living nature. At the same time, its capacity to grow and expand when aided by other elements usually make those dominated by its influence do things on a grand scale. Wood people are also excellent at creating teams, and they have good management and executive skills. They are usually successful in corporate situations, where building, growth and expansion situations come into focus.

Wood is generally an excellent additional element for those born under the influence of fire, since wood feeds the fire, making it burn brightly. Too much fire however creates excess energy, which under certain circumstances could be harmful. Wood is not good for those born in earth years, although a bit of wood is considered favourably since this allows the earth to create something living ... just ensure there isn't too much.

For those born in wood years, all other elements are excellent. There should be a mix of the five elements, nothing should predominate, and fire is necessary to ensure that all projects succeed. The Chinese say that the *flower cannot bloom without the sunlight* ! Thus fire is necessary.

✳ If you need to enhance your relationships with the wood symbol, wear greens and browns; carry something that's made of wood on your body, and live with lots of wood paneling, or have wallpaper in your rooms.
Put your photograph into a wood picture frame; place a wooden sculpture next to your bed and display lots of plants in your home.

THE FIRE ELEMENT

Fire is an element which everyone needs if they wish to shine or to have the energy and stamina to succeed. Fire is the also the only element that does not exist on earth of its own accord. Apart from the sun, fire needs to be created or produced everytime it is needed. And fire cannot be stored. It does not really have a tangible form. Yet it is all powerful, being the source of heat, light and energy. Without this light and warmth, plants cannot bloom or reproduce itself; water cannot be harnessed into steam energy, and earth itself cannot even be produced ! Without fire, metal cannot be transformed into useful implements. Fire is thus a vital element that transforms or enhance the other four elements.

People born under the influence of the fire element in their birthcharts are usually decisive and confident ... they know instinctively that people are drawn to their aura of power, in the same way the moth gets drawn to the light bulb. Fire influenced people are natural leaders, have fairly aggressive temperaments and often demonstrate great courage and tenacity. They are ambitious, and their brilliance inspires and motivates others. These are the positive aspects of fire people.

But it is also important to remember that fire must always be controlled. In terms of destructive capability, fire has the most frightening potential to get out of control, and to be destructive. The nuclear bomb symbolises this point eloquently. Too much fire is dangerous and wreaks havoc, showing us the dark side of excess ! If your mate has too much fire, (e.g. born in the summer months, in the year and hour of fire and perhaps having fire in the name and always wearing red !!!) encourage him/her to drink lots of water, wear blues and blacks, and to strenuously avoid reds and greens, (since wood produces more fire). Remember that an excess of fire leads to abrasive behaviour, extreme self centredness, and even a tendency to violence.

Fire is generally an excellent additional element for any of the other elements, but especially for wood, since fire gives light and warmth to plants, symbolically helping wood to bloom and reproduce itself ... Fire is not good for metal dominated people, although in small quantities, it aids in making metal more valuable. Without heat, metal cannot be manufactured into something useful and beautiful.

✱ If you need fire to enhance your relationships, wear the colours, red and orange; keep all your rooms brightly lighted; display potted flowers and hang pictures of sunrise in your room.

THE METAL ELEMENT

Metal is the only lifeless element. Of the five, this is the one that suggests a coldness and a hardness that comes from it being completely deficient in spirit and movement. It is devoid of the vitality of fire, the flow of water, the growth of wood, and the quiet breathing of the earth. Metal is totally inanimate. It thus symbolizes a rigidity that is resolute and unbending Metal dominated people are therefore (unsurprisingly) one dimensional, are impossible to influence, persuade or coerce, and who are noticeably stubborn and dogmatic.

Nothing can bring metal to life. But it can be transformed into the most magnificent of tools, and the most stunningly beautiful of objects and accessories. It is there to be used or admired. Think of the coldness of steel; of gold and silver, and think of chain saws, and hammers and nails.

Metal is best seen as a symbol of material wealth, something that adorns and is made used of. It is sought after for what it adds to one's life, and as a resource to be mined and utilized. Without metal, buildings cannot get constructed. Transportation comes to a standstill, and the implements of modern communication disappear. Even the human body needs mineral nutrients to survive ! In short, metal is the one vital ingredient needed for sustaining life and progress. Seen in this light, it is easy to understand the vital importance of metal in its interaction with the others.

Metal is supposedly the element that produces water, and is thus an excellent additional element for those born in water years. But it is also a necessary supplement (in small quantities) for the other elements since it represents a valuable resource that can be turned into productive and beautiful objects. It is also great for making people lacking in determination and will power, more decisive and resolute !

In this connection, one must make a distinction between big metal and small metal, a difference best demonstrated in an example. Small metal symbolize implements that transform logs into furniture. Big metal cuts down trees and destroys wood altogether !

✳ If you need metal to enhance a weak willed personality, wear gold accessories; and develop a preference for metallic colours. Paint your rooms white; use the name *Kim* ... it means gold !

153

 THE EARTH ELEMENT

The Earth element dominates the world. In terms of supply, there is more of this element than any other, and it is also deep and awesome, full of things the mind cannot yet fathom. The earth element is tangible and solid, usually lying silent and still for centuries. The only time it blows its top is when the element of fire cause volcanoes to erupt and earthquakes to rumble. Most of the time however the earth element symbolizes the kind of strength that comes from being dependable and reliable.

People dominated by this element in their birthcharts, are usually outstandingly pragmatic. The term *being down to earth* applies, and the implication is that having one's feet planted firmly on the ground suggests a practical, no nonsense personality that one can almost always rely one. But it is a personality that perhaps lacks for imagination and humour. These attributes will have to be supplied by the other elements !

Earth people are usually highly disciplined and honest. They have a solid moral code of conduct, and while these attributes may seem to suggest something of a dull and plodding personality type ... lest we forget, the earth is also deep, mysterious and unfathomable ...

Earth is the element that produces metal, and is thus an excellent additional element for those born in metal years. But earth is also a necessary supplement (in small quantities) for wood, for without it, wood would have a hard time attempting to survive and flourish.

Earth makes for pragmatism and discipline and would be a most valuable addition for those whose lively and restless natures need to be contained. Couples whose combined birthcharts lack this element should take corrective measures. Earth is not good for those whose dominant element is water since the destructive cycle comes into effect when the two mix. Earth also exhausts those born in years of the fire element.

✳ If you need to supplement your relationship with a dose of earth element, do invest in a natural crystal, either to wear as an accessory, or merely to place next to your bed or on your table. Other symbols of earth are the beautiful Chinese landscape paintings of mountains, and pictures of famous peaks like Mount Fuji and other snow clad scenery of the Swiss Alps ... in fact these mountain pictures and paintings are a wonderful feng shui tool. Placed behind you, it symbolizes solid support for all your endeavours.

INTERPRETING AND USING THE ELEMENTS

To interpret the interaction of the elements correctly, the true nature of the two cycles must be understood. And also, that a proper <u>balance of all five elements is more important than any single element on its own</u>. No single element is ever better than the other. They have real meaning only when viewed as being interactive. Since everything and every date has element components, it is important to give <u>proper weighting</u> to the correct set of elements. The year elements are the most important. Next comes the hour, then the season (month) and then the day. If you wish to go deeper, you can investigate the other symbolic meanings of the elements, particularly as it pertains to other important aspects of life ... things like flavours, senses, colours, energy types, emotions, mental attributes and morality. Use the table below to make your detailed analysis.

	FIRE	METAL	WOOD	EARTH	WATER
Flavour	bitter	hot	sour	sweet	salty
Sense	taste	smell	sight	touch	hearing
Emotion	joy	sadness	anger	nostalgia	fear
Voice	laughter	crying	shouting	singing	groaning
Energy	directing	physical	psychic	archaic	creative
Main Fault	greed	stubborn	hostile	ambitious	desire
Intellect	spiritual	romantic	rational	tranquil	desperate
Morality	humility	integrity	charitable	trusting	wisdom
Climate	heat	dryness	wind	humidity	cold
Colours	red	white	green	yellow	black

<u>Example:</u> From the productive cycle: you can deduce that in the realm of emotions, *joy* (fire) creates *nostalgia* (earth) which creates *sadness* (metal) which creates *fear* (water) which creates *anger* (wood) which creates *joy.*
<u>Example:</u> from the destructive cycle, you can also deduce that *laughter* (fire) opposes *crying* (metal) which opposes *shouting* (wood) which opposes *singing* (earth) which opposes *groaning* (water) which opposes *laughter.*
<u>Or, in the realm of emotion,</u> note that *joy* destroys *sadness, sadness* destroys *anger, anger* destroys *nostalgia, nostalgia* destroys *fear,* and *fear* destroys *joy !*
And finally, do note that the subtlety of the five element theory is complicated by the fact that every element has a YIN and a YANG aspect ! Thus the yang aspect of metal is acute stubbornness and rigid inflexibility, while the yin aspect is being firm and dogmatic, but not unbending. Elements generate and destroy each other in continually moving cycles ... how strong the energies released depend on their yin or yang aspects.

USING FENG SHUI
TO ACTIVATE YOUR LOVE LIFE

156

Can romance and marriage be made sweeter with Feng Shui ??
Can this thousand year old science jazz up your love life, rekindle the faded embers of a marriage gone sour, or even, bring you the man or woman of your dreams ?

Indeed it is not only possible, but also highly probable that when the marriage and romance corners of your home or room are properly aligned, and suitably activated, your chances of finding marital happiness will be vastly improved. And not just that ... you could actually be staying in a room where certain aspects of furniture arrangement, or layout design may be hurting your marriage feng shui ... thereby spoiling your potentially favourable relationships, and creating havoc in your love life .... this happens if you are inadvertently creating *shar chi* which spoil all your chances at finding romance, or worse still, causing you and your spouse to quarrel, or to attract a third party to enter the picture and cause you heartbreak.

There are several things you can do to activate your marriage feng shui. This involves identifying the relevant corner or sector of your room and house to activate, and for this there are two methods, one based on the Eight Life Situations method which assigns a specific corner for marriage which needs to be activated; and the other, which is based on your date of birth. This latter method is highly potent, as it aligns the individual chi with that of the environment; and is part of the Pa Kua Lo Shu formula.

✿ The complete Pa Kua Lo Shu formula of the Compass School Feng Shui, together with details on all other practical applications can be found in the author's red book **APPLIED PA KUA LO SHU FENG SHUI**. For love and romance, the formula given in the following pages of this book is more than adequate !

There are also several feng shui taboos you must be aware of, and which you must correct if you want to have a better social life thereby activating the *sheng chi* which makes it easy for you to meet a potential mate. Bad marriage feng shui cause husbands to stray; wives to find lovers; sex life to be bad; communication to be nil ... and just about everything going wrong with the marriage. For singles, bad feng shui makes it tough, sometimes even impossible, to get married. Relationships break off for no apparent reason, or obstacles get created which hamper marriage prospects ...

THE UNIVERSAL MARRIAGE CORNER

This is based on the Eight life situations feng shui where the 8 sided
Pa Kua is superimposed onto the room or house. Then standing in the
centre of the house, a compass is used to identify the Southwest location.
This is the universal marriage and family corner for the room/house, and is
applicable for everyone. It is necessary to locate this corner standing in the
centre of the house because in dealing with location, rather than direction,
taking one's bearing from the centre is deemed to be more accurate.

Having located the Southwest corner, the next thing to ensure is that the
toilets, bathrooms, garages, kitchens or storerooms, must not be located
here. The worst situation is when the toilet is located here, since all
marriage opportunities and happiness simply get flushed down the toilet !!
This rule of feng shui is sometimes inadvertently broken by families, so that
the sons and daughters of the family have difficulty in getting married, or in
staying married. If you discover that there is a toilet located in the marriage
corner of your home, and you are having problems in your social or love
life, you will be well advised to try and stop using this toilet altogether. Or
like a very close friend of the author did, just relocate the toilet elsewhere !

This corner should also be activated to attract good marriage and
romance feng shui. The tools that can be used for activating this corner
are many, but if you have a toilet, kitchen or storeroom here. It is best to
first relocate these unsuitable rooms. If for instance you activate the corner
(e.g. by placing flowers there) and the toilet is still there, you might attract
potential suitors but for the most part, they will be unsuitable !
It is necessary therefore to first open up the marriage corner before
attempting to activate it. Under this method of feng shui, the way to
activate the corner is based on it being the Southwest corner, which
according to the Later Heaven arrangement of the Pa Kua has an earth
element. Thus symbols associated with earth should be used. The best
method really is to use natural quartz crystals. Place them on a table with a
marble or stone top. Or hang a painting which shows mountains and
beautiful scenery to symbolize earth. Keep the corner well lighted always,
since fire produces earth. Other fire symbols can also be used quite
effectively, e.g. you can place porcelain figures of horse and snakes since
these two animals symbolize the fire element.
Or place a red lantern or lampshade in the corner !

YOUR PERSONAL MARRIAGE CORNER

In the Pa Kua Lo Shu method, the *personal marriage corner* of individuals can be determined according to one's date of birth. Let this feng shui method play cupid in your life .... to do this, first determine the lunar year of your birth which generally corresponds to the western calendar except that you will need to adjust for the Chinese New Year date of your particular year of birth. Check against the tables presented in Pages 8-13.
Then use this formula to determine your KUA number:

FOR FEMALES: TAKE THE YEAR OF YOUR BIRTH;
Add the last two digits; Reduce to a single number;
Add 5 and the answer is your KUA number.
Example: year of birth 1945. Thus
4 + 5 = 9; 9 + 5 = 14: 1 + 4 = 5. So the KUA is 5

FOR MALES, TAKE THE YEAR OF YOUR BIRTH:
Add the last two digits; Reduce to a single number;
Deduct from 10. The answer is your KUA number.
Example: year of birth 1936. Thus
3 + 6 = 9; and 10 - 9 = 1   So the KUA is 1

Check your personal marriage corner from this table

YOUR KUA NUMBER	YOUR MARRIAGE CORNER
1	SOUTH
2	NORTHWEST
3	SOUTHEAST
4	EAST
5(MALES)	NORTHWEST
5(FEMALES)	WEST
6	SOUTHWEST
7	NORTH EAST
8	WEST
9	NORTH

Once you know your personal marriage corner, try to make sure that neither the toilet nor the kitchen nor the storeroom is situated in that corner.
These press down on your marriage luck. Also make sure you do not place things like brooms and mops in this corner. Instead, you should think about activating this corner, and the following pages tell you how !

CAN'T SEEM TO MEET ANYONE SUITABLE ?

Perhaps your marriage/romance corner in your bedroom or house is missing ? Or maybe the toilet is located there ? Or perhaps the elements symbolized by things you have in that corner are clashing badly with the element of that corner. All these situations can be a) corrected and b) activated with the use of feng shui activators.

Firstly to correct:

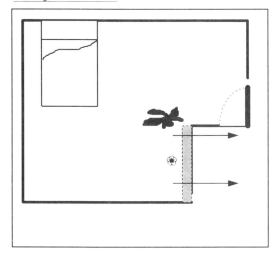

If the corner is missing altogether, as shown here in this sketch, marked with a ✸ the thing to do is to use mirrors to create an illusion of additional space. This should however only be done in such a way that you will not see the mirror when you sleep since mirrors in the bedroom are not advisable. In the sketch, a plant has been used to shield off the wall mirror which has been installed to extend the wall in the direction of the missing corner. Usually the missing corner can be an attached toilet or bathroom, in which case the vital marriage corner has been occupied by a toilet. You are then strongly advised not to use the toilet or bath, and instead turn it into a dressing and make up area only.

Secondly to activate:
The important thing to remember about activating any corners, including the romance and marriage corner is that there are two types of symbolic objects that can be used. The first are universally accepted symbols of love, marriage, conjugal bliss and so forth while the second depends on element compatibility. Some of the universally accepted symbols shown here can be placed in the marriage corner to attract that man/woman into your life !

Mandarin ducks   Love birds   Double happiness   Valentine card   Roses

ACTIVATING YOUR NIEN YEN CORNER

Your personal marriage corner is known, in feng shui terms as your *Nien Yen* corner. This is the corner AND also the direction (see page 158) which affects everything to do with your love life and family happiness. When this corner is properly oriented and is activated, it makes for harmonious family relationships, bringing marriage opportunities to those who are single and of marriageable age; brings children to those who may be childless; and generally improves relationships between husband and wife, and between all members of a household. Loosely translated it means *Longevity with rich descendants*. Once you know your Nien Yen directions and corners, expressed as one of the eight compass directions, you should seek out that corner of the room or home which represents your Nien yen and activate the corner by placing any of the symbols suggested.

Mandarin Ducks are the Chinese symbol of conjugal bliss and is often representative of young love. Place a pair of carved wooden ducks (easily available in any Chinese emporium) in this corner ... or if you like place a whole family of ducks ! You can put them on a table or on a floor *swimming* on a square sheet of mirror to simulate water !

Love birds or Budgerigars may be substituted for mandarin ducks ... you can use a picture of a pair of budgies, or carved versions of these beautiful birds. It is not advisable to keep the real thing in cages since keeping birds in cages do not bring good luck as it represents a lack of freedom.

The double happiness sign is the symbol of happy occasions, what the Chinese refer to as *hei see*. Look for a large version of this sign in Chinese emporiums or draw it out yourself, but make it red ! This signifies marriage and should be effective for singles who can't seem to meet the right one !

Valentine cards or other symbols of love and romance are also excellent activators.... it is perfectly acceptable to use your imagination. You can use wall paper with *heart* designs; or place a heart shaped picture frame, or a heart shaped musical box ... or you can use a Chinese love knot !.

Roses signify the universal expression of love and are great for the *Nien Yen* corner. It is not necessary to use real roses. Beautiful silk ones will do just as well, and indeed are to be preferred since they never fade ! If you are placing real roses in this corner, do throw them out the instant they fade. Faded flowers are a source of *shar chi* which is inauspicious. The Chinese prefer the use of the peony or *moutan* flower to symbolize marriage. These are found in paintings and screens and can also be used.

YOUR BED AND YOUR SLEEPING DIRECTION

Armed with your personal *Nien Yen* direction, you must also try to select that corner of the house or apartment which represents this direction as your bedroom. Obviously if this is not possible, it is not the end of the world. Indeed it is seldom possible to get everything right in feng shui since we all have space and money constraints. But what you can do is make sure you sleep with your head pointed to the *Nien Yen* direction, e.g. if your *Nien Yen* is North, then sleep with your head pointed North ! This is shown in the sketches below. Do note that the arrows point to your *Nien Yen*. Do note also that sometimes this requires the bed to be placed in an unconventional way. The sketches below indicate acceptable placements.

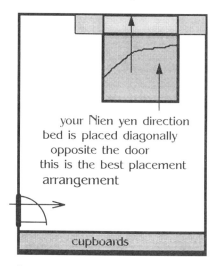

your Nien yen direction
bed is placed diagonally
opposite the door
this is the best placement
arrangement

cupboards

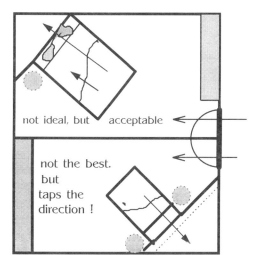

not ideal, but   acceptable

not the best.
but
taps the
direction !

If, for some reason. you cannot sleep with your head pointed in your *Nien Yen*, the next best thing to do, is to ensure that you DO NOT sleep in any of your inauspicious directions. How do you determine this ?

Look at the table below, you will see two sets of directions. Everyone belongs to either the East group or the West group. Each group has four auspicious and four inauspicious directions. Once you know your *Nien yen*, you will also know what group you belong to. The Table above shows you the East and West group auspicious directions. If you cannot orientate your head to your *Nien Yen*, select from the other three directions that make up your group and strenuously avoid the four directions of the other group.

WEST GROUP DIRECTIONS	West, Southwest, Northwest and Northeast
EAST GROUP DIRECTIONS	East, Southeast, North and South

BEDROOM TABOOS

Is your marriage going sour ?
Does your husband have a roving eye ?
Could he be having an affair ?
Is your wife flirting too much with her colleagues ?
Is your sex life going to the dogs ?
Are you and your spouse always quarreling ?

When things seem to go wrong and keep going wrong between you and your husband or wife, for no apparent reason; when love seems to have flown out of the window suddenly ... especially just after you have moved into a new apartment or home, it is not a bad idea to check and see whether both of you are being attacked either by bad feng shui or by killing breath i.e. shar chi caused by any number of things. These are what I term the bedroom taboos, which can be corrected with little difficulty.

MIRRORS facing the bed are terribly harmful to a marriage ! Whether they are facing you directly, i.e. they are in front of the bed ... perhaps on the doors of cupboards; or they are by the sides of the bed, or if they are above the bed ... my advice is get rid of them immediately. Mirrors in the bedroom are usually bad feng shui, unless you cannot see the mirror when you lie in bed. In a marriage bed, mirrors are supposed to cause friction between the couple because of the appearance of a third party ... thus either the husband or the wife could find love with someone else ! These guidelines on mirrors is illustrated in the sketch below. The thick black lines indicate where mirrors should NOT be placed.
The dotted lines are where mirrors will do no harm.

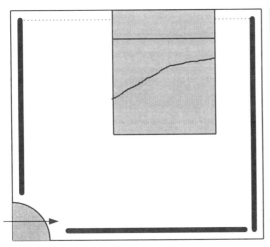

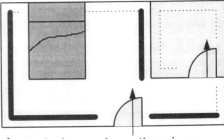

In the bedroom above, there is an attached bathroom, and mirrors should be placed in the bathroom or the dressing area.

BEDROOM TABOOS

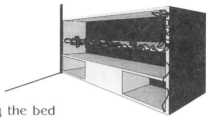

<u>OPEN BOOKSHELVES</u> directly facing the bed
create *shar chi* for the couple, and often cause migraine and headaches.
These shelves represent sharp knives cutting at you and should best be
closed up with a door or if that is too expensive, place artificial creeper
plants (as shown) to deflect the knife like edges of the shelves. This rule of
feng shui should also be observed for offices and study rooms.

<u>WALLPAPER</u> with sharp pointed designs, checks, stars or abstracts. These
merely serve to create inauspicious *chi* flows inside the bedroom (or indeed
anywhere else) and is best avoided.

<u>PAINTINGS</u> in the bedroom should symbolize auspicious and happy
occasions. Sunrise scenes are better than sunsets for obvious reasons.
Flowers are better than animals (do avoid fierce animals like tigers !)
And do avoid also abstract paintings that show distorted views of people
and buildings ... these cause bad vibes in the bedroom and will definitely
affect the couple's well being. And finally avoid anything frightening !

<u>BEDROOM TELEVISION</u> is often discouraged
by feng shui Masters on the grounds that TV screens are
in actual fact mirrors. Thus if you need to have a TV in
the bedroom, observe the same rules as for mirrors.
Make sure the screen does not directly face the bed.
If your bedroom is too small to accommodate this, far
better not to have a TV !

<u>POINTED CORNERS</u> cause *shar chi* and should be
deflected with plants and creepers. Shown here.

ACTIVATING THE ELEMENTS IN THE BEDROOM

There is a second method of activating good feng shui in the bedroom, thereby ensuring a balanced and harmonious relationship between the couple. This makes use of the Theory of Five Elements , i.e. using good luck emblems and tokens that symbolize Fire, Earth, Metal, Water and Wood, and then placing them in the four sectors which represent your auspicious corners. Before proceeding to do this it is important to first check what your *Nien Yen* direction is from the formula on Page 158 and your other directions are from the Table in Page 161. This allows you to determine whether yours are West group or East group directions. In case you and your spouse belong to different groups, the Chinese conventional recommendation is that the husband's directions be followed.

The FIRE corner is South. This is an East group direction. The best objects that symbolize fire are lamps, lights and chandeliers. Make certain the South corner of your room is always brightly lit. Fire is also great for any of the earth corners and for the centre of the room which is deemed to be of the earth element. This is because fire produces earth.

Other ways of activating Fire is to display paintings of sunrises. A picture of a sunrise is excellent feng shui as it symbolizes a new beginning ... and it also represents the start of a new day, when there is much to look forward to. Sunsets on the other hand (though sometimes more beautiful) symbolize the end of a day, when things are finished and completed. Sunsets should thus be avoided, especially in the bedroom.

ACTIVATING THE ELEMENTS IN THE BEDROOM

The EARTH corners are Southwest and Northeast. These are both West group directions. Earth also represents the centre of the room. The best objects that symbolize earth are crystals and chandeliers. As with the fire corner, make certain the Southwest and Northeast corners of your room are brightly lit, because fire is also good for earth. Do invest in beautiful man made cut crystal objects or in natural crystals like quartzes, amethysts and citrines. The uncut version ... i.e. in their natural state, when displayed in earth corners cause harmonious *chi* to be created. Since earth produces metal, earth symbols are also excellent for metal corners.

Man made crystals come in various shapes and they are all suitable.

The METAL corners are West and Northwest. These are also West group directions. The best symbols to use in the bedroom to symbolize metal are clocks, metal chests, pcfax machines and electrical appliances like radios and hi fi sets.

Bells and windchimes are also great purveyors of good and harmonious *chi,* but do make sure windchimes are made from hollow metal rods (copper aluminum or steel) and that they are not too large. Windchimes are also excellent to use to deflect any exposed overhead beams which may be present in the bedroom. Such beams cause severe headaches and you should not sleep directly under them. Those designer type bedroom suites often come with overhead protuberances that seem to hang above your head. These are bad feng shui and are best done away with. The sketch here also shows another way of deflecting the *shar chi* ..i.e. by using creepers (can be artificial) to block the sharp edge of the beam.

ACTIVATING THE ELEMENTS IN THE BEDROOM

The WATER corner is the North This is an East group direction. The best objects to use in the bedroom for symbolizing water are actually pictures of water views or paintings that depict beautiful waterfalls or other water scenery. This is because, unless you have a really large bedroom, aquariums are not that suitable. You can if you wish have a small goldfish bowl but keeping fish in the bedroom is not highly recommended. Since metal produces water, all the metal symbols mentioned earlier can also be placed in the water corner with some success, but the best is still to hang a water picture or painting

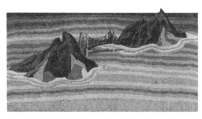 A water picture is ideal for the water corner.

The WOOD corners are the East and the Southeast. These are East group directions. Wood corners are best activated with wooden paneling, wallpaper that have flower or plain colour designs (paper is regarded as wood); all shades of the colour green ... in case your windows are in the wood corners and you need to make curtains ! Wood is also represented by plants and flowers and these can be placed in the bedroom to great effect. Do however avoid prickly plants like cactus as these are unfriendly and possess hidden poison arrows. The Chinese are fond of displaying paintings of auspicious flowers in the wood corners of the room. Suitable flowers include the peony and the chrysanthemum, and suitable plants are those with broad leaves. Avoid bonsai (stunted) plants, and plants that have needle like leaves.

Good feng shui plants

Not recommended for feng shui

FENG SHUI ADVICE FOR WOMEN

It is important for women who practice feng shui to remember that this is an ancient science from China. In the old days good feng shui creates wealth, success, happiness and prominence to families, and particularly to the family patriarch. In the old days also, success for a man was often measured by the number of *concubines* he had. Indeed men of stature often had an entire harem of wives ! Thus when you introduce feng shui inspired changes to your house, particularly those that involve the use of water (which signifies wealth) it is prudent to be careful.

Perhaps one of the most important tips passed on to me by Taiwan feng shui Masters skilled in the practice of water feng shui, was that pools of water in the vicinity of homes should NEVER be located on the right hand side of the main front door. Whether the pool of water is inside or outside the house, it should be on the left hand side of the front door. Otherwise although your husband will be successful and grow wealthy, he will also take additional wives, and while this may be have been quite acceptable in the old days, it is by no means acceptable today. Wives should thus ensure that this guideline is followed if they do not want their husbands to stray !!
The way to determine the location is to stand inside the house looking out. The pool should then be on your left ! See sketches below where both the pools, indoor and outdoor (A and B) drawn in, are on the left hand side of both doors ! The main door is marked M and the side sliding doors are marked S. Notice that the orientation is taken from inside the house.

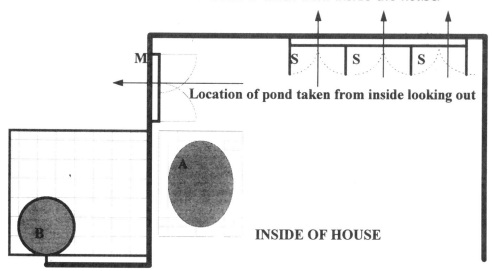

Location of pond taken from inside looking out

INSIDE OF HOUSE

CHECKING COMPASS COMPATIBILITY
EAST AND WEST GROUP PEOPLE

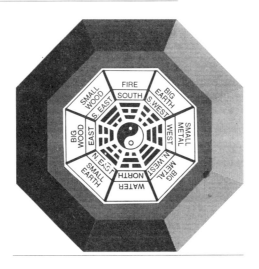

One of the best ways of investigating compatibility, a method which can be used to supplement the animal readings of compatibility is to see whether two people belong to the same grouping based on the Pa Kua Lo Shu method of feng shui, which divides people into two groups, East and West. This depends on your KUA numbers, which in turn is determined or calculated according to a formula that uses the individual's year of birth. This formula is given on page 158. Once you have your KUA number, please note whether you are West Group or East Group according to the following Table.

KUA NUMBERS	DIRECTIONS	GROUP
1, 3, 4 and 9	South, Southeast, East & North	East group
2, 6, 7, and 8	Northwest Southwest Northeast and West.	West group
5 (for females)	West	West group
5 (for males)	Northwest	West group

✿ As a general rule, it is highly recommended that people should marry someone from the same group. When an East group person marries a West group person, the compatibility is seriously reduced, and depending on the individual KUA numbers of both, the incompatibility can be quite severe and extremely serious.

INVESTIGATING DEGREES OF COMPATIBILITY

Based on the Pa Kua Lo Shu formula of feng shui, all those who belong to the East group have the East group directions as their auspicious directions; and the West group directions as their inauspicious directions.

The converse of that also applies so that those who belong to the West group have the West group directions as their auspicious directions, and the East group directions as their inauspicious directions.

According to this same formula, we can determine the AUSPICIOUS and INAUSPICIOUS pairings. Based on a formula that is too complicated to present in full, a Table has been prepared to indicate the degrees of compatibility between people of different KUA numbers. These compatibility ratings are based on eight descriptions viz.:

AUSPICIOUS AND COMPATIBLE

Sheng Shi: Extremely compatible. Your mate will bring you excellent luck.
Tien Yi: Very Compatible. Your mate will look after your health very well.
Nien Yen: Extremely compatible. A most harmonious relationship.
Fu Wei: Very compatible. Your mate will be supportive and encouraging.

 INAUSPICIOUS AND INCOMPATIBLE

Ho Hai: Incompatible. Your mate will cause you accidents and mishaps.
Wu Kuei: Very incompatible. You will have lots of quarrels and anger.
Lui Sha: Extremely incompatible. Your mate will cause you grievous harm and heartbreak. This is the six killings description.
Chueh Ming: Totally and Irretrievably incompatible. Your mate will ruin your name, cause you loss of wealth and break your heart totally.

In the table on the next page, the KUA numbers are matched against each other and you can use it to investigate the various permutations of compatibility based on this method. The key to unlocking the meanings in the Table will be your KUA number, and from there you can find out who are those compatible or not compatible with you.

 THE COMPATIBILITY TABLES

TABLE ONE
KUA NUMBERS THAT ARE COMPATIBLE WITH YOURS

Your KUA NUMBER	sheng chi compatibility Kua number	tien yi compatibility Kua number	nien yen compatibility Kua number	fu wei compatibility Kua number
1	3	4	1	9
2	7	8 only (m) 8 and 5 (f)	5 and 2 (m) 2 only (f)	6
3	1	9	3	4
4	9	1	4	3
5 ✿	7(m) 6(f)	8(m) 2(f)	5(m) 5(f)	6(m) 7(f)
6	8 only (m) 8 and 5 (f)	7	6	2 and 5(m) 2 only (f)
7	2 and 5 (m) 2 only (f)	6	7	8 only (m) 8 and 5 (f)
8	6	2 and 5 (m) 2 only (f)	8 only (m) 8 and 5 (f)	7
9	4	3	9	1

✿ Males with KUA number 5 please follow the number(s)with (m) after it
 females with KUA number 5 please follow the number(s) with (f) after it

Note: The numbers in the grid refer to KUA numbers that are compatible to your KUA number. Note East group always pairs with East group numbers and West group always pairs with West group numbers.

Example: If your Kua number is 8, then the best match for you is someone with the KUA number 6 as this represents the *Sheng chi* match for you. Also people with Kua numbers 2, 8 and 7 are also compatible, and for males, a woman with KUA number 5 is also suitable.

Example: if your Kua number is 1, then the best match for you is someone whose Kua number is 3, but those with Kua numbers 4, 1 or 9 are also suitable.

 THE COMPATIBILITY TABLES

TABLE TWO
KUA NUMBERS THAT ARE INCOMPATIBLE WITH YOURS

Your KUA NUMBER	ho hai Kua number	wu kuei Kua number	lui sha Kua number	chueh ming Kua number
1	6	2 and 5 (m)	7	8 and 5 (f)
2	9	1	3	4
3	8 and 5 (m)	7	2 and 5 (m)	6
4	7	8 and 5 (f)	6	2 and 5 (m)
5	9 (m) 3 (f)	1 (m) 4 (f)	3 (m) 9 (f)	4(m) 1
6	1	9	4	3
7	4	3	1	9
8	3	4	9	1
9	2 and 5 (m)	6	8 and 5 (f)	7

✤ Males with KUA number 5 please follow the number(s)with (m) after it
   Females with KUA number 5 please follow the number(s) with (f) after it
Note: The numbers in the grid refer to KUA numbers that are incompatible to your KUA number. Note East group are always incompatible with West group numbers and West group are always incompatible with East group numbers. These numbers refer to Kua numbers and not anything else.

Example: If your Kua number is 9, then the most incompatible match for you is someone with a KUA number 7, but those with KUA numbers 8, 6, 5 or 2 are also very incompatible and should be avoided.
Example: If your KUA number is 2, then the worst match for you is 4 but those with KUA numbers 1, 3 and 9 are also bad for you. Better to avoid.

NOTE: The above Table was extracted from
the Pa Ku Lo Shu formulas, and were compiled in the following manner:
(i)The respective ho hai; wu kuei, lui sha and chueh ming directions were
first obtained by checking against the original formula. (ii) Each of these
directions were then counter checked against their corresponding Kua
numbers using the matching respective *sheng chi* numbers. (iii) Further
checks were made against the matching male and female Kua numbers
according to the directions.

USING THE I CHING
TO INVESTIGATE FURTHER

The seasoned wisdom of thousands of years has gone into the makings of the I Ching, and you can use this wonderful Book of Oracles to further investigate various aspects of your love life and marriage.

Both branches of Chinese philosophy - Confucianism and Taoism have their common roots in this ancient classic, and it alone, among all the Confucian classics escaped the great burning of the books under the Emperor Chin Shih Huang Ti in 213 B.C. The origins of the I Ching go back to mythical antiquity, as a book of divination and as a book of wisdom.

All that is great and significant in Chinese cultural history takes inspiration from the I Ching - aspects of the many related principles and symbols of Chinese predictive sciences, its view of the Trinity of luck, (Heaven, Earth and Man luck), Yin and Yang concepts, balance and harmony, positive and negative forces, good fortunes and misfortunes. These and much more are collectively derived from interpretations of the text and judgments of the I Ching's 64 hexagrams.

The I Ching's hexagrams are each made up of six lines, one placed above the other. These lines may either be broken (▬ ▬) lines (yin) or they may be unbroken (▬▬) lines (yang). These lines may also be changing or unchanging, i.e. a broken yin line can change into an unbroken yang line and vice versa. The key to comprehending the I Ching is in interpreting its answers is in understanding the placement of broken and unbroken lines in relation to each other. In general also, changing lines offer specific predictions to specific questions.

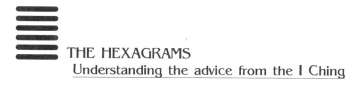

THE HEXAGRAMS
Understanding the advice from the I Ching

The Hexagrams of the I Ching originate from three lined Trigrams i.e. by doubling the Trigrams. There are 8 possible combinations of broken and unbroken lines when arranged in sets of three lines. There are thus 64 Hexagrams because 8 X 8 makes 64. When placed in <u>sets of six lines</u>, there are altogether 64 possible combinations of broken and unbroken lines. Each of the 8 Trigrams symbolize different meanings; and their positioning contain suggestions of good or bad luck. This aspect of the I Ching's text is what has made it China's premier classics on divination.

The I Ching's Hexagrams contain symbols and ideas from nature, society and the individual. For those who consult the I Ching before deciding on some action, the Hexagrams offer wisdom, warnings, and also specific predictions on outcome, thereby giving guidance on whether to proceed, to wait, or not to proceed at all.

The Hexagrams also advise on timing, behaviour and attitudes directly related to the specific question asked. It may counsel further preparation, or advocate patience or even warn of misfortune hidden in apparent good fortune and vice versa. Favourable or unfavourable conditions are described, and difficulties, at the beginning and at the end are revealed.

The six lines of the Hexagrams contain a symbol, an event and a judgment. The Hexagram itself represents overall indication of the situation. Each Hexagram contains four Trigrams, two primary Trigrams and two <u>nuclear Trigrams</u>, and each has something to say about what is being asked. Thus:

Primary Trigrams refer to the circumstances of the situation while Nuclear Trigrams usually reveal the predicted outcome, often providing precise details for judging the nuances of the divination. Much depends on how the reader reacts and responds to what the I Ching says, to get the full benefit of its counsel. It helps if one is already familiar with the meanings and symbolism of the 8 Trigrams, upon which the meanings of the Hexagrams are derived. This greatly facilitates the understanding of the I Ching's language of prediction.

CONSULTING THE I CHING
Focusing on the questions to ask

It is important to treat the I Ching with respect. When constructing your question, the more serious and concentrated you are, the more accurate and precise will be the answers revealed. Successful consultations with the I Ching are often preceded by some effort to quiet the mind, perhaps through meditation. At the same time, consultation must be made in a tranquil atmosphere where one is not disturbed by excessive noise or distractions. Some moments should also be spent reflecting upon the question beforehand so that the frame of mind is serious.

Tips on I Ching consultation

✿   When consulting the I ching, it is important to be very specific with your question. Formulate your inquiry very carefully and concentrate on it for sometime before proceeding with the consultation. Never ask, *"who is better for me ? "* and expect the I Ching to tell you ... rather you should phrase the question like this *"Will so and so be good for me"* ... *" will I have a future with so and so ?"*   If you are trying to decide between two boyfriends for instance, ask the same question about both separately and then compare the answers and judge for yourself by interpreting what the I Ching says !

✿   Do remember that answers received pertain ONLY to the specific question asked. Thus if you receive something that implies bad luck, relate it only to the question asked , and NOT to your entire life !!

✿   Write down your question in a notebook and reflect upon it. If necessary, rephrase your question so there is little room for ambiguity. Ask one question at a time. Keep a record of all questions asked and predictions received so that you can check on them from time to time. With practice you will become very adept at it since your mind would be tuning in to the I Ching regularly.

✿   Put a date to your question and wherever possible, include a time frame or period to your question. Never leave questions open ended.

✿   Do not ask the same question over and over again. This will be viewed as being frivolous and the answers you obtain will not be accurate. You could also end up getting Hexagram Meng which means immaturity ! So do remember to be respectful, the I Ching is a serious Oracle. !

CONSULTING THE I CHING
Interpreting the answers

❀ Always remember that the hexagrams reveal a specific answer to a specific question. If you obtain a negative answer do not fret unnecessarily. The answer refers only to the question asked.

❀ Always analyze the symbols represented by the lines of the Primary and NuclearTrigrams, as well as their relationship with each other. Often, insights will come to you as you reflect upon the symbols. If in doubt, refer to the texts, and you can also refer to more detailed works on the I Ching.

❀ When there are changing lines, these indicate specific predictions which may come in the form of encouragement, or as serious warnings to be careful, or to be patient. But it refers only to the question asked.

❀ If there are changing lines, two hexagrams will be indicated. The first describes your present situation and the second contains a predicted outcome which must be read in conjunction with the changing lines of the first Hexagram. If you require clarification to answers given, ask the I Ching for a clearer explanation !

❀ Sometimes the I Ching offers a time reference e.g it may refer to Spring, or Summer ... in which case it may be telling you to wait.

Examples of questions to ask:
On Marriage and family:
✤ Can my marriage problems be resolved ✤ Will my husband succeed in his plans ? ✤ Can our family difficulties blow over? ✤ Will he/she be a good son or daughter in law ? ✤ Will the affair last ✤ Has my husband/wife stopped loving me ? ✤ Will I have problems with my in laws if I marry this man/woman ? ✤ Is there a bright future if I marry this person ? ✤ Should I seriously encourage my son/daughter in this relationship ? ✤

On Love and Romance.
❀ Will he/she always love me ? ❀ Can our relationship improve ? ❀ Will he/she go out with me if I ask ? ❀ Should I marry him/her ? ❀ Will I be happy with him/her? ❀ Is this a good year for me to get married ? ❀ Is this man/woman meant for me? ❀ Does he/she love someone else ? ❀ Is he/she the faithful type ? ❀ Can I trust this person ? ❀ Will life with this person be happy ? ❀ Is he/she keeping secrets from me ? ❀ ❀ Is he/she seeing someone else ? ❀

TOSSING THE COINS
To construct the Hexagram

An extremely good method to use in I Ching Consultation is the tossing of three coins, six times in a row. Based on the way the coins fall each time, the lines of the Hexagram get constructed until all six lines are done. The resulting hexagram(s) can then be interpreted for answers to questions.

> It is good to select these three coins carefully. Serious practitioners prefer ancient Chinese coins, which in Asia are not difficult to find. These old coins are round with a square hole in the centre; the round shape symbolizes heaven (Chien) while the square hole stands for the Earth (K'un). They Yang or positive side has four characters. The Yin or negative side has two characters. Together, the four plus two characters add up to the six lines of the Hexagram. Using three coins symbolize the Trinity of heaven, earth and man, and also the three lines of the Trigrams.

If old coins are not available, it is perfectly acceptable to use normal everyday coins. Heads stand for Yang (positive), while tails stand for Yin (negative). But it is advisable to set aside three coins for frequent usage so that over time they become closely associated with I Ching consultation. Before tossing the Coins, calm your mind and focus inwards.

Then proceed to toss the coins. Put all three coins in a container, shake vigorously, and toss them onto a clean piece of fabric. It is acceptable to shake the coins in one's hand but this is not as efficient. While shaking three coins, concentrate on the question and ask for a clear, easy to understand answer.
You must toss the three coins six times to obtain the six lines of the Hexagram. After each throw analyze how the coins fall. Each throw of the coin represents one line of the Hexagram. The way the coins fall will tell you the kind of line it is; i.e. whether it is a yang line (unbroken) or a yin line (broken); and whether it is a changing or an unchanging line.

> **━━━━━**   A young Yang line is unbroken and unchanging
> **━━━━━** ✳ An old Yang line is unbroken but changing
>
> A young Yin line is broken and unchanging **━━ ━━**
> An old Yin line is broken but changing   ✳ **━━ ━━**

 CONSTRUCTING THE HEXAGRAM

The Hexagram is constructed from the bottom up. The first line is the bottom line, and each line is determined by the way the coins fall after each throw. The coins are thrown six times, with the first throw representing the first line, the second throw is the second line and so on.

Each time the coins fall there are four possible combinations.
Learn this formula !

● *one yang and two yin* (Or one head and two tails)
represents an unchanging unbroken line (young Yang)   ▬▬▬▬

● *three yang* (Or three heads)
represents a changing unbroken line (old Yang)   ▬▬▬▬ ✳

○ *one yin and two yang* (Or one tail and two heads)
represents an unchanging broken line (young yin)   ▬▬ ▬▬

○ *three yin* (Or three tails)
represents a changing broken line (old yin)   ▬▬ ▬▬ ✳

Construct the hexagram based on theabove formula for the lines.

THE CHANGING LINES:
Each time the coins fall and display either three Yang or three Yin sides, the particular line it represents is referred to as a *changing line*. These lines may change from Yang to Yin or from Yin to Yang i.e. from broken to unbroken and vice versa. Whenever changing lines are indicated, two things must be noted :

✱   A new Hexagram is formed so that there are now two Hexagrams in answer to your question. the first Hexagram describes the situation, while the second Hexagram describes the outcome if the situation.

✱   The changing lines themselves indicate the prediction of the first Hexagram. Thus, if the second line is a changing line, read the prediction represented by the second line. If there is more than one changing line, read all predictions indicated and try to formulate a pattern to the message being given. Mark your changing lines with an asterisk ✳

IDENTIFYING THE HEXAGRAM

Now that you have constructed the predictive Hexagram(s), the next stage is to <u>identify</u> the Hexagrams. Use the table below to do this. You now have the I Ching symbols which contain the response to your inquiry. The next step is to understand what these symbols (lines and Trigrams) are telling you. This is done by reading the sections on the Trigrams and the Hexagrams in this book. Interpret the Primary and Nuclear Trigrams in relation to each other, and in conjunction with the changing lines. Also read the judgments, symbols and text associated with each of the Hexagrams. Only by combining all the messages given can you formulate a suitable interpretation of the answer. If you like, you can extend your reading by consulting other books on the I Ching which contain more detailed insights on the Hexagrams. The descriptions in this book were extracted from scholarly translations of the I Ching texts and should really be adequate.

IDENTIFYING THE HEXAGRAMS

upper trigram / lower trigram	chien	chen	kan	ken	kun	sun	li	tui
chien	1	34	5	26	11	9	14	43
chen	25	51	3	27	24	42	21	17
kan	6	40	29	4	7	59	64	47
ken	33	62	39	52	15	53	56	31
kun	12	16	8	23	2	20	35	45
sun	44	32	48	18	46	57	50	28
li	13	55	63	22	36	37	30	49
tui	10	54	60	41	19	61	38	58

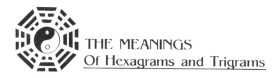

THE MEANINGS
Of Hexagrams and Trigrams

The meanings of the 64 hexagrams are connected to the symbols associated with their base Trigrams. The attributes of these 8 Trigrams give clues to the meanings of the Hexagrams. Thus:

1. CHIEN the creative, is yang, associated with the father, the leader and the patriarch. It signifies heaven, the sky, power, brightness, energy, strength and perseverance. Getting Chien means *heaven is helping,* or *some force is lending a hand.* It indicates good fortune and success. Its element is big metal, it is totally positive and its direction is Northwest.

2. KUN the receptive, is yin, associated with the mother, with female, the maternal and devotion. It is yielding, and is the perfect complement to Chien. Signifies nature, the earth, and productive compliance. Southwest.

3. CHEN the arousing, associated with eldest son, vehemence, shock, decisions, and thunder. Suggests Spring's luxuriant growth, the Dragon, big wood. Implies caution as the path to good fortune. Inner fortitude. East.

4. SUN the gentle, associated with eldest daughter, with indecision and the wind. Suggests three benefits, profits, success and luck. Southeast

5. TUI the joyous, represents happiness, the youngest daughter, a beautiful lake. Tui is small metal, the mouth that speaks, a petite woman, a concubine, someone outwardly weak and inwardly stubborn. Autumn. West.

6. KEN the mountain, keeping still. There is mystery in the depths. Suggests period of transition. Waiting. Time for reflection. Link between the end and the new beginning. Small earth. Northeast.

7. KAN the abysmal, representing danger. Carries connotations of warning.   If your hexagram contains this trigram, be wary The warning of Kan must be taken seriously. Also signifies hardship, toil and melancholia. A certain frustration. Not a happy prediction. Blood. North.

8. LI the clinging, fire, representing the sun, intense brightness, lightning, heat, and warmth. Suggestive of tough exterior hiding weakness inside. Someone with no substance but full of gloss and glamour. Middle daughter. Suggest dependence. But also denotes great potential. Li can light up the world and set it resoundingly on fire ! Summer. South.

 CHIEN THE CREATIVE

This Hexagram stands for heaven, leader, father. All four Trigrams are Chien indicating strength, energy and movement. This is the strongest hexagram; the advice is to use strength with caution and without arrogance.

THE JUDGMENT: Great and strong success. Benefits through perseverance.
THE SYMBOL: Heaven moves powerfully.
THE CHANGING LINES :
Line 1: Not a good time to act or commit to anything. Prepare. Rest. Romance moves slowly But family relations are good.
Line 2: A time of development. You will get help from superiors. Excellent opportunities are coming. Women will become prosperous through marriage or on their own. Success in exams indicated.
Line 3 : Be cautious. A busy time. Relationships will suffer. Prospects bad.
Line 4 : Hard times ahead. Some good short term luck. Lucky for women.
Line 5 : Excellent fortune. Mentors appear. Power increases. Promotions.
Line 6 : Arrogance leads to trouble. Marriage indicated. Loss of friendship.

 KUN THE RECEPTIVE

Kun means earth, mother. All four Trigrams are Kun - The Yin Principle dominates. Yielding overcomes strength and endures. ExcellentHexagram.

THE JUDGMENT: Great success. Benefits come from perseverance. All undertakings are successful, peacefulness and harmonious relations. Good fortune in all things.
THE SYMBOL: Greatness and genuine strength which comes from non resisitance. And with the character to endure anything.
THE CHANGING LINES :
Line 1 : Beware of gossip/jealousy. Women will bring prosperity to family.
Line 2 : Everything benefits. Promotions. Recognition and prosperity.
Line 3 : Time of quiet success. Excellent fortune for men or women. But stay very low profile. Wealth is indicated. Success in romance.
Line 4 : Time to be watchful. Act with caution. Better to be inactive. Wait.
Line 5 : Everything goes smoothly. Money. A time of great success.
Line 6 : Expect danger. Loss. Lawsuits. Quarrels. Exam results uninspiring.

3. CHUN Difficulty in the Beginning

Signifies difficulty, confusion and danger at the start but improvements later. Upper trigram is Kan, water, clouds, rain. Lower Trigram is Chen, thunder and movement. Together they signify disorder, a harsh time. But later sunshine comes. Prepare.

THE JUDGMENT: Difficulties at the start. Later great success comes. Proceed despite problems. Continue and it will benefit.

THE SYMBOL :The superior man makes order out of disorder. Difficulties can be overcome. Need to persevere. Have faith in yourself.

THE CHANGING LINES   :

Line 1 : Good fortune indicated. Careers, relationships, studies have excellent prospects. Do not doubt yourself. Proceed decisively.

Line 2 : Many difficulties, much patience required. Can benefit from career change. Good time for marriage. Some obstacles.

Line 3 : Refrain from action. Proceeding leads to misfortune. Stop ! Students encounter obstacles.

Line 4 : Good fortune for everything. Marriage prospects. Goals achieved. Promotion and recognition at work. Good job available.

Line 5 : Good fortune in small things. Misfortune in big matters. Plan with care. Do not be too trusting.

Line 6 : Beware. Extreme misfortune indicated. Stay out of it !

4. MENG or YOUTH

Youthful folly and immaturity indicated by Meng. the Trigrams, upper and lower, are Ken and Kan, i.e. Mountain over water. Extreme foolishness. The I Ching says *"first time he asks, I answer, but if he asks again and again,......no answer"*. Be thoughtful and generous.

THE JUDGMENT: It is annoying to be asked the same question.

THE SYMBOL: Spring at the foot of the mountain. Youthfulness. Grow up!

THE CHANGING LINES   :

Line 1 : Develop discipline to succeed. Good indications for students. Will pass well and find a good job. Quarrels indicated in friendships.

Line 2 : Excellent predictions for marriage. Perhaps a child is born. Peaceful time coming. Powerful friends. A satisfying period.

Line 3 : Caution. Failure indicated. Reduce drinking and womanizing.

Line 4 : Confusion and humiliation. Troubled times. Bad luck. Obstacles

Line 5 : Good fortune. Goals can be achieved. Proceed !

Line 6 : Time of quarrels, lawsuits. Auspicious for students. Goals achieved.

5. HSU the WAITING

Hsu means waiting, nourishment or necessity. Upper diagram Kan means water or danger; Lower trigram Chien denotes strength. Image is water in heaven i.e. clouds & rain. One should wait and prepare. Nourishment is opportunity. Be ambitious. Perseverance brings success. you have inner energy and there is sincerity. Success will be glorious.

THE JUDGMENT: Continueing bringssuccess. Benefits to cross waters.
THE SYMBOL: Enjoy life, but prepare. Opportunities are coming soon.
THE CHANGING LINES :
Line 1 : Time to consolidate. Wait before proceeding. Plan carefully.
Line 2 : Agitation/Gossip. But good fortune. No need to fret !
Line 3 : Be careful of loss. Caution in travels. This person not good for you.
Line 4 : Situation can improve slightly but no great success is possible.
　　　　Not a good idea to take risks. Do not make the first move.
Line 5 : Good fortune. Can gain property and profit, Or get married. All the
　　　　indications are excellent and spell potential success..
Line 6 : Unexpected guests. Treat them well. They bring good fortune but
　　　　proceed slowly. Refrain from aggressive behaviour.

6. SUNG the CONFLICT

Sung indicates disputes, arguments, and opposition. Chien above Kan denotes conflicting forces. Old man vs Young man. This hexagram warns against undertaking big ventures. Maintaining the status quo brings good fortune. Indications for marriage or love affairs are inauspicious.

THE JUDGMENT: You are sincere but others are not. Withdraw. Stop.
　　　　　　　　　If you proceed, misfortune. Better to pause.
THE SYMBOL: Different views and opinions. Analyse well before starting.
THE CHANGING LINES :
Line 1 : Gossip, Lawsuits and disaster. Ignore them all.
　　　　In the end everything is resolved in your favour.
Line 2 : Retreat. Avoid conflicts. Stability and money indicated for those
　　　　who hold steady. So have faith in yourself.
Line 3 : Not a time to be ambitious. Wait. Strongly advocate patience.
Line 4 : Losses can definitely be recovered. Do not worry.
Line 5 : Help from an influential person. Recognition and promotion.
Line 6 : Some success some failure. For students, the line predicts
　　　　excellent grades. In romance a frustrating time. Be patient.

7. SHIH the ARMY

Shih denotes battles, competition and business rivalries. Kun above is earth. Kan below is water - together the lines indicate powerful forces. Water can overflow causing damage. The single yang line represents a great general or leader. He dominates. On him will depend success or failure.

THE JUDGMENT: The army requires a strong leader.
                    Good fortune comes with him.
THE SYMBOL: A respected General brings prosperity to his people.
THE CHANGING LINES   :
Line 1 : Be smart. You can make money, gain favours, achieve your goals.
          But arrogance leads to failures. Control your temper.
Line 2 : Excellent fortune. Honours and rewards predicted.
          Everything will be easily successful.
Line 3 : Misfortune. A time of sudden mourning. Luck is bad for most.
Line 4 : Avoid reckless actions. Compromise. Do not be arrogant.
Line 5 : Money comes. Goals achieved. But trouble for youngest son.
Line 6 : Much prosperity for all. Success indicated. Avoid over confidence.

8. PI or UNION

Pi means harmony, cooperation, mergers. Kan above Kun. Water above earth denoted bonding and power. The single yang line is in a high position. He is strong and generous. This hexagram is favourable for marriages, love affairs and business joint ventures.

THE JUDGMENT: Good fortune. Greatness and prosperity for those who
                proceed with sincerity. Hesitation may lead to bad luck.
THE SYMBOL: Union, Expansion, Growth.
THE CHANGING LINES   :
Line 1 : Proceed with confidence. Help from friends. Unexpected promotion
          and openings. New opportunities. Will meet someone else better !
Line 2 : Help from superiors. Scholarships and recognition indicated.
          Women will find good husband. Ambitions are achievable.
Line 3 : Union with wrong people. Sad outcomes. Loss of money and
          opportunities. Danger from jealousy. Health declines.
Line 4 : Excellent indications for success
Line 5 : Honour. Happiness. Good fortune. Success. Everything smooth.
Line 6 : Misfortune. Trials and difficulties. Health is poor. Quarrels.
          No support is forthcoming. It is best to retreat.

9. HSIAO CHU or Taming the small Powers

This hexagram implies rest and preparation. Sun, wind above and Chien, sky below with the nuclear Trigrams also symbolizing sun and clouds. Meaning : The wind blows the clouds to cover the sun. Soon it will rain. But the sun will come out after the rain. You will meet with difficulty at first but success will come later.

THE JUDGMENT: Eventually success will surely come.
THE SYMBOL: Winds blow across the skies. Improve and prepare.
THE CHANGING LINES   :
Line 1 : Peace. Difficult decisions. But success is just around the corner.
Line 2 : Good influence brings good fortune. Promotions. Recognition.
Line 3 : Marital problems. Be prepared for setbacks and separations. Illness.
Line 4 : Friends give good recommendation. Romance is in the air.
Line 5 : Can expect help and cooperation from others.. Will make gains.
Line 6 : Beware of traps. Withdraw. Troubles await, but can avoid them.

10. LU the TREADING

This hexagram predicts inactivity. Only in seclusion and careful planning can there be good fortune. The lower Tui, gentle daughter and upper Chien, father represents gentle obedience to experience, Tui is also tiger and lake; so avoid danger by being careful.
THE JUDGMENT: The Tiger does not bite those who step on its tail.
THE SYMBOL: Treading with care. Be respectful. Not impulsive.
THE CHANGING LINES   :
Line 1 : Continue. Can expect success. Can make money. Good fortune.
Line 2 : Caution brings extreme good fortune. Good time to rest awhile and enjoy a relaxing period. Build your energy. Slow down !
Line 3 : A dangerous time. Watch out for conflicts, even loss of money, job and position. Slander and gossip will hurt. Stay low profile.
Line 4 : Disaster and troubles threaten. Be careful. Marriage under stress but for students it is a good time. High grades possible.
Line 5 : Don't rush. Don't be careless. Even if you work hard you will not be rewarded. Your time has not come yet.
Line 6 : Great fortune. Expect to receive money and property. Success. Be confident. In love you will have your way. Smile !

11. TAI or PEACE

This is a hexagram of great good fortune. Kun, yin above Chien, yang, denoting perfect balance and harmony. Flexibility with strength and compromise with energy. This is an excellent Hexagram to get ! The nuclear Trigrams are also favourable ... denoting growth and harvest.

THE JUDGMENT: The small departs. The great arrives. Huge success.
THE SYMBOL: Heaven and Earth cooperates, bringing peace and harmony.
THE CHANGING LINES   :
Line 1 : Cooperation brings great prosperity and happiness. At work
          the boss is pleased and at school the teacher is impressed.
Line 2 : Support from influential mentor. Great success is achieved in
          business, work. And relationships. There is peace !
Line 3 : Problems are superficial. Do not worry. Things will work out and
          everything will come right in the end.
Line 4 : New ventures could fail. Be careful.
Line 5 : A time of great fortune. Everything will succeed brilliantly.
          Prospects for marriage are excellent. Money flows in.
Line 6 : A bad time. Slander and Gossip. Avoid disaster by being generous
          and kind. But do not fret. Troubles soon blow over.

12. P'I or STAGNATION

This hexagram denotes poverty and hard times. Chien above Kun, is unnatural and disharmonious. Strength at the top but weakness below, something which collapses easily. There is no foundation. But do not be discouraged. In misfortune there can be good fortune. Work hard. Be diligent and do not give up.

THE JUDGMENT: The great departs. The small arrives.
                    Symbolizing stagnation.
THE SYMBOL: Disharmony. Neither wealth nor honour is yet possible.
THE CHANGING LINES   :
Line 1 : Be careful. Avoid bad company. Stay reserved.
Line 2 : Be cautious and circumspect and wait for more auspicious times.
Line 3 : Some humiliation could come. Bear with it. Stay low profile.
Line 4 : A good line. Friends rally round to help. Small successes.
Line 5 : Bad times are coming to an end. Rivals will be silenced. bad luck
          turns to good luck. Unexpected gains are made.
Line 6 : Bad times ended. What has failed, now succeeds. Illness is cured.
          The small goes away making way for the great ! Smile !

13. T'UNG JEN or FELLOWSHIP of MEN

This hexagram has <u>Chien</u> above and <u>Li</u>, fire below. It represents a group of people working effectively together. The Trigrams denote brightness shining in heaven i.e. clarity with strength and decisiveness. Great skills in leadership are indicated. The nuclear Trigrams are <u>Chien</u> meaning energy and fire. Stay calm. Stay in control. Do not get over confident.

THE JUDGMENT: Everything benefits.
THE SYMBOL:The heavens burn brightly. Symbolizing energy and strength.
THE CHANGING LINES :
Line 1 : Good fellowship and cooperation indicated. A long trip.
   A new opportunity. Do not miss this chance !
Line 2 : Conflicting opinions lead to trouble.
Line 3 : For some, a period of difficulty lasting three months or three years.
   For scholars and young people, an excellent time.
Line 4 : New responsibilities lead to success. But take care. Be wary.
Line 5 : Both good and bad times. Publicity brings good fortune.
Line 6 : Do not change jobs now as it will lead to unhappiness.
   Be contented. Let sleeping dogs lie.

14. TA YU or GREAT POSSESSIONS

Great riches, wealth and prosperity are all indicated ! Bright and glorious <u>Li</u> on top and strong and sturdy <u>Chien</u> below signify honour and recognition. Nuclear Trigrams signify gold. So much good fortune is indicated. But beware. Those already successful must remember that the sun can set on those who are arrogant and indolent. Stay humble, and refrain from aggressive behaviour.

THE JUDGMENT: Great Possessions
THE SYMBOL: Destiny brings success.
THE CHANGING LINES :
Line 1 : If there are problems, resign, walk away. Your luck is shining.
Line 2 : Success in investments and business.
   If engaged in a battle you will surely win.
Line 3 : Rich people will get richer. Working people will get promoted.
Line 4 : Your success is definitely assured. Your good fortune will continue.
Line 5 : Great good fortune. Be confident in whatever you undertake.
Line 6 : Blessed by heaven! Everything benefits. Prosperity, high positions
   and influence all come your way unceasingly.

15. CH'IEN or MODESTY

This hexagram describes a successful but modest person. Kun, earth above Ken, the mountain. The single yang line is in the third position signifying undue modesty. This is something rare and it attracts good fortune.

THE JUDGMENT: Modesty allows success to be maintained.
THE SYMBOL :The mountain in the earth calls for reducing the excess and
increasing that which is lacking. Equalize all things.
THE CHANGING LINES   :
Line 1 : Travel and new responsibilities indicated, both leading to success.
Your abilities are recognised. Continue.
Line 2 : Some more good fortune. To act or not to act will bring the same
benefits. But plan carefully.
Line 3 : Undertakings will be profitable, and opportunities for further
advancement come your way. Be bold and grab them.
Line 4 : A good time to consolidate and take stock. Not a time for
advancement. Patience.
Line 5 : Immense benefits and great success come your way from
influential people. But be discreet. Or you could lose everything.
Line 6 : Avoid remorse by being aware of your weakness.

16. YU or HAPPINESS

Happiness and enthusiasm. Chen above and Kun below. A time for new ventures and undertakings. The period between winter and spring. A time for planting the seeds !This hexagram advises preparation and planning before embarking on something new.

THE JUDGMENT: It benefits to commence a new venture. Build a
business. Get started on a new relationship. Growth.
THE SYMBOL : Thunder awakens the Earth. Signifying great happiness.
THE CHANGING LINES   :
Line 1 : Boastful behavior cause jealousy. Curb your enthusiasm.
Scholars will achieve sudden recognition. Romance blossoms.
Line 2 : An excellent prediction. Proceed. Decide quickly. Do not hesitate.
Line 3 : Sudden setbacks bring remorse.. Delays cause problems.
Line 4 : Great pain forecasted in matters of the heart.
Line 5 : Will find difficulty in getting started. Ventures cannot take off.
Seek assistance from someone powerful or influential.
Line 6 : If you are insincere or dishonest, you will be found out.
This is a dangerous time.

17. SUI or FOLLOWING

The hexagram depicts a young man wooing a pretty girl. He is successful. But Tui the upper trigram also symbolizes a sunset. Night time approaches. Beauty fades. If you get this prediction, avoid new entanglements. Stay faithful, and resist the temptation to stray ... or you could lose something.

THE JUDGMENT: Initially great success.
THE SYMBOL: Having achieved success, follow up with rest. Retire. Enjoy.
THE CHANGING LINES
Line 1: Good fortune comes again and again. Social life is enjoyable.
    Business brings profits. Everything succeeds easily.
Line 2: A young person causes anguish and scandal.
    Watch your behaviour carefully.
Line 3: You must choose one or the other. You cannot have both.
Line 4: A powerful man brings good fortune, saving you from ruin.
    Recognition comes. Be grateful.
Line 5: Honourable behaviour brings great good fortune. Success comes.
Line 6: Some danger from envious people. Stay low profile.

18. Ku or WORK after SPOILING

Bad times now. But things will improve. The wind, Sun, below blows at the mountain Ken above, destroying the vegetation. But later, the plants grow once more. For business and politics, this Hexagram predicts grave misfortune. In love affairs, a young man loves an older woman. Or an old man is involved with a young girl. Both situations are difficult.

THE JUDGMENT: Bad times do not last long. only three full moons.
THE SYMBOL: During bad times, it is necessary to work and persevere.
    And to cultivate good virtues. Then success comes.
THE CHANGING LINES:
Line 1 : Get help from your father or family. There is danger but difficulties
    will resolve. Stay committed and strong.
Line 2 : Hardwork is necessary for success. Relationships die without care.
Line 3 : Do not be over ambitious or hasty. Pause and take stock.
Line 4 : A period of difficulty when everything goes wrong. you will be
    strongly criticized. Perhaps with justifiable cause. Look within.
Line 5 : A good time. Remorse vanishes. Marriage indicated. Students and
    managers start new careers and advancements.
Line 6 : A good time. But not for new ventures or start new
    careers or fresh entanglements. Patience !

19. LIN or APPROACH

This hexagrams depicts a mother/daughter relationship. Kun above, and Tui below. Guidance, wisdom, kindness and experience are all suggested. The two yang lines at the bottom signify growth and vitality, indicating good fortune and high hopes for achievements. But be wary of the eighth month which comes later.

THE JUDGMENT: It is beneficial to continue.
THE SYMBOL: Earth above lake signifies positive reaction,
      a successful approach.
THE CHANGING LINES :
Line 1 : Success in work or studies. Help comes from a person in power.
Line 2 : Excellent outcomes for all your undertakings. Especially good for
    careers. You have reason to be cheerful and happy.
Line 3 : A boring and unsuccessful time. Bear with it !
Line 4 : Harmonious relationships bring good cheer and happiness.
    Opportunities abound. Grab them !
Line 5 : Excellent prospects for everyone and everything.
    Plans go smoothly. Success.
Line 6 : Great good fortune in all your endeavors. Success is implied.

20. KUAN or OBSERVATION

This Hexagram signifies dust being blown by the wind and it settles in a far away mountain. Sun above Kun. For businessmen, success must be sought elsewhere. Patience is necessary before targets can be achieved, but in matters of the heart, perseverance and sincerity will bring triumphs. It is a good time to go slowly, and for study and to learn meditation.

THE JUDGMENT: The sacrifice is still to come. Sincerity of self is required.
THE SYMBOL:The wind blowing signifies the need to observe and to learn.
THE CHANGING LINES :
Line 1 : Your efforts do not bear fruit. Betrayals. Limited opportunities for
    advancement. A most difficult time.
Line 2 : Good time for women to achieve their goals, but for men it is a
    frustrating period. You will have no luck with the girls.
Line 3 : A time for ups and downs, highs and lows. A need for caution.
Line 4 : Business travel augurs well. Going overseas brings good luck.
Line 5 : The predictions for this line are good. Success indicated. Births.
Line 6: The waiting is at an end. It is time for new beginnings.

21: SHIH HO or CHEWING

This hexagram predicts obstacles and quarrels. The lines are shaped like a mouth, with words or food inside. Only by chewing can there be nourishment. So it indicates success through hard work. The bottom three lines indicate hardships at the start. But then there is a breakthrough and the next two lines indicate good fortune. For marriages, someone is coming between the husband and wife. But... with sincerity, there is a happy ending!

THE JUDGMENT: Success from chewing
THE SYMBOL: Ancient Kings brought justice
THE CHANGING LINES   :
Line 1 : Caution avoids personal disaster
Line 2 : Gossip, sickness, injury, frustration, and difficulties are all indicated.
Line 3 : Success is tough to come by even in small things.
            There is also danger. Beware.
Line 4 : Breakthrough! Good fortune comes. Love smiles again.
              Promotion, honour and profits roll in.
Line 5 : Further good fortune. Like gold at the doorstep,
Line 6 :Misfortune. Humiliation. Troubles. This is an insecure period for you.

22. PI or GRACEFULNESS.

Beauty, grace and decoration are indicated. The sun is shining on the mountain in the evening and lighting up the flowers and trees. Ken above, and Li below ! The Trigrams also represent a handsome couple, vivacious, elegant and happy. This Hexagram indicates success and happiness, but only in small things. The time for greater things has not yet arrived ...

THE JUDGMENT: Grace. Beauty. Success.
THE SYMBOL :Fire illuminates the mountain and makes it beautiful
THE CHANGING LINES   :
Line 1 : If you want to succeed you must be action oriented and work hard.
Line 2 : A good opportunity is coming. Be alert. Someone will help you.
Line 3 : Success is easily achieved. But also be careful.
Line 4 : A white horse brings good fortune. In the midst of sadness there is
            happiness. Early opposition transforms into harmony.
Line 5 : You will have a series of little successes, nothing huge.
Line 6 : Simple undertakings bring satisfaction.
            Overall good fortune in most things.

23. PO or DECAY

A miserable hexagram indeed. Disintegration and misfortune are indicated by Po. Mountain, <u>Ken</u>, above <u>Kun</u>, the earth, stands exposed to the wind and rain. The Hexagram itself does not look solid. It has no support. There is nothing within. For romance, it indicates too many girlfriends for the man and lots of gossip for the woman. Most inauspicious.

THE JUDGMENT: Decay. It is most unfavourable to undertake anything.
THE SYMBOL: The mountain is in decay.
THE CHANGING LINES   :
Line 1 : Discord amongst relatives, and between lovers. Relationships spoil.
Line 2 : So much bad luck everything goes wrong. Plans go awry.
Line 3 : Everything falls apart. Friends desert you. Romance goes sour.
Line 4 : Enormous danger. Lawsuits. Bad luck cause difficulties to escalate.
Line 5 : Success come from a woman's help. Women will enjoy good
         fortune and success. It will also be a good time for scholars.
Line 6 : Honourable men will achieve success. Dishonesty is punished.

24. FU or REVIVAL

Bad times get better. What seems cold and lonely is really full of light and energy. There is warmth underneath all that cold, as symbolized by the one yang line at the bottom of the hexagram. Chen below <u>Kun</u>. Prepare now for a wonderful opportunity. A second chance. Reunions. Second Marriages. Money. All are indicated. Success will creep up and surprise you.

THE JUDGMENT: Multiple benefits arrive
THE SYMBOL:Thunder in the earth announce the arrival of good fortune.
THE CHANGING LINES   :
Line 1 : Great good fortune. Profits expand. Romance flourishes.
         If you want marriage you can have it too !
Line 2 : If in danger, you will be saved. If sick you will be cured.
Line 3 : Changing times. Success comes but slowly. Persevere.
Line 4 : This is a time to improve yourself. There is much waiting.
Line 5 : Success in careers, but a personal tragedy could occur. Sorry!
Line 6 A time of danger and defeat.
         Stay inactive and lie low for awhile.

25. WU WANG or UNEXPECTED

Wu Wang signifies the natural order of things. It advocates adapting to circumstances, and advises one not to struggle against nature. The Trigrams show Chien, heaven, father above and Chen, thunder, son below. When it is time to rain, nothing can prevent it. The son should obey the father. Nature must follow its course.

THE JUDGMENT :The unexpected brings sublime success.
                          Perseverance benefits.
THE SYMBOL : Cultivate virtue and use it at the appropriate time..
THE CHANGING LINES   :
Line 1 : Profit for all. Harmony. Good fortune.
Line 2 : Fame, money and property are predicted. Great good luck!
Line 3 : Good fortune for those in business, but for lovers itís a trying time.
Line 4 : Good fortune for everyone. Projects succeed. no one loses money.
Line 5 : Success in your plans. Advance with confidence. Plan a family.
Line 6 : If you are not careful, you will suffer misfortune.

26. TA CHU or TAMING THE GREAT POWERS

This Hexagram predicts a successful, bright future, the storing of great internal strength for a large undertaking. Ken above denotes stillness and resilience. This is a Hexagram to encourage you to strive and persevere despite difficulties. There is something great and wonderful in store for you. Many people will assist you. Do not falter in your ambitions and dreams.

THE JUDGMENT: Persistence benefits. Cross the great waters and succeed
THE SYMBOL :The superior man tames the great powers, and improves.
THE CHANGING LINES   :
Line 1 : In the face of danger, pause. Wait. The danger will pass.
Line 2 : Watch your health. Go slow. Do not be in too much of a hurry.
Line 3 : A time to advance. Seek new avenues for growth. You will succeed.
Line 4 : Unrestrained success. Great good fortune is coming.
              Expect all the best things. And great on the romantic front.
Line 5 : Happiness and extreme good fortune now comes your way. You will
              be offered a very high position. Proceed with confidence.
Line 6 : Success in everything. Nothing can stop you for heaven is solidly
              on your side. You will be blessed with auspicious luck !

27.  I or NOURISHMENT

An open mouth with the jaws chewing food give nourishment to the body. In eating there must be moderation. The mouth represents speech. Idle chatter can cause problems. For young people this Hexagram is quite favourable because they have the energy required. For older people it is better to retire. Dirty old men should not fool around !

THE JUDGMENT: Good fortune comes from good nourishment
THE SYMBOL :The superior man is cautious in his speech.
THE CHANGING LINES   :
Line 1 : Indicates a possible disaster due to the arrogance of the speech.
Line 2 : The venture will be unsuccessful. It is necessary to be very careful.
Line 3 : Misconduct is strongly predicted. Take control of yourself !
Line 4 : A hungry man hunts strenuously for food. But success is indicated.
Line 5 : Travel by the ship or plane could be disastrous.
         Otherwise, good fortune. Proceed with your plans.
Line 6 : Nourishment is found. Great success abounds, and it continues.
         Jobs and promotions available. Grades are excellent.

28.   TA KUO or GREAT EXCESS

The image is one of trees under water, a flood. The hexagram itself has two weak points supporting the strength inside (as depicted in the nuclear Trigrams which are both Chien). This signifies that one's ambitions surpass his abilities. It also means over expansion in business and difficulties in matters of the heart. Tui, the lake is above Sun ! This is also a warning to be cautious.

THE JUDGMENT: Great excess
THE SYMBOL : The Lake waters rise above the trees, flooding the
                surrounding landscape. There is danger !
THE CHANGING LINES   :
Line 1 : Slow and steady wins the race. Do not be too great in a hurry.
         Gain some experience. In love, dont be such a fast worker huh !
Line 2 : Success in romantic matters even though one is much older than
         the other. But calls for genuine patience and understanding.
Line 3 : Misfortune. One cracks under pressure. Humiliation. Setbacks.
Line 4 : Good fortune comes with compromise.
Line 5 : An older woman causes problems.
         Difficulties encountered are not resolved.
Line 6 : A time of sadness. Misfortune. Perhaps heartbreak !

29. K'AN or WATER

This hexagram is warning of grave danger, misfortune and involvements in difficult entanglements. Water doubled means many situations of danger surrounding you. Beware of deception and trickery. For young couples this is not an auspicious time. For singles, this hexagram warns of entanglements that will lead to grave danger. Be very careful !

THE JUDGMENT Sincerity overwhelms the danger.
THE SYMBOL : Water flows unceasingly bringing grave danger
THE CHANGING LINES   :
Line 1 : Misfortune from excessive drinking . At work and at school there is
        risk of demotion and severe reprimand.
Line 2 : A time to keep your ambitions on a back burner. Stay low profile.
Line 3 : Great difficulties and conflicts. You need to be tough and resilient.
Line 4 : A time for marriage and socialising. Not for serious work.
Line 5 : The water is under control and it brings good fortune. The danger
        has receded, Opportunities can be obtained. Tread warily.
Line 6 : Bad vibes. Grave misfortunes. Avoid entanglements at all costs.

30.   LI or FIRE

The double fire, signifying bright sunlight, but the fire is unstable and can be explosive. It also indicates a successful woman, beautiful both inside and outside. It is great if you can win her ! Young courting couples who are passionately in love should marry soon or lose the opportunity to do so. This is not the time to hestitate.

THE JUDGMENT: Fire brings success.
THE SYMBOL : Double brightness illuminates the
                four corners of the universe
THE CHANGING LINES   :
Line 1 : Proceed with caution. Or you could get burnt. A confusing time.
Line 2 : Sunlight represents great, good fortune. It shines brightly.
Line 3 : The sun has set. It is the twilight of one's years and fortunes are
        on the decline. Relationships are ending ... there is nothing to be done.
Line 4 : Insolence and arrogance cause conflicts. Beware of ill tempers.
Line 5 : A period of mourning but good fortune is just around the corner.
        However, do not expect much. Only small triumphs.
Line 6 : A lucky period. Success is easy but loneliness may overshadow
        achievements and material gains. Choose wisely.

31. HSIEN or STIMULATION

Also means attraction and affection. The image is of a joyous young woman and young man. The couple are strongly attracted to each other. This hexagram is favourable for marriage. There is harmony and expansion. For those seeking guidance on relationships check the changing lines carefully.

THE JUDGMENT: To marry the girl is good fortune. Brings success.
THE SYMBOL: Attraction is strong
THE CHANGING LINES   :
Line 1 : Wait patiently and choose your time carefully before proceeding.
            Your prospects are favourable, and you can expect to succeed.
Line 2 : Good fortune lies in inactivity. Transfers lead to misfortunes.
            What you have is better than what you crave !
Line 3 : Luck is only average.There is stimulation but no attraction.
Line 4 : Minor success. Not resolute enough. Try harder !
Line 5 : Strong opinions cause discord. Tone down !
Line 6 : Small success only. Too much talking leads to conflicts and
misunderstandings. Beware of gossip. Repair the situation quickly !

32. HENG or DURATION

This hexagram signifies a strong enduring marriage. Chen, above and Sun below spells long term success. This hexagram also predicts a happy time of high profits for business people and a release from difficulties and entanglements. It also teaches perseverance for excellence in academia.

THE JUDGMENT :Everything succeeds.
THE SYMBOL: Thunder, Wind. Standing firm. Without changing direction
THE CHANGING LINES   :
Line 1 : It is not necessary to be too hard or be too insistent.
            Nothing benefits. Go slow.
Line 2 : Remorse disappears. Stability is now achieved.
            Past failures are now corrected. All is well again.
Line 3 : Do not bring misfortune on yourself. Offending people is bad !
Line 4 : A difficult situation. Improve your present situation before thinking
            of expanding. There is a real risk of loss.
Line 5 : For women, this is a successful time. But for men, misfortunes.
Line 6 : Aim for modest successes only. It is a difficult time for finding
            proper solutions to your dilemma. Just wait for the right time.

33. TUN or WITHDRAWAL

Tun advocates compromise. Avoidance of direct confrontation. The Hexagram symbolises a hermit in the mountains - it is a favourable time for retirement and retreat. For those in business, this Hexagram advises closing down and cutting losses. Not a good time to start new ventures except perhaps in the entertainment and restaurant businesses. For marriage difficulties, wait and let the bad times pass ... or things just get worse !

THE JUDGMENT: To persist is of benefit
THE SYMBOL: Keeping one's distance
THE CHANGING LINES   :
Line 1 : Retreat. Danger. Avoid engaging in conflicts. You will lose.
Line 2 : Expect contentious behaviour from friends and associates.
         But do not respond. YOu are weak at the moment !
Line 3 : Good fortune comes only if you can withdraw without
         entanglements. There is danger. Be careful.
Line 4 : Your troubles are not over. You are advised to surrender. Preserve
         your strength for another battle when luck is with you.
Line 5 : You are blessed with good fortune, and your luck improves.
         But only in small doses.
Line 6 : Everything is beneficial. But working people experience problems.

34. TA CHUANG or GREAT POWER

Thunder in the sky. Power. Force. Speed. Like a strong horse galloping, the young man's energy and enthusiasm for action bring him success. Temper force with compromise and haste with patience and you will be most successful. In romance yes get sewpt off your feet !

THE JUDGMENT : It benefits to continue
THE SYMBOL: Thunder in the sky above symbolises awesome power.
THE CHANGING LINES   :
Line 1 : Not a time for hasty action. Wait. you are not ready to proceed.
Line 2 : Persistence benefits and you will achieve your objectives.
Line 3 : Be cautious. There is disaster lurking in the background. Conflicts.
Line 4 : Act now, say yes ! Yield and you will succeed beyond your dreams.
Line 5 : Not a lucky time. More failures than successes. Obstacles.
Line 6 : Your problem is your terrible arrogance. Misfortune, even disaster,
         will visit you if you don't change your attitude.

35. CHIN or PROGRESS

A time for beginnings. There are bright prospects for the future. Business experience growth and expansion, and achieve a high degree of success. For career professionals, promotions are on the way with added incomes. Chin is also favourable for marriage and moving to a new home. The only problem lie in the potential problems in interpersonal behaviour but these too can be resolved.

THE JUDGMENT :The king bestows honours on the Marquis three times
THE SYMBOL:The sun rising above the earth brightens the horizon.
THE CHANGING LINES   :
Line 1 : Obstructions block one's way. But persistence dissolves problems.
Line 2 : Help comes from your mother or your wife. Small successes.
Line 3 : Friends help to bring success. Value them !
Line 4 : Too many conflicts. Stay cool. Do not get into new entanglements.
Line 5 : Remorse vanishes. Everything succeeds. Big profits are possible.
Line 6 : Incomes increase. Students are successful.
        Awareness of risks brings rewards. No blame is attached.

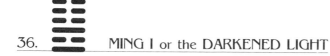

36. MING I or the DARKENED LIGHT

Earth above the sun. Darkness is everywhere. Evil conditions exist. It is time to sleep and wait for the dawn. Be patient even when there is danger. Hide your wisdom and ability. Jealousy causes extreme problems.

THE JUDGMENT: Carry on through hard times. Do not give up.
THE SYMBOL:The sun sinks beneath the earth.
            It's time to hide your brightness.
THE CHANGING LINES   :
Line 1 : A mixed time. Be aware of danger and of being harmed.
        But also expect honour and prestige to come to you.
Line 2 : You will obtain a powerful position.
Line 3 : Take your time to act. Be careful.
Line 4 : Success comes with the goodwill of others. You can get sons.
        Transfers bring good fortune, and an opportunity comes.
Line 5 : Success achieved in a foreign land.
Line 6 : Early triumphs give away obstacles. Do not be indifferent or
        unconcerned. Apathy brings misfortune and losses.

37. CHIA JEN or THE FAMILY

This hexagram stresses the importance of family in society. Sun, above and Li below predicts happiness for those who contemplating marriage, or an alliance of some kind involving the emotions. Married couples will be blessed with children if they wish to start a family.

THE JUDGMENT: A woman benefits the family
THE SYMBOL: Wind from the fire symbolises the family.
                    Conduct should be enduring
THE CHANGING LINES   :
Line 1 : Expect success. Marriage is likely. Romace will endure.
Line 2 : Success and increase in family wealth are indicated.
Line 3 : Goodwill towards each other benefits everyone. But be sensible.
Line 4 : Great good fortune. Incomes and wealth increase. Popularity soars.
Line 5 : Patronage from men of power and influence bring wealth and great
             good fortune.
Line 6 :Sincerity and dignity bring good fortune.
         Reputation will reach heights.

38. KUEI or OPPOSITION

Indications here of opposition and strong conflicts and contradiction. Li, is above and yet fire burns upwards; Tui or the lake is below, and yet water flows down ‐ the elements are in opposing directions, an inauspicious indication. Water dampens the fire. Not a good hexagram for marriage, friendships or joint business ventures. If you get this hexagram, better to break off the relationship ... there will be too much opposition.

THE JUDGMENT: Opposition dampens enthusiasm.
THE SYMBOL: Water and fire opposes each other. No success !
THE CHANGING LINES   :
Line 1 : Discord at the start but later there is harmony.
             There is progress but it is slow.
Line 2 : Can expect help from friends. Line indicates good fortune.
Line 3 : Misfortune in the beginning but later things improve. Some danger.
Line 4 : Indicates good fortune. Obstacles are overcome. Marriage possible.
Line 5 : Benefits come.. Marriage is indicated. Promotion possible.
Line 6 : Early losses but profits later. Confusion clears up, and ventures
             proceed smoothly, Watch out for gossip and slander.

39. CHIEN or OBSTRUCTION

Difficulty and danger are predicted, by this Hexagram which has kan, water above and Ken, mountain below, a sign of danger ! It is a cold barren period when water causes damage. If planning a venture, postpone it for awhile. It is also not a good time for marriage and love affairs as it is a time of many misunderstandings. Communications is difficult. In travels, avoid the Northeast direction. Southwest is better.

THE JUDGMENT: The Southwest is of benefit
THE SYMBOL: Water on the mountain. Danger.
THE CHANGING LINES :
Line 1 : Remain inactive. Don't relocate and don't start a new venture.
Line 2 : There are many obstacles to overcome. Poor health is indicated.
Line 3 : Caution prevents loss or injury. A good time for marriage.
Line 4 : Perseverance and hardwork will be rewarded but there is danger of lawsuits. Stay aloof from other people's conflicts.
Line 5 : Despite strong opposition you will succeed with help from influential friends.
Line 6 : Recognition and progress are around the corner. Good fortune. Powerful support from a great man. Beneficial to ask.

40. HSIEH or LIBERATION

Freedom from all obstructions! Upper trigram Chen is Spring and lower Kan is water. They present an image of springtime when ice melts and water is free to flow again. Complicated and difficult problems get resolved. Time for expansion and growth. Marriage and Romance blooms !

THE JUDGMENT: If there is somewhere to go, going quickly brings fortune.
THE SYMBOL:Thunder and rain symbolises a new period of growth.
THE CHANGING LINES :
Line 1 : Success indicated. If you are single you are likely to get married.
Line 2 : Continue with what you are doing or planning. Great good fortune comes your way. Incomes increase. Like finding gold !
Line 3 : If your luck seems bad now, don't fret, just be cautious.
Line 4 : Trust your associate. But be wary of the new friends
Line 5 : Good fortune is indicated. Ventures become profitable.
Line 6 : Major leaps in income and prestige. Great good fortune.

41. 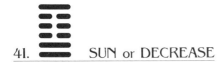 SUN or DECREASE

This hexagram indicates a monetary loss, a contraction in business and even severe financial problems. If you get this Hexagram, watch your expenses and lie low. Wait for a more auspicious time. For marriages and studies however, this is a good time. But do not expect budding romances to quite take off yet ! Be patient.

THE JUDGMENT: Decrease comes but sincerity transforms it into great good fortune. One may then proceed.
THE SYMBOL : The mountain slowly crumbles into the water.
THE CHANGING LINES :
Line 1 : Work out your budget carefully, Do not expand or over commit.
Line 2 : Not a time for change or new activity. Maintain normal routine.
Line 3 : Good social interface indicated. Friends come to your assistance.
Line 4 : Good fortune is coming. Plans in hibernation can be re‑explored.
Line 5 : Great good fortune. Unexpected windfall. Benefits are forthcoming.
Line 6 : Help from friends play a big part in your success.
       It is a good time. Proceed.

42.  I or INCREASE

An active period for those in business. Sun, above and Chen below indicates prosperity and expansion. It is also an excellent time for marriage. Even if others advise against your plans, follow your own instincts. Luck is with you. Be confident. This is a very good time for long term commitments.

THE JUDGMENT: It benefits to set forth.
THE SYMBOL :Wind and thunder symbolize increase and great prosperity.
THE CHANGING LINES :
Line 1 : Sublime good fortune. Everything proceeds smoothly. Good period.
Line 2 : Magnificent good fortune. Success in whatever you do.
Line 3 : Even with setbacks you can succeed. Promotions, honours, wealth.
Line 4 : You will be given a brilliant opportunity. Be ready for it !
Line 5 : You will become an outstanding leader.
       Your achievements will be recognized and strongly rewarded.
Line 6 : There is jealousy and betrayal. Be careful. Do not respond.
       Just be cautious. You will succeed.

43. KUAI or DETERMINATION

Chien below and Tui above signifies a firm decision. This Hexagram advocates dealing decisively with life's opportunities in order to succeed. The five yang lines indicate willpower, and also strength of character. Success and triumphs are indicated, but mainly in business and careers, not so much for marriage or love affairs.

THE JUDGMENT: Strength creates success.
THE SYMBOL: Lake ascends to heaven, and Man accumulates his wealth.
THE CHANGING LINES   :
Line 1 : Determination can breed arrogance. If so there will be cause for
          much regret. Good fortune turns into misfortune.
Line 2 : A sudden crisis of confidence, but overcome it. Be determined.
Line 3 : Don't be over confident. Even good fortune requires humility.
Line 4 : Small setbacks. But don't let them hold you back.
          Success comes with resolve.
Line 5 : Difficulties discourage you. Stay resolute.
          In the end you will succeed.
Line 6 : Misfortune is indicated. Withdraw. Go back to original plan.
          Your difficulties unfortunately, will be severe.

44. KOU or ENCOUNTERING

Accidental meetings bring new opportunities. New situations arise without warning. Chien above, Sun, the wind below. One yin line shows a woman with many boyfriends. Marriage is not indicated. Love affairs will deteriorate into discord and gossip. Stay cool and above the fray.

THE JUDGMENT: The woman is not for marrying.
THE SYMBOL: Wind under the sky symbolizes a chance encounter.
THE CHANGING LINES   :
Line 1 : Legal problems indicated which drag on. Good time for births.
Line 2 : Can expect benefits and favours. Personal efforts cannot succeed.
Line 3 : At work there are problems and disputes. Studies lead to success.
Line 4 : Danger at work. Politicking and back biting cause distress.
          Health may decline. Love brings heartaches.
Line 5 : Excellent. Help from a powerful person. Achievements are brilliant.
          Childless couples conceive. Happiness !
Line 6 : Moderate success. Some difficulties.

45. TS'UI or GATHERING

A celebration, a party, a festival. All are indicated in this hexagram. Tui, the joyous is above, and Kun, the receptive is below, indicating that business prospects are predicted to be excellent and that marriage is favoured. This Hexagram signifies good fortune.

THE JUDGMENT: It benefits to see the great man and to proceed with undertakings. Continuing benefits.
THE SYMBOL: The lake in earth symbolizes a happy and joyous gathering of people.
THE CHANGING LINES   :
Line 1 : Caution is advised because initially there will be problems. Success comes later.
Line 2 : Introductions lead to profit making ventures. Efforts will be successful.
Line 3 : Moderated success indicated. Some setbacks.
Line 4 : Great good fortune. But too much on your plate. Be more focused.
Line 5 : Credibility problem.. But with effort you will succeed.
Line 6 : Unlucky developments & bad luck cause distress. Health suffers.

46. SHENG or ASCENDING

An excellent prediction is contained in this Hexagram. Kun above and Sun below is excellent. Promotion, prosperity and expansion are signified by trees blossoming and bearing fruit. Continue but also temper progress with good sense. Gradual, solid growth is better than sudden advancements. Sheng is favourable for marriage, careers and business expansion.

THE JUDGMENT: Ascending. Great success.
THE SYMBOL: The plant matures, flowers bloom and fruits ripen.
THE CHANGING LINES   :
Line 1 : Fantastic luck ! Everything is successful. Everything is achieved. If in a relationship, go for it ! Luck is with you.
Line 2 : Bad luck is transformed into good luck. Things move smoothly. A bad relationship will improve. You will make good decisions.
Line 3 : Careers take off. A new job offer brings more money and prestige. You will also be lucky in marriage.
Line 4 : Good time for careers and travel. Will befriend a powerful man.
Line 5 : Steady steps up the corporate, academic and business ladder. Great success is in store for you. Romance is beneficial.
Line 6 : Some obstacles and setbacks. But there is still good fortune.

47. KUN or OPPRESSION

This Hexagram predicts difficulty in growing and development. Kan, the dreaded trigram of warning is below, and Tui, the lake is above, indicating a huge excess of water ... There are obstructions everywhere. Danger, quarrels and shortage of money. Kun strongly advises extreme care and caution; perhaps it is beneficial to change jobs, or business or direction. If you get this Hexagram, do not proceed with any of your plans. Lie low for awhile.

THE JUDGMENT: Oppression requires persistence and patience.
THE SYMBOL: A lake with too much water.
THE CHANGING LINES   :
Line 1 : A dark period. Three years of bad luck. Stay very quiet.
Line 2 : Better to postpone all decisions. If you do nothing, it is beneficial.
Line 3 : Misfortune. Loss. Sadness. Try to be strong ...
Line 4 : There is danger. Be very very careful indeed.
Line 5 : Need for sacrifices in the beginning. Much hard work. Benefits are
         small. But this is better than nothing. Don't be ambitious.
Line 6 : No way out. Hampered by obstacles all the way.
         Better to make drastic change. Or do nothing ... yet.

48. CHING the WELL

The image is water in wood. Kan, water is above, while Sun, is below, indicating a well. If the well is clean, the water is pure and tasty. If it is neglected, the water is murky and dirty. But dilapidated wells can be repaired and made productive. So it is with life, and with business And with relationships. Nurturing brings its own rewards.

THE JUDGMENT: The rope breaks. you cannot get water.
THE SYMBOL: The superior man improves himself and works diligently.
THE CHANGING LINES   :
Line 1 : The well is old. It needs repair. Business is bad.
         Improvements are required.
Line 2 : The well is dry and the jug leaks. A very bad time for relationships.
         Situations are tense. You need to do some repair work.
Line 3 : Circumstances improve. Ideas are sound. But much work to do.
Line 4 : A period of learning and preparation. Wait but be prepared.
Line 5 : Success. Efforts are rewarded. Profits flow in. You gain respect.
Line 6 : Great good fortune. Income increase. Recognition. Rewards.
         Everything succeeds. The well is flowing again.

49. KO or REVOLUTION

Situations of conflict leading to major upheavals. Fire in the lake. Li below, and Tui above. This Hexagram symbolizes people who really cannot get along. Disagreements and violent friction leading to clashes and strife. There is a need for change. But there is only danger.

THE JUDGMENT: Revolution. Change.
THE SYMBOL: In the lake there is fire - an impossible situation.
It is time for a change.
THE CHANGING LINES :
Line 1 : Guard against over ambition. Improve yourself.
Don't depend on luck alone.
Line 2 : You are ready. It is time for action. There is good fortune ahead.
Line 3 : Confusion.Things turn nasty. Stay calm.Rise above petty squabbles.
Line 4 : A leader emerges. Remorse and regret disappears. Great good luck
brings new opportunities to those who are prepared.
Line 5 : A great man. Like a tiger. Highly respected. Dynamic. Brilliant.
Proceed with confidence !
Line 6 : Don't change course. To persist brings good fortune.
Writers will gain recognition. Stay within the law.

50. TING the CALDRON

The Hexagram looks like a caldron, with Li, fire above, and Sun, wood below. The nuclear trigram is water. The fire boils the water to produce steam. The meaning is creation of energy and nourishment. Good fortune.

THE JUDGMENT: Great good fortune. Success.
THE SYMBOL: The superior man creates his own destiny.
THE CHANGING LINES :
Line 1 : Indicates the concubine, but also good fortune. Happiness emerges
from sadness. Initial disappointment. Later triumphs.
Line 2 : Plenty of food. Prosperity and success. There is envy. Be careful.
Line 3 : A very trying time at first. But upsets become success. There are
new opportunities. Be cool.
Line 4 : Misfortune. Loss. Injury. Illness. Better to stay queit.
Line 5 : Brilliant indications of success. Everything works and takes off.
Line 6 : Great good fortune! Jade and gold indicated. Everything succeeds.

51. CHEN the THUNDER

Thunder creating shock and fear. It stirs people, opens their eyes and shakes them into action. <u>Chen</u> doubled, predicts favourable luck for those in entertainment and publicity related industries. There is merrymaking and plenty of energy. But restraint is necessary.

THE JUDGMENT: Thunder brings success.
THE SYMBOL:Thunder doubled brings shock, fear and caution.
THE CHANGING LINES   :
Line 1 : Good fortune. You may feel threatened but there is no need.
Line 2 : The danger is real. Loss of wealth. Sickness. But later you recover.
Line 3 : Being cautious and circumspect will protect you from injury.
Line 4 : You are stuck in a rut. Better do nothing.
            Boredom is better than danger.
Line 5 : Neither good nor bad. Do what you presently do. Don't take risks.
Line 6 : A dangerous time. Be careful.
            Avoid getting entangled in new situations.

52. KEN or STILLNESS

Ken is *"mountain doubled"* stressing immobility, stillness, control. It suggests a time for reflection and meditation; for planning, for depending on yourself. Not a time for beginnings, new ventures or new affiliations. There is already harmony in existing relationships. Be patient. This is a time of waiting.

THE JUDGMENT: A time for keeping still.
THE SYMBOL:The superior man's thoughts are turned inwards.
THE CHANGING LINES   :
Line 1 : No threats to existing situations but not a good time to pursue
            new ventures, nor to start new relationships.
Line 2 : Tiredness and lethargy makes concentration difficult. Stamina and
            energy is also lacking. A most apathetic period.
Line 3 : A case of trying too hard at a time when it is better to relax.
Line 4 : Do not be aggressive. Progress and advancement is not possible.
Line 5 : A breakthrough. Success. A time to seek new opportunities.
Line 6 : Good fortune. Expect gains in investments, recognition and
            improvements. Expect progress also in all relationships.

53. CHIEN or GRADUAL DEVELOPMENT

The image is of trees growing slowly on the mountain. The Trigram <u>Sun</u> above and the Trigram <u>Ken</u>, below. Good fortune comes to those who are patient. Despite obstacles, plans will eventually succeed. Goals will be achieved. In love, business, careers, studies; there is good fortune to come, but consider alsothe specific predictions of the changing lines.

THE JUDGMENT: Good fortune
THE SYMBOL: A tree on the mountain
THE CHANGING LINES   :
Line 1 : Difficulty. the boy is in danger. But ultimately, good fortune.
Line 2 : Good luck in everything and plenty to eat.
         A comfortable and successful prediction.
Line 3 : Misfortune. Ventures cannot succeed. Buds cannot open.
         Romance is missing. Pregnancy terminates.
Line 4 : Harmony at home but difficulties in dealing with people. Small
         misunderstandings cause irritations. Minor good fortune.
Line 5 : Three years of waiting and preparation are over. Good fortune now
         comes. He could propose and she could say yes !
Line 6 : Significant success, sometimes unexpected. Important opportunities.

54. KUEI MEI or THE MARRYING GIRL

This hexagram predicts marriage or a final resolution of a relationship, but there will be little long term permanence. Unhappiness and misfortune soon follows. Even separations and scandals. The Trigram above is <u>Chen</u>, and the one below is <u>Tui.</u> Happiness cannot last and will give way to heartaches. This Hexagram is a warning to be cautious, especially in relationships.

THE JUDGMENT: Undertakings get unfortunate results.
THE SYMBOL: Thunder above lake. There is danger.
THE CHANGING LINES:
Line 1 : Mixed fortunes. A mentor appears. A new love interest excites !
Line 2 : Unspectacular period. Neither a time of loss or of gains.
Line 3 : Sudden advance, sudden misfortune. Things are not what they
         seem. Beware ! Be alert to betrayals.
Line 4 : Wait. A better opportunity comes later. Good time for travel.
Line 5 : Favourable indications for success and glamour.
         Good fortune is genuine. There is much to celebrate. Applaud !
Line 6 : Empty promises. A bad time. Cannot expect success or sincerity.

55. FENG or GREATNESS

The promise of brilliant success and prosperity are predicted by this Hexagram, which has the Trigram Chen above, and Li below. This symbolizes a couple in their prime; or a businessman with plenty of cash. But guard against being over confident. Handle your affairs with care.

THE JUDGMENT: Attainment of greatness.
THE SYMBOL: Lightning brings brilliance.
THE CHANGING LINES   :
Line 1 : Goals achieved easily. Influential people help you. But be careful.
Line 2 : Success under adverse conditions. Things appear to look bad, but your luck is excellent. It is unnecessary to worry
Line 3 : Something blocks your success. But stay confident.
Line 4 : Hard work leads to achievement, but there is misunderstanding.
Line 5 : Power and influence are indicated. Time of great good fortune.
Line 6 : A time of decline for rich man. But for lovers a brilliant period.

56. LU the EXILE

A favourable hexagram for those who travel but it is unfavourable for marriage, new ventures or partnerships. Both parties will change their minds. This Hexagram indicates loneliness and separations. Li, fire and lightning above, and Ken, the mountain below symbolizes fire over mountain.

THE JUDGMENT: Small success
THE SYMBOL: Fire over mountain. Wandering. A sense of being alone.
THE CHANGING LINES   :
Line 1 : Lack of energy and will power. Small success at best but misfortune at worse. Perseverance is required.
Line 2 : Recognition is attained away from home. Travel or transfer brings good fortune. Marrying someone from another country bring benefits and good fortune..
Line 3 : Fire will bring disaster. A time of danger. Be prepared for troubles.
Line 4 : Success in another city, and another country. If marriage takes you to another country, it brings great good fortune.
Line 5 : Attainment of brilliant success. Recognition brings satisfaction. There is power and influence indicated for the exile.
Line 6 : Misfortune. There is risk of loss. Things seem wonderful but there is betrayal and ill fortune later. Guard your words and deeds.

57. SUN the WIND

Sun indicates success by following a great man. Good strategy brings a good fortune. Prosperity is achieved by those who travel, live or invest abroad. Sun is wind doubled, and it symbolises great success.

THE JUDGMENT: Seeing the great man, or going somewhere leads to
                great success.
THE SYMBOL: The wind scatters the seeds which take root, producing
                plants and trees, symbolizing growth
THE CHANGING LINES:
Line 1 : Some ups and downs. Some gains and some losses.
          But in the end, success.
Line 2 : Honesty brings rewards. Good fortune. But don't keep asking.
Line 3 : Travel indicated. But there is humiliation and sudden loss.
Line 4 : Remorse vanishes. Benefits and good fortune are in store for many.
Line 5 : Everything benefits. Your abilities and contributions are recognized.
          Great success.
Line 6 : Wealth is lost. Persistence leads to misfortune. Loss and sickness
          indicated. But from misfortune, sometimes good fortune arises.

58. TUI or JOYOUSNESS

This Hexagram indicates great happiness and implies success and beauty. Benefits and prizes are coming. Especially good predictions in store for those in the glamour professions. But Tui is also "gold doubled" indicating a great deal of wealth for all.

THE JUDGMENT: Good fortune brings smiles to faces.
THE SYMBOL: Plants thrive along the lake.
THE CHANGING LINES   :
Line 1 : Harmony and joy. Great happiness.
Line 2 : The path is clear and smooth.
Line 3 : Small obstacles irritate. A pot of gold at the end of a rainbow.
Line 4 : Great material success attracts envy. Harmony is elusive but
          advancement is certain.
Line 5 : You have an enemy who tries to undermine you.
          Be wary of slander/gossip.
Line 6 : Someone works against you. But help comes from someone
          influential. Success is yours !

59. HUAN or DISPERSION

Separation is indicated. Travel. Dispersion. It is good to expand or go overseas for business, career or studies. The Trigram <u>Sun</u> is above, and <u>Kan</u> is below. None of the lines indicate misfortune but they advise one to be careful and diligent. Love life is nil.

THE JUDGMENT: Dispersion brings success, and it benefits to cross the great water.
THE SYMBOL: Boats on the water blown by the wind.
THE CHANGING LINES   :
Line 1 : Approvals and benefits received. Success in your projects indicated.
Line 2 : Peak of attainments. Great success. You become the boss, gain power and influence. Applaud.
Line 3 : Transfers and opportunities. A good time for beginnings and start up ventures. A new romance is in the air.
Line 4 : You become a leader after some struggle. Obstacles are overcome.
Line 5 : Job search brings success. Hard work necessary but you have determination. Faint heart never won fair lady !
Line 6 : There is danger but you cope with it.

60. CHIEH or LIMITATION

Guard against loss of control. Plan carefully before deciding. This Hexagram advocates compromise, the middle ground. Avoid extremes. Be thrifty. But stay confident. <u>Kan</u> above, and <u>Tui</u> below spells good fortune.

THE JUDGMENT: Maintain your success by being careful.
THE SYMBOL: Water above the lake. Ensure the water does not overflow.
THE CHANGING LINES   :
Line 1 : Not a time to take risks. Be satisfied with your present situation.
Line 2 : Be alert to opportunities. Take action, but cautiously. But success for you is definite.
Line 3 : Guard against over indulgence. There are enemies in your midst. Be alert. Love knows no bounds but be careful.
Line 4 : Through sound strategy you achieve success from circumstances.
Line 5 : Good fortune. Undertaking brings honour. Work brings success.
Line 6 : A good time to be positive and move ahead. But stay in control at all times. Love life starts to take off !

61. CHUNG FU or INNER TRUTHS

Sun above and Tui below conveys good fortune. Sincerity. Someone one can trust and depend on. There is harmony between the members of a family, all indicated by the primary and nuclear Trigrams. And also between boss and subordinate. Success and cooperation. But beware of over confidence.

THE JUDGMENT: It benefits to cross the great waters.
THE SYMBOL: Wind over lake. Kindness.
THE CHANGING LINES
Line 1 : Work hard and diligently, for hidden in your good fortune lurks
        some risks. Also be alert.
Line 2 : Happiness all around. You will have sons, and live a long life.
Line 3 : Good fortune turns bad, then good again. This is the I Ching !
Line 4 : Professionals are promoted; But married people lose their spouses.
Line 5 : Great good fortune. Opportunities abound. Goals achieved.
Line 6 : Beware entanglements with strangers which bring misfortune.
        Mentors help.

62. HSIAO KUO or SLIGHT EXCESS

This Hexagram says that sometimes small mistakes can hamper the achievement of great things. Examples are stinginess, excessive negativism and lack of purpose. To be successful you must be confident and generous. Accept opportunities.

THE JUDGMENT: Continuing brings success
THE SYMBOL: The conduct is overly humble. In mourning,
                the lament is too loud.
THE CHANGING LINES   :
Line 1 : Rapid advancements at the beginning, but severe humiliation later.
Line 2 : Many influential and helpful friends.
        Good luck is very much on your side.
Line 3 : Misfortune. Someone may stab you in the back.
        Beware of sweet tongued villains.
Line 4 : Be content with present situations.
Line 5 : Not a time for taking risks. Accept present conditions.
        Otherwise misfortune befalls you. .
Line 6 : Beware of ambition. Don't over stretch yourself. Otherwise disaster.

63. CHI CHI or COMPLETION

This Hexagram has Kan water, above and Li, fire, below, and it indicates something successfully achieved or accomplished. A project. A business deal. A university degree. Pursuit of a girlfriend or boyfriend. It also indicates harmony and balance in situations. Almost ideal. But stay alert to danger. Take precautions.

THE JUDGMENT: Success in small things. But disorder brings disaster.
THE SYMBOL: Water above fire. Attainments with hidden dangers
THE CHANGING LINES   :
Line 1 : Caution makes one prepared. Ultimate success is difficult.
Line 2 : Don't let early setbacks discourage you.
          Success does come later. Persevere.
Line 3 : Difficulties to tax even the most determine person. Don't despair.
Line 4 : Be very cautious. With preparation you can overcome adversity.
Line 5 : Success in small projects. Disaster in grand schemes. Influential or
          prosperous people will attract destructive jealousy.
Line 6 : Danger in travel and at work.

64. WEI CHI or BEFORE COMPLETION

This Hexagram, with Li (fire) above and Kan (water) below, predicts a time of strenuous efforts, just before something is achieved. Everything is about to start. Be fully prepared. This Hexagram implies great success for the future. Accept advice from a woman.

THE JUDGMENT: Before completion. There is success.
THE SYMBOL: Fire above water.

THE CHANGING LINES   :
Line 1 : Goals cannot be achieved. Humiliation. Obstacles. Difficulties.
Line 2 : Small successes are possible but even these are hard to achieve.
Line 3 : Initial frustration. Travel bring some success in small ventures.
Line 4 : Good fortune. Difficulties are overcome with unexpected help.
Line 5 : Proceed with confidence. Good fortune brings success. Promotions.
Line 6 : There is escape from a dangerous situation and advancement is in
          store for you.

THE SCIENCE OF FENG SHUI
with LILIAN TOO on Internet
http://www.asiaconnect.com.my/lillian-too

THE GEOMANCER on Internet
http://www.wwwmktg.com/client/feng shui/

Trade Inquiries may be addressed to the following:

UK & EUROPE
MILLBANK BOOKS
The Courtyard, The Old Monastery,
Bishops Stortford, Hertfordshire,
CM23 2PE, United Kingdom.
Tel: 44 1279 655 233
Fax: 44 1279 655 244

AUSTRALIA & NEW ZEALAND
ORIENTAL PUBLICATIONS
16 Market Street,
Adelaide South Australia 5000,
Australia.
Tel: 618 212 6055
Fax: 618 410 0863